THE
FOOTBALL
RAMBLE

MARCUS SPELLER

LUKE AARON MOORE

PETE DONALDSON

JIM CAMPBELL

THE FOOTBALL RAMBLE

By Four Men Who Love
The Game They Hate

CENTURY

5 7 9 10 8 6 4

Century
20 Vauxhall Bridge Road
London SW1V 2SA

Century is part of the Penguin Random House group of companies
whose addresses can be found at global.penguinrandomhouse.com

 Penguin
Random House
UK

First published in Great Britain by Century in 2016

www.penguin.com/

A CIP catalogue record for this book
is available from the British Library.

ISBN 9781780896342

Typeset in India by Thomson Digital Pvt Ltd, Noida, Delhi

Printed and bound in Great Britain by Clays Ltd, St Ives plc

Penguin Random House is committed to a sustainable future
for our business, our readers and our planet. This book is made
from Forest Stewardship Council® certified paper.

For anyone who has ever downloaded
a *Football Ramble* podcast.

Contents

FOREWORD

Ladies and gentlemen, welcome to *The Football Ramble*. It's lovely to have you here. Presumably you've bought this book because you love football as much as we do.

In April 2007, after David Nugent stole his only international goal from Jermain Defoe against Andorra during England's doomed quest to qualify for Euro 2008, *The Football Ramble* was born as a podcast. Along with Luke, Pete and Jim, I've been writing and talking about the game ever since, covering ten domestic seasons and five international tournaments, and we are proud to now bring you our first book, highlighting everything we love (and loathe) about our national sport.

Football can be unbelievably good. Football can be bloody awful. Football can be mysterious, but also painfully obvious. Football inspires us to throw an impromptu party at someone else's house but also convinces us to cancel our mother's birthday celebrations – when Paul Gascoigne scored that famous goal against Scotland at Wembley in 1996, my brother and I hugged each other in jubilation because, as English boys living north of the border, we knew we were off the hook with our Scottish classmates.

Alternatively, when England laboured to a pathetic 0–0 draw against Algeria at the 2010 World Cup, I was so low I didn't attend my friend's birthday party that night. My friends and I simply didn't have the energy or desire to do anything after what we'd just witnessed and, what's more, we genuinely feared we'd bring the overall mood down with our attendance. In hindsight, he wasn't that good a mate anyway – I've barely seen him since. You just can't trust a man whose birthday falls on such a depressing day.

Football is also reassuringly constant. It's never-ending. 'Off-season' still has the word 'season' in it. It can inspire you to behave in the most surprisingly hilarious ways. For example, do you remember when and why you last skipped in public in a fit of gay abandon? I do. It was on 31 May 2002. I had just handed in my final assignment at the end of my first year of university and then watched world champions France lose 1–0 to World Cup debutants Senegal. Now, I have nothing against France and I have no reason to support Senegal. Despite this, as three friends and I left the pub that day we all began skipping and dancing with glee along a busy road in Farnborough at what we'd just seen and became giddy at the thought of a month's worth of World Cup action to come. Fortunately 'Billy Elliot' was still in the public's psyche so perhaps it wasn't too shocking for those who saw us, but the point is *that's* what football can do to you.

The next morning I was up at 7 a.m. Why? Because two teams I'm completely impartial to in the form of Ireland and Cameroon were kicking off at 7.30 a.m. as the tournament was being hosted by Japan and South Korea. Like most students, I usually hated getting up early.

Of course, although we love watching it being played, there's a lot more to the game than what 22 men do between the white lines of a football pitch. Football is a culture, a never-ending circus of drama and comedy, and we – fans, media, players, managers, officials and administrators – are all actors in this, the world's biggest play. Football is comprised of many wonderful and curious things that guarantee our interest will never wane and, without the inherent ridiculousness of our national sport, *The Football Ramble* would have no reason to exist. We hope you're as thankful as we are that it does.

For instance, have you heard about Romário's latest tirade from Brazil, where he has hung up his boots and is now forging an unlikely career in politics? Do you really know what Sven-Goran Eriksson is getting up to in Asia years on from his stint as England manager? Or even why Kevin Keegan regularly comes out with stuff like: 'It's like a toaster, the ref's shirt pocket. Every time there's a tackle, up pops a yellow card.' If the answer is 'no, but I'd like to', *The Football Ramble* is for you.

Football continues to throw up countless players, managers, moments, matches, teams, venues and tournaments that have captured fans' and the media's attention, and in this book we explore it all in as much detail as we can readily muster.

So, without further ado, here's our take on this irresistible, glorious, addictive sport that we all have running through our veins, whether we like it or not. In the words of the great Barry Davies, 'away we go!'

Marcus Speller, October 2016

1. History

Jim Campbell

There's something irresistible about balls. If a ball is nearby then every atom of you is compelled to bounce it, throw it or kick it. It calls to you like a mysterious orb made of pure fun. You don't know why, you sometimes don't even notice it happening, but you just need to play with it.

Much is written about how football began, about who invented it and at what point it became enough like the game we have today to be considered football. Maybe it exists because it has to. Something about us *needs* to kick around a spherical object and football has evolved so that we can satisfy this urge. It's true beginnings probably come from our ancient ancestors kicking fruit about because when there's a roundish object on the ground something inside us just has to absolutely leather it. Even as a 34-year-old man I'm still tempted by every stray bottle cap I come across. In fact I once broke my toe attempting to kick one, but that's a story for one other book. Kicking things is fun. Throw in an objective like scoring to give it some competitive purpose and you have a sport.

To people like ourselves, football is a big part of our lives that has always just been there. We've been meeting since 2007 to enthuse and despair about it into microphones then release our thoughts into the wild simply because we're hooked. All fans have a history with it, yet it has a long history without us. Of course it hasn't always just been there. It's evolved over time to become the behemoth it is now. However it started, it's been quite a journey . . .

Early doors

Football was formalised in England in 1863 when the Football Association got together in a pub and decided on a definitive set of rules for the sake of practicality. This is often considered to be the birth of the modern game but the true history of football goes back a lot further than that no doubt drunken afternoon. The Chinese have such a legitimate claim to have invented it that FIFA recognise one of their ancient sports, *cuju* – the literal translation of which is 'to kick a ball' – as being the earliest form of football.

The first written reference to *cuju* came more than 2,000 years ago during the Han dynasty (206 BC–AD 220). It began as military fitness training but became popular among the aristocracy, with games providing entertainment at the Emperor's birthday celebrations and other formal occasions. It's hard to overstate how similar it became to modern football both in terms of the game itself and the role it played in society. It wasn't simply a primitive, lawless kickabout. It was a properly organised, competitive sport. Initially it was played with teams of twelve to sixteen players facing off on a square court, with six crescent-shaped goals at either end. Over time it evolved to become like a cross between volleyball and headers and volleys, played with a single goal located in the centre of the pitch. Players scored by shooting the ball through a hole in the middle. It had referees, penalties and many other things that are integral to the modern game. Maybe it even had frustrated tablet warriors, bashing abuse into bits of stone and chucking them at players after they'd had a bad game.

During the Han dynasty, Emperor Wudi loved it so much that he had his servants write articles about it in what may have been the first examples of minute-by-minute reports. They're hard enough on a laptop, let alone on a piece of parchment when you have no access to replays and face the very real threat of execution if you happen to miss who actually scored because you were finishing off a sentence about who conceded the corner.

During the Song dynasty (970–1279, as if you needed reminding) the sport was so popular that many major Chinese cities had their own fully professional *cuju* clubs, playing in a nationwide league called the *qiyun she*. These are considered to be the first sports clubs of any kind.

It was a big deal, so much so that around this time the Emperor Taizu became known for his freestyle *cuju*, in which he'd perform tricks as modern exhibition players do, except much better because it was like the Queen doing it.

As with football centuries later, commercialisation followed this popularity. It's not as if players were endorsing ancient bamboo-flavoured soft drinks but many were fully fledged professionals who became rich and famous through their skill. Female *cuju* players were also popular, with records showing that a seventeen-year-old girl once beat an entire team of soldiers in what is perhaps the earliest and most authentic recorded result of Chinese whispers. One women's game is believed to have featured 153 players, playing in front of tens of thousands of fans.

Sadly, the game went into decline during the Ming dynasty (that's 1368–1644), possibly because everyone was getting really into vases instead. As a sport it became associated with brothels and vice, with teams of prostitutes organising and playing games to attract customers, which seems both coy and forward at the same time. This reputation diminished its popularity so much that it ceased to exist at all, though at one point during the Qing dynasty (1644–1912, obviously) it was modified to be played on ice skates in what was effectively a spin-off. That's some pretty modern thinking. If this has happened before, and as football becomes more like a product than a sport, then it can be only a matter of time before we get 'The Premier League – On Ice!' or perhaps a World Cup in Antarctica. It makes as much practical sense as a World Cup in Qatar, more so if you factor in global warming.

So football, this mad and addictive game that we all love, that is ours, *has happened before*. As a fan it's hard to get your head around that, especially as it was popular over a period of twelve centuries, far longer than football as we know it has existed. Maybe *cuju* wasn't even the first time it had happened. The dinosaurs at the top of the food chain must have needed something to do when they weren't eating. Tyrannosaurus rex would have had the pace for it and their tails would have provided a useful extra limb – with arms as rubbish as that they wouldn't have been playing basketball, for God's sake.

Dinosaurs aside, *cuju* definitely wasn't the first competitive ball game. Many were played throughout the ancient world and some outdate *cuju*, though these weren't nearly as similar to football and FIFA certainly don't recognise them. Probably because of all the violent deaths . . .

The oldest ball game historians know of is broadly known as the Mesoamerican ball game, which was really many similar games played in the ancient cultural region that stretched from modern Mexico down into Central

America. The Mayans called their version *pok-a-tok*, the Aztecs knew it as *tlachtli* and the game that is still played today is called *ulama*. The oldest court discovered has been dated to 1400 BC and courts have been found as far south as Nicaragua and as far north as Arizona. Interestingly, records of both *cuju* and the Mesoamerican games include references to a mysterious, nomadic figure known only as 'Kanu', something that has baffled historians.

A common objective of the games was to keep the ball off the ground without using your hands, a point being scored when the other team failed to return the ball. The Mayans added stone rings that hung high on the court walls and were used as goals. In most versions players had to use their hips rather than their feet. This would be unwieldy enough with a modern ball but these players used a solid rubber thing about the size of a basketball. It was also played on a stone court, meaning players would end up bloodied and bruised from simply playing the game as it was supposed to be played. There are many accounts of players dying from internal bleeding caused by the injuries they sustained.

It's all pretty horrifying and that's before we even get to the human sacrifice. If you didn't die from playing the game you could be killed for losing it, with the captain of the vanquished side, or sometimes the entire team, offered up as a sacrifice for the gods. I would definitely have died doing this were I around at the time. Games had a religious significance, with the ball representing the movement of celestial bodies. Those that ended in sacrifice correlated with the cycles of the sun and moon. This was because the Mayans believed that two of their gods – the twins Hunahpu and Xbalanque – had travelled to the underworld to battle death gods called Xibalbans in a booby-trapped ball game. They were victorious and eventually transformed themselves into the sun and the moon, meaning that sacrifices must be made so that both could rise each day. It all seems so obvious once you know that.

What's particularly galling about this is that evidence for the sacrificial element appears fairly late in the archaeological records, at which point those in charge had surely figured out that the sun comes up every day regardless of what you do. The late addition suggests it was intended as an improvement, like it was goal-line technology or vanishing spray. Perhaps the authorities had a hidden agenda: 'That Axayacatl was terrible today. This team will never win anything with him as captain. By the way, how's your maize doing? Mine is awful. The gods must be seriously displeased.'

'Mine is exactly the same. Hang on. I've got an idea . . .'

Much of the art depicting the sacrifices made at the games shows decapitation, leading some scholars to believe that the newly available supply of heads were then used as balls. At least the rubber balls didn't have teeth. The pressure must have been unbearable – Sam Allardyce bellowing at you for not tracking back is one thing; making sure you don't get your head lopped off as the only alternative to the sun disappearing for ever is something else.

Though *ulama* is still played, it is done so only in a few places in Mexico. When the Catholic Spanish conquistadors arrived in the sixteenth century they suppressed the game because of what they considered to be pagan elements – and because they favoured a high-pressing, quick-tempo passing game – and the gruesome practice of human sacrifice came to an end. Recently it has been reintroduced in preparations for the 2022 World Cup.

The ancient Greeks had a game called *episkyros* and the Romans had an equivalent, known as *harpastum*. Much of what is known about both has been pieced together from poems, stories, paintings and vases. The European Cup features an image of a man balancing a ball on his knee that originally appeared on a marble vase from ancient Greece. Ornaments were the highlights packages of the time. Where modern footballers can simply record themselves scoring on *Match of the Day*, the Greeks and Romans would have to sit eagerly by the kiln to see if their goal was as good as they remembered.

Both *episkyros* and *harpastum* bore similarities to rugby. It's thought that the aim of both was to keep the ball in the air and on your side of the pitch while the opposition attempted to steal it and get it on to theirs. It sounds almost jolly and twee – the kind of thing you might do with your partner if you existed solely in a yoghurt advert – but as with everything that ever happened in the ancient world it was punctuated by extreme violence. One of the rules of *harpastum* was that only the player with the ball could be tackled. Imagine having to specify that. It'd be like managing Lee Cattermole. As if everyday life wasn't risky enough back then, the Greeks also played their version naked, just for the added frisson of some testicular or vaginal jeopardy.

Harpastum was popular among Roman children, who would play it in the street. We know this because Cicero, the Roman philosopher, politician and lawyer, wrote of a court case in which a barber accidentally slit the throat of a man he was shaving after he was struck by a wayward ball. Hitting your neighbour's window is bad enough but causing a man to execute a customer in his admittedly poorly conceived outdoor barber shop doesn't bear thinking about. I can only conclude that the victim must have been an ancestor of Kevin Keegan to have suffered such a slapstick death. That, or Rome's answer to Sweeney Todd simply murdered a man in broad daylight and blamed it on those pesky kids.

What's striking about so many of these games is that they had structure and organisation, although not so much in Britain, where chaos reigned supreme. The early history of football and its ancestors often seems like it was full of violence as we know about it only through records that were primarily related to crime or medical emergencies. However, in some cases this is simply because it *was* incredibly violent.

Mob football began in the Middle Ages and is where the modern game has its roots. It was a combination of football, rugby and rioting. The number of players was unlimited as sides were made up of entire towns rather than teams. You could use your hands and essentially do anything as the only rule was that you couldn't kill anyone. Imagine having to specify that. It'd be like managing Lee Cattermole. Terrible injuries occurred all the time but people simply got on with it. If you severed a leg while playing you merely slapped some leeches on the wound, played on, then spent the next month dying an agonisingly slow death.

The 'goals' were markers at the far ends of each town and everywhere was part of the game – from paths and squares to hedgerows and rivers – inevitably leading to significant property damage. In some cases the game was won when one team managed to kick the ball on to the neighbouring town's church balcony.

This may sound chaotic but it also sounds brilliant. Were it reintroduced today, say as a one-off Tyne-Wear derby, it would attract record viewing figures. The full squads, the management staff, season-ticket holders, casual fans, bystanders caught up in the thrill of it, pets, everyone, just going at it for bragging rights as the drone cameras fly overhead.

The first record of a game that featured the exclusive kicking of a ball in England is from 1280, in Ulgham, Northumberland, noted because a player died after he ran into an opponent's dagger, of course. Daggers must have been an essential part of the kit back then. 'Honestly ref, he just ran into my knife.'

The first time it was actually referred to as football came in 1314 when London Mayor Nicholas de Farndone banned it. There were thirty bans between 1314 and 1667 because football was – and this will come as no surprise – really violent. James I of Scotland banned it in the Football Act of 1424, which featured the words 'na man play at the fut ball' in a dialect still spoken there today.

Henry VIII was another notable figure to ban it, in 1540, though he must have liked it at some stage. In 1526 he ordered the first known pair of football boots, from the Great Wardrobe. This was the store in which his clothing was kept and not, disappointingly, what he believed in a gout-induced fever to be a magical cupboard that spoke only to him. When ordering some footwear he sent for '4 velvet pairs and 1 leather pair for football', possibly for use on one of his many, many stag weekends. Tu-dor! Tu-dor!

Evidently, William Shakespeare was also not a fan, with his character Kent using the term 'base football player' as an insult in *King Lear*. This is disappointing as it's nice to think that, as observers of people, he and his bard pals would have watched the chaos unfold from the sidelines, perhaps biting their thumbs and chanting 'Who art thou?! Who art thou?!' at bloodied rival towns-people after a few meads.

It's understandable that people took issue with foot-ball. It sounds like it was a genuine public menace, with games leaving a trail of destruction in their wake. If I was a market trader just trying to make a living by sell-ing my pewterware and a football match came along and smashed up my business I know I wouldn't be happy. Games were even organised as a pretext to riot-ing. Despite all this the bans were difficult to enforce as people simply ignored them and a crude set of rules began to take shape.

Around 1660 Francis Willughby wrote his *Book of Games*. It was the first account to describe fundamen-tals such as scoring, goals themselves, tactics and rules. He described an early version of the outlawing of high tackles, which had typically gruesome results: 'They often break one another's shins when two meet and strike both together against the ball, and therefore there is a law that they must not strike higher than the ball.' Well over 350 years on some players still struggle with this.

The chaos continued regardless, so much so that people seemed to think it was a good idea to play on roads. Eventually the Highway Act of 1835 was passed, introducing a fine for anyone still mad enough to use a road as a football pitch. Football and disorder went hand in hand. What this game needed was some good old British rules . . .

Standardisation

England was the first country to have codified rules and this came to be because public school teams wanted to play each other. This proved problematic as they all used different rules, like men in pubs who make you play them at pool when you really don't want to and suddenly it's for cash and then the rent is gone again.

The Cambridge Rules were created in 1848 to unify them all but there were still other sets that followed. Sheffield FC had their own rules – which, as they were the first officially founded football club, started in 1857, isn't as weird as it sounds. For a while they must have had only themselves to play so could do whatever they wanted. They killed the time spent waiting for other clubs to form by coming up with things like crossbars, free-kicks and half-time.

In 1862 a man named J.C. Thring created the Uppingham Rules, number three of which gives an exasperated insight into the approach many players still favoured at the time: 'KICKS must be aimed only *at the ball.*'

Those italics are Thring's. When the Football Association was founded in 1863 they decided to put an end to all this piffle and poppycock by agreeing on a definitive set of rules. The Laws of the Game of Association Football were drawn up by a man called Ebenezer Cobb Morley, who, despite sounding like a heavy handed parody of a Charles Dickens character, honestly did exist. In fact, the FA was formed in the first place only because Morley wrote to a London news- paper called *Bell's Life*, proposing the idea of a governing body for football. That led to a meeting in a London pub called the Freemasons' Tavern where, by the sound of it, very serious men arrived on penny farthings, stroked their undoubtedly impressive waxed mous- taches and defined the foul throw. Huzzah! The meeting was attended by representatives from a number of now defunct clubs, including some jokers called No Name Club of Kilburn, who sound like a pub quiz team who blagged their way into the discussions. It was decided that elements such as hacking – kicking your opponent's shins – and carrying the ball would be outlawed. Those who disagreed with these changes broke away and went on to form rugby union, probably chanting about how ungentlemanly it all was while daring each other to down pints of their own piss. In time this also led to American football and Aussie rules. As afternoons in the pub go it was a productive one.

This is not to say that the game immediately became the sport we know today. When Sheffield FC visited London for a game in 1866 they were roundly mocked for using their heads, which unless the crowd was made up of doctors who specialised in the long term effects of head trauma now seems embarrassingly short-sighted.

A loose version of the offside rule was introduced in 1867 and this led to a host of new tactical innovations. Like passing. Before this the most common tactic was for a player to kick the ball forward and everyone else to charge after it. The exact origins of the passing game are difficult to determine as they provide an early example of England and Scotland's sporting rivalry. Legend has it that, in 1867, Scotland's Queen's Park met to create a style that would give them an advantage over the English, whom they were mostly smaller than. In England the ever-present Sheffield FC and Royal Engineers AFC also lay claim to pioneering this style. If there's one thing the English and Scots can agree on it's that the other is wrong. Wherever it started, the new style became known as the Combination Game and, adorably, Scientific Football.

Sheffield continued to innovate, giving the world its first cup competition in the same year. It was stubbornly played under the Sheffield Rules and was won by local side Hallam, who defeated Norfolk by two rouges. Not goals, rouges. The goals in the Youdan Cup format were four yards wide and a rouge was scored if the ball missed the goal but would have gone in had it been twelve yards wide. They were used to settle a game in the event of a draw. People complain that penalties aren't a fair way to decide a game but they seem a lot fairer than basing the result on what might have happened in a parallel universe.

In 1871 the whole cup thing was attempted again with the first nationally organised competition, the FA Cup. It was an instant success. It was easier to follow as it featured events based solely in this dimension.

This period also saw the first international match. It was set up by an Englishman named C.W. Alcock, who placed an advert in a Glaswegian newspaper challenging the people of Scotland to produce a team to play England. He received no responses. Undeterred, he simply arranged a match with a team of London-based Scots, which England won. He kept putting adverts in newspapers in an attempt to goad players down from Scotland, eventually giving up and instead taking an English team to Glasgow in 1872. This is the first official, FIFA-recognised international. It was a 0–0 draw and, given most of what was to come for both nations, it's perhaps fitting that nobody won.

Things were at a point where they were getting serious but not yet professional and this was becoming a bone of contention. Those in Scotland and the north of England wanted the game to become professional as they couldn't afford to take time off work for games, whereas those in the south, where it was a more moneyed pursuit, favoured keeping it amateur. Professionalism won and, in 1888, the Football League was formed by Aston Villa director William McGregor to provide regular competitive matches. Doing nothing for future stereotypes, no sides from the south initially took part, at least being consistent in throwing an entirely unprofessional collective strop.

Going Global

Such was the popularity of the game among Britons that they began to take it abroad and force it on other people, as they had previously done with imperialism and subsequently with Coldplay. In Switzerland, Lausanne Football and Cricket Club was formed in 1860 by English students doing joint degrees in timekeeping and money laundering, though it's thought that they began as primarily a cricket club. In France a club is believed to have been founded by the English as early as 1863. A report from *The Scotsman* said that this team managed to 'surprise the French amazingly', though this could have been confusion caused by nearby mimes. They always look surprised. It's somehow their job.

In Germany Dresden English Football Club was founded in 1874, though the Germans didn't need the British influence for long. They formed a gigantic amount of amateur local leagues with regional champions then competing in play-offs to reach a national final in a typically rigorous test of a team's championship credentials. It wouldn't be until 1963 that the *Bundesliga* was formed, by which time they'd already won the World Cup. It would be unbelievable were it not so German.

In Italy a man named James Richardson Spensley introduced a football section to Genoa in 1886, who until then had been a cricket club set up to represent England abroad. Chaps on tour, what what! Another outfit, Torino Football and Cricket Club, arrived the next year. Concerned by the gulf in quality between foreign and Italian players, the powers that be split early Italian tournaments into two competitions: the Federal Championship, in which foreign players who lived in Italy could play; and the Italian Championship, in which only Italian players could compete. The Federal Championship's prize was the Spensley Cup. In 1908 this cup should have been won by Juventus but previous champions AC Milan simply refused to give it to them, confusingly handing it to Genoa rather than keeping it. Thankfully Italy's football authorities are now a bastion of credibility and have never since been associated with anything so completely and utterly ridiculous.

British workers also introduced the game to Spain. Legend has it that Seville were founded in a café on Burns Night, 1890, by a group of Scottish ex-pats and Spaniards after 'a deal of talk and a limited consumption of small beer', in a rare example of British people actually playing down how much they've had to drink in Spain.

In Bilbao groups of British steel and shipyard workers and Basque students returning from studying in England formed Bilbao Football Club, who would go on to become Athletic Bilbao. The club now famously employs the *cantera* policy of allowing only players born in the Basque region to represent the club, in a foreshadowing of future Brits abroad being kicked out of ex-pat bars for no doubt disgraceful behaviour while on holiday. That's more like it.

Football was taking hold everywhere. The first recorded match outside Europe was played in Buenos Aires, Argentina, in 1867 between two teams of British merchants. The first match in Brazil was arranged by a Scotsman named Thomas Donohoe in 1894. Soon after that Charles William Miller, the Brazilian-born son of another Scottish immigrant, returned from studying in Southampton armed with some footballs and a rule book. He introduced the game to São Paulo Athletic Club, one of many clubs that played a number of sports, founded a league and installed himself as their main striker. This may seem egotistical but, to be fair to him, they won the first three championships. Sports clubs were common in Brazil and Flamengo's football team came to exist only because a group of rowers from Fluminense decided they'd rather be footballers. The board told them they couldn't, not unreasonably, and they presented their proposal to Flamengo, who were fine with the idea. It's a tactic the modern player can't be far away from adopting . . .

'Boss, this season is getting really tough, so I've spoken to the lads and we've decided to become hoverboard racers instead.'

'Saido, get off that thing and give me forty press-ups.'

The Football League Kicks Off

Back in Blighty, the soft southern clubs were still in a huff about all this professionalism balderdash. Everyone else just got on with it. Preston North End were crowned champions of the inaugural Football League in 1889 without losing a game and also won the FA Cup, immediately setting an impossible standard for their sulky southern rivals.

Familiar names were starting to appear. In 1892 a second division was added to the league system. Woolwich Arsenal became the first London club to join the party and would later have the dubious honour of being supported by me. Liverpool entered the league in the same year. Tottenham Hotspur became the only ever non-league FA Cup winners, in 1901. Sheffield continued to be a hotbed of activity, with success coming for The Wednesday, as Sheffield Wednesday were then known, and Sheffield United – not Sheffield FC, in fact suggesting a lack of unity in the city's footballing circles. Newcastle United and Sunderland AFC were successful while Manchester City looked like they might become a powerhouse only for it to turn out that they'd been paying players £7 a week when the national wage limit was £4. This may not sound like a lot but it was still double what a skilled tradesman could earn. Complaints of footballers earning too much are nothing new. The FA sacked five of their directors and banned four players from ever playing for them again. This was a much harsher punishment than certain clubs receive for financial irregularities now, which basically amount to a framed certificate that says: 'Don't do it again £lol.'

International fixtures were also becoming increasingly popular, with the home nations regularly playing each other in highly competitive games. The FA were the only governing body in the world at the time and an invitation was extended to them to become part of a wider, international body. They rejected it out of hand, cocking a snook at such bunkum. Undeterred, the plucky, heroic administrators who'd made this invitation decided to go it alone. It was time for the real heroes of the piece to emerge . . .

Rules Are Rules

FIFA was founded in 1904, when Sepp Blatter was merely a twinkle in the eye of his father, Cthulhu Blatter. The FA would eventually accept FIFA's authority and join them only to leave again in a further row about professionalism. Great Britain had won Olympic gold in 1908 – fielding only English players – and again in 1912. In 1920 they lost to Norway after selecting a team of amateur players, whereas the Norwegians simply picked the best players they had available, the absolute dicks! The FA wanted the Olympics to remain amateur, FIFA wanted to push on and have a fully professional tournament of their own. The row got so bad that Great Britain didn't enter teams in the 1924 and 1928 tournaments. Eventually things settled down. Olympic football did remain amateur, for a time, FIFA got their tournament and they and the FA lived happily ever after. Sort of.

The FA certainly were stuffy back then. In 1921 they banned women's football because: 'The game of football is quite unsuitable for females and ought not to be encouraged.' Sadly, attitudes like this were common. In 1931 a Norwegian women's team, IF Fløya, wrote to the Norwegian FA asking to stage a series of fund-raising games. They received no reply so played one anyway, then swiftly received a haughty response saying: 'Ladies should not play football . . . the ladies could also get injuries that destroyed their reproductive organs.' Presumably back then all male Norwegian players had to wear penis guards as the male reproductive organs are at far greater risk.

War Stops Play

Some things are more important than football, like massive wars. On 4 August 1914 the First World War broke out, though it wasn't called that at the time. It later became known as the Great War, which is also inaccurate as by all accounts it was seriously shit for everyone involved. Incredibly the 1914/15 league season and FA Cup were played as normal despite outcry. It was widely believed that if football carried on then men of fighting age would prefer playing or watching it to living in a ditch and being shot at all day and night.

In the end there was, in fact, a whole battalion made up of footballers, called simply the Football Battalion. Bizarrely, they were formed after Arthur Conan Doyle, the creator of Sherlock Holmes, appealed specifically to footballers to enlist. They were led by one-time Aston Villa player Frank Buckley, who estimated that 500 of the 600 men who originally joined the battalion died. A modern equivalent would roughly be Benedict Cumberbatch convincing Gabby Agbonlahor to sign up to such responsibility. He's bad enough at closing down defenders.

For the rest of the war the FA suspended the league but allowed clubs to organise regional competitions, with every opportunity taken to convince those taking part to enlist. It became an effective propaganda tool. A children's football-themed pinball game from the time even featured the strange aim of getting the 'football' through the trenches and into Kaiser Wilhelm II's mouth. That showed him.

On Christmas Day, 1914, arguably the most famous game in history took place as troops from both sides met on no-man's land during an all too brief truce. The story goes that someone produced a ball from somewhere and a game ensued. Some historians are sceptical but there are accounts from both sides describing something similar. It even seems that this may have happened in a number of places across the battlefield. Soldiers did play behind the lines as a method of staying fit and keeping up morale so it's entirely possible that there would have been a ball to hand. While it's impossible to know, it's safe to assume that if any of these games did take place then Germany would have won. It's lucky that war can't go to penalties or the world might be very different.

The war ended in 1918, definitely ending all war for ever, everyone hoped. Football picked up where it had left off. In England the league system continued to expand and, in 1923, Wembley Stadium was opened. The first FA Cup final played there was between West Ham United and Bolton Wanderers and is known as the White Horse Final, not because either side featured a goal-scoring horse but because the match was so over-crowded that police had to intervene and an image of a no doubt confused white police horse was particularly striking. The official attendance was 126,047, with esti-mates of the actual figure being closer to 300,000. Bolton won 2–0 with many a thrown cap lost in the throng.

One of the scorers on the day, David Jack, would later move to Arsenal to play under one of the innovators of the time. Herbert Chapman won two league titles and one FA Cup with both Huddersfield Town and Arsenal and was one of the first managers to have full control of team affairs. Before this teams had largely been chosen by board members. Chapman also intro-duced numbered shirts, added hoops to Arsenal's socks so that the players could pick each other out – crucial in a time when everything was in black and white – and was an early advocate of floodlights, installing them at Highbury in 1932 despite them not being officially sanc-tioned for use in matches until the 1950s. He was also a pioneer of what might loosely be termed transfer shenanigans. In 1928 he set a world transfer record when he signed Jack from Bolton for £10,890. He held the negotiations in a hotel bar and instructed the staff, whom he knew, to give the Bolton representatives doubles of whatever they ordered while he drank gin and tonic that, in fact, contained no gin. As the Bolton men got increasingly drunk Chapman used the advantage of his sobriety to haggle them down to a price he considered to be a bargain. It was all a bit of a lark, and possibly a crime.

The first World Cup took place in 1930 in Uruguay. England refused to take part, believing it beneath them, and Uruguay went on to win it. The second World Cup took place in 1934 in Italy. England refused to take part, believing it beneath them, and Italy went on to win it. The third World Cup took place in 1938 in France. England refused to take part, by now probably realising that they should but not wanting to look silly, and Italy went on to win it, again. There would not be another until 1950 because, in 1939, that absolute prick Adolf Hitler rolled into Poland and the Second World War began. Football was officially suspended in September 1939, all players had their contracts terminated and the majority of clubs shut down. Regional leagues were set up to keep some semblance of the game running but few even completed a season. Stadiums were even repurposed to aid the war effort. Arsenal's Highbury was used as an Air Raid Precautions centre so they and Tottenham Hotspur had to share a ground in just one of the many tragedies of war.

Perhaps the most famous story of football in World War Two is that of the 'Death Match' involving FC Start, a team made up of former players from Dynamo and Lokomotiv Kyiv. There are many versions of the story, including one that features Sylvester Stallone in goal if the movie *Escape to Victory* is to be believed. What does seem clear is that the Start players worked in a bakery under occupation and beat a Nazi side called Flakelf 5–1. A rematch was ordered. The most well-known version of the story says that during the half-time break the players were threatened with execution should they win. Defiant, they won 5–3. One Start player rounded the German keeper, stopped the ball on the goal-line, turned around and kicked it back down the pitch in a show of contempt. Days later the players were arrested and shot. Various accounts say that there were no such threats and that, though some of the players were later arrested, this was not as a result of the match. Regardless, many were sent to camps and whatever the truth it makes a wet and windy, clichéd night in Stoke seem comparatively appealing.

The world took time to recover and so did football, naturally, it being part of said world. In 1950 the first post-war World Cup was held in Brazil, with Uruguay victorious in a final the hosts assumed they would win. Their disappointment led to what can only be described as a state of mourning, with some distraught fans even committing suicide. The experience gave rise to a phenomenon called the Phantom of '50, a fear of failure that strikes Brazil when they face Uruguay. Amongst it all a young Pelé promised his tearful father that he would win the World Cup for Brazil, which eight years later he did.

Despite not winning their maiden World Cup, England still considered themselves to be the global leaders of the game. This idea would come under intense scrutiny in 1953 when they hosted Hungary at Wembley. Known as the Mighty Magyars, the Hungarians were ranked first in the world but England, then third, had never lost to a team from outside the British Isles at home. The press dubbed it the Match of the Century. Hungary scored in the first minute. With twenty-seven minutes gone they were 4–1 up and they went on to win 6–3. Upper lips unstiffened, mouths sat agape and pipes teetered redundantly upon them. England had suffered a right old bamboozling and no mistake! It wouldn't happen again, though. They organised a rematch, in Hungary, only this time they'd be ready for the Magyars and their fancy tactics! They lost 7–1. It's said that the English players simply weren't as technically competent with the ball as their foreign counterparts, the correction of which the FA will be getting around to any day now.

At a stretch England could actually lay some claim to have influenced the style that had so roundly beaten them. An Englishman named Jimmy Hogan had been coaching in Austria when the First World War broke out and then spent time coaching the Hungarian side

MTK. He was known as a tactical innovator and his methods helped shape the football Hungary later played, itself a precursor to the Total Football that would later emerge. For his efforts abroad he was seen by some as a traitor. Great work everyone. Sándor Barcs, president of the Hungarian Football Federation, said after the game: 'Jimmy Hogan taught us everything we know about football . . . When our football history is told his name should be written in gold letters.' That Jimmy Hogan is largely unheard of is probably Barcs's fault. Gold lettering is prohibitively expensive. Sorry Jimmy, you're just having normal ink here, but well done all the same.

Eurovision

In 1948 Chile hosted the *Campeonato Sudamericano de Campeones*, or 'South American Championship of Champions' in English, which sounds lame and slightly wacky in comparison to its suave Spanish cousin. It was the precursor to the *Copa Libertadores*. French journalist Jacques Ferran was covering it for the newspaper *L'Equipe* and hit on the idea of doing exactly the same thing in Europe. UEFA loved the idea and with the trademark speed they still display today the first European Cup kicked off in 1955, a mere seven years later. Hibernian, made the semi-finals but the FA refused to allow England's champions,

Chelsea, to enter, reasoning that it could be bad for English football in general. In the short term they may have had a point. Real Madrid kept up a tradition left over from the days of the Franco regime by murdering everybody, winning the first five. They were finally defeated in Europe by Barcelona in the first round of the 1961 competition. Their fierce rivals would go all the way to the final before losing to Benfica at the Wankdorf Stadium in Bern, which it is absolutely necessary to mention here. European football became truly continental.

The fifties had been a tough time for English football. As well as international humblings from Hungary and the USA, the Munich air disaster claimed the lives of twenty-three people when Manchester United were returning from a European Cup match with Red Star Belgrade in 1958. Many of those who died were part of the team known as the 'Busby Babes', owing to manager Matt Busby's influence in ushering through the talented young players who made up much of the squad. They'd been expected to dominate for years to come. Recovery would be a long and difficult process.

English teams did begin to have some success in Europe, with Spurs becoming the first English team to win a European trophy with their Cup-Winners' Cup triumph in 1963. Two years earlier Spurs had become the first English side in the twentieth century to win the league and cup double. That year, 1961, was significant also because it marked the end to the cap on footballers' wages. Jimmy Hill, then head of the players' union, the PFA, had campaigned hard for this and the impact was immediate. So immediate that Hill's then Fulham team-mate Johnny Haynes became the first £100-a-week player (up from £20 a week) within hours of the rules changing. I hope he at least bought Hill a pint afterwards.

In international football 1960 brought the introduction of the European Championship, just forty-four years after those crazy, disorganised South Americans held their first *Copa América*. The four-team tournament was won by the Soviet Union. Brazil then won their second consecutive World Cup, in 1962, and in a little-remembered piece of classic pub quiz trivia England actually won the World Cup on home soil in 1966. This was obviously huge for England as, until this point, we'd been telling everyone that we were the best in the world at this game and we now finally had the proof to back it up. It still resonates now because we're part of a select few who've actually won the World Cup and it feels like if we did it once we can do it again . . . right? We're going to win it again before I die, right? Please? *Oh God, please let us actually win something else one day.*

In European club competitions, Spain, Portugal and Italy dominated until 1967, when Celtic beat Internazionale to became the first British club to win the European

Cup. Inter went 1–0 up with a seventh-minute penalty then set up to defend for the rest of the game, employing their famous *catenaccio* style. Undeterred, Celtic had a massive forty-three attempts on goal, eventually winning 2–1. All but one of the fifteen players in their squad had been born within ten miles of Celtic Park and the team earned the nickname of the Lisbon Lions. It is just one of many examples of football's weird obsession with comparing men to lions. Lions and eagles. You'd think they were the only hard creatures. The under representation of bears and sharks in particular is yet another illustration of how football still has a way to go before it can consider itself truly inclusive.

A year later the 1968 European Cup final was contested between Benfica and Matt Busby's Manchester United, ten years on from the tragedy of Munich. Survivors Bobby Charlton and Bill Foulkes featured and United also had a 22-year-old George Best in the team. They beat the Portuguese side 4–1 at Wembley. If the events of 1958 were a reminder that football is ultimately unimportant, 1968 was a reminder that it can still be incredibly powerful.

The World's Favourite Game

Football was now in a golden period in terms of both popularity and quality. Brazil again won the World Cup in 1970 with a team widely considered to be one of the most entertaining of all time. In the Netherlands, Ajax gave us Total Football. It's worth pointing out here that if you add the prefix 'Dutch' to anything it makes it sound dirty – a Dutch tango, a Dutch car park, a Dutch penis – so you're just going to have to be mature for a bit.

Ajax held a Dutch carnival (behave) between 1971 and 1973. They won the European Cup in 1971 and '72 – a year in which they won four trophies overall – winning every single home game they played in both seasons, then won their third European Cup in a row in '73. Their style was simple in theory but difficult in practice. Allow me to explain. Every player is absolutely brilliant in every position so they're completely comfortable in any situation and then you're brilliant and you win everything. That is as sound a tactical summary of it as you're ever likely to read. The Dutch linchpin (stop it) was Johan Cruyff. One of the most technically gifted players ever, Cruyff was ostensibly a forward but had so much ability that he could damage teams all over the pitch. Jan Olsson, the Swedish defender he tricked with his famous Cruyff turn at the 1974 World Cup, said: 'That moment against Cruyff was the proudest moment of my career . . . I was not humiliated. I had no chance. Cruyff was a genius.'

Evidently, Cruyff tricked him so comprehensively that he immediately fell victim to a very appropriate kind of Stockholm syndrome.

Ajax boss Rinus Michels built his side in such a way that Cruyff's team-mates would always be ready to accommodate his roaming. They refined the system to perfection and the rest of the world gawped on in envy, unable to do anything about it. Until the Germans did. No doubt irked by this Dutch threesome of European Cups (come on . . .) they ruined it by beating them in the 1974 World Cup final. Bayern Munich then followed Ajax's treble by winning three European Cups in a row themselves, before a period of English dominance it's hard to believe was real. English teams won the next six finals. Liverpool, who established themselves as one of the most dominant sides ever, won two in a row, Nottingham Forest then did the same, Liverpool won another and then Aston Villa rounded it off.

Even having lived through a period in which English clubs had sustained success in Europe earlier in this century it's hard for someone of my generation to fathom this, especially based on the reputations players had then. If the stories are to be believed they were basically drinking clubs that liked a bit of football as a livener before they got down to the serious stuff.

The 1970s were a successful – and boozy – period in English football but things were far from perfect. Rarely will you hear the words 'West Bromwich Albion made history' but West Bromwich Albion made history in 1978 when they became the first British team to field three black players in the same side: Laurie Cunningham,

Brendon Batson and Cyrille Regis. That seems ridiculous now, because it was. Their manager Ron Atkinson dubbed them the Three Degrees, which sounds un-PC but was sadly just the tip of the idiotic mahogany iceberg. They were subjected to regular abuse – they would have fruit thrown at them and Cunningham even had a petrol bomb thrown through his front door – but with an incredible defiance all three played with a skill and dignity that helped pave the way for the more multicultural game we now have.

Time rolled on into the 1980s and this was another turbulent period. In England hooliganism was such a problem that the popularity of the game began to decline, in part because of the not unwarranted negative associations. At the 1985 European Cup final thirty-nine people died at the Heysel Stadium in Brussels when a wall collapsed before Liverpool and Juventus played out one of the most haunting games in the history of sport. The aftermath led to English teams being banned from European competition for five years, with Liverpool banned for six. It is understandably looked upon as a very dark period, probably not helped by movies that romanticise the act of kicking someone's head in because of the colours of their scarf.

Thankfully, when things are looking grim domestically, there's always the World Cup. The 1986 version produced one of the defining individual tournament performances from the magical feet and dastardly hands of one Diego Armando Maradona. Even with a great such as Johan Cruyff still large in the memory, the received wisdom was that Pelé was the greatest player of all time. Diego was not having this. His genius cannot be put into words, squeezed into YouTube clips or demanded by final notices from the Italian government, who, in 2013, reckoned he owed them £33 million in unpaid taxes. He was worth it. At the 1982 World Cup in Spain he'd been repeatedly kicked out of games by opponents eager to nullify him. In 1986 he had something to prove and this was when he was at his most dangerous. In the quarter-final against England he famously punched one goal into the net then dribbled the ball around half the team from the halfway line for another. In a sense the national team are still recovering from being mugged off to this almost celestial standard.

Back in Italy he immediately led unfashionable Napoli – it was the eighties, all shoulder pads and mullets, everyone was unfashionable – to the *Serie A* title, beginning the most successful period in their history. In brilliantly Italian style Napoli fans held mock funerals for Juventus and AC Milan, burning coffins just in case their message was too subtle. Milan survived, though, becoming the last side to win back-to-back European Cups, which they did in 1989 and 1990 under former shoe salesman Arrigo Sacchi, who built a defence as impenetrable as the Roman army's.

In 1989 tragedy would strike English football again when overcrowding led to a crush that saw 96 Liverpool supporters lose their lives during an FA Cup semi-final between Liverpool and Nottingham Forest at Sheffield Wednesday's Hillsborough stadium. It is endlessly appalling that blame for the tragedy was placed on the very people it struck owing to the incompetent and reprehensible actions of South Yorkshire Police. It's a disaster that still looms large over football and yet the truth has only recently been admitted. The tragedy led to the Taylor Report, which in turn led to the all-seat stadiums of today. Football is still not perfect but it is much safer now than it was then, both in terms of the stadiums in which it takes place and the atmosphere inside them. So English football was in a difficult period but it wouldn't last . . .

In the early 1990s Italy was still the place to be. Italia '90 had been a great success – Gazza's tears, England's glorious failure and, to a lesser degree, Gary Lineker literally shitting himself against Ireland helped to restore interest in the game in England.

In 1992 came the formation of the Premiership, as the Premier League was then called, and the European Cup became the Champions League. Sky TV struck an exclusive deal to show the games and suddenly there was blanket coverage and swooshing noises to accompany replays, as long as you were willing to pay to have a satellite dish stuck on your house. Back then most people had only four TV channels, unimaginable now. If you were lucky enough to get Sky you instantly had hundreds of channels to explore, ones that featured weird shopping channel hosts, loads of sport and *The Simpsons*. It was like suddenly being American.

This is when my clearest memories begin, which I guess makes me a child of the Premier League generation, as many of you will be. Leeds United were the last team to win the First Division and I have no memory of it at all. Sorry about that Leeds, though, to be fair, you have bigger problems. We all lived this and you'll have your own highlights and lowlights of this period but let's indulge in some nostalgia. Maybe put on '*Three Lions*' or something. This is how I remember it happening . . .

Alex Ferguson's Manchester United dominated the decade despite resistance from Arsenal and Blackburn Rovers, who, with one title-winning season, doomed a generation of glory hunters who couldn't locate Blackburn on a map to a lifetime of regret.

In Europe Johan Cruyff was back, moulding Barcelona in his image and creating the Dream Team, featuring Romário, Hristo Stoichkov, Michael Laudrup, Ronald Koeman and Pep Guardiola. They played an updated type of Total Football that led many to declare them the greatest Barcelona team ever. Guardiola had even bigger plans.

The celebrity footballer was nothing new but in the nineties it reached a different level. George Best had been known as 'El Beatle' in the sixties and in the seventies Kevin Keegan even released a number of singles – one of which charted at number two despite a midweek lead of twelve sales points, probably, before later being withdrawn as it was made of highly flammable asbestos, probably – but in the nineties the David Beckham effect gave birth to the cult of celebrity we still have. He combined an awareness of his own brand with actually being really good at football and became a phenomenon. He married a pop star, wore a sarong and now we have Martin Skrtel and Adam Lallana trying to flog us moisturiser. Thanks, Dave.

Not that it was all easy. At the 1998 World Cup Beckham was sent off against Argentina for kicking out at Diego Simeone, who appeared to think he'd stepped on a landmine, and the press vilified him. *The Sun* used the headline 'Ten brave lions, one stupid kid'. Again with the lions. He would bounce back, winning an historic treble the next season, before Ferguson kicked a boot into his face and sold him. Odd how things pan out.

Beckham would move to Real Madrid in 2003, becoming part of one of the most significant projects of the decade, the *Galácticos* – which, let's be honest, is just a slightly different way of saying 'Dream Team'. Madrid's president Darth Florentino Pérez would add one expensive star to his team each year, with Beckham joining Ronaldo, Luis Figo, Roberto Carlos and Zinedine Zidane at the club. During the *Galácticos* era Madrid were successful – they won the Champions League in 2002 as well as a number of *La Liga* titles – but they were also farcical. Hell-bent on dictating transfer policy, Pérez was like a kid entrusted with the big shop, just buying sweets and crisps, neglecting to even look at the defenders aisle and letting the perfectly good Claude Makélélé he had in the fridge go to waste.

As Madrid descended into farce Barcelona regrouped through the brilliance of Ronaldinho, apparently rejected by Real Madrid as he was 'so ugly he'd sink you as a brand' if a newspaper quote attributed to 'an associate' of Pérez is to be believed. It probably isn't but it genuinely reflects the way Madrid did business at the time.

In 2005 Liverpool shocked the world by rolling back the years and coming from 3–0 down to win the Champions League final in one of the most memorable feats of the decade. It came just a year after Greece provided the other one by inexplicably beating Portugal on home soil to win Euro 2004, introducing the world to the phenomenon of Cristiano Ronaldo crying after losing a big match, which happened a lot for a while.

English teams began to find success in Europe, though that has not been so much the case in recent years, and the Premier League continued to grow in popularity to firmly establish itself as the monster it is today. Clubs started to go on pre-season tours of far-flung places to get new fan bases hooked on the product. In Spain, Barcelona and Real Madrid moved into the Lionel Messi v Cristiano Ronaldo era that will surely be viewed with astonishment in the future. They've each set so many records during their intense rivalry that it can't be long before we see Messi attempting to become the first player to score a hat-trick while wearing a beard of bees or Ronaldo trying to devour the most hot dogs ever eaten in one sitting while setting a record for kick-ups with the world's biggest rubber band ball during half-time of *El Clásico*.

It took football a long time to turn into the global phenomenon it is today. It's hard to know what the future holds. Perhaps the Premier League's riches will make things like Leicester City's incredible title-winning season of 2015-16 the norm. Maybe it will just inflate the transfer market and leave things exactly as they are but with more zeroes on the end. Perhaps the much-touted European Super League will become a reality. Maybe the rich, emerging leagues in China and the Middle East will start to become major players on a global scale. The Chinese may well want their game back, after all. Whatever happens, however different the game may become, those of us who are hooked will remain hooked, that's how it works. There's just something irresistible about balls.

2. Media

Luke Aaron Moore

In the beginning, football was pure and true and, one assumes, uncorrupted by such trivialities as media commitments, image rights and TV deals. Well, one doesn't need to assume because obviously none of those things existed. For years, details of results, scorers and league tables were communicated to cloth-cap-wearing manual labourers by eight-year-old newspaper boys shouting 'Read all about it!' in a high-pitched voice with a cockney accent, and the best way to see an interview with a player was to head down to his local and buy him a pint of mild. But not too late, mind. He'd be up early to head down the pit and couldn't stay out all night chatting.

Then something seismic happened on 1 January 1927 – the BBC received a Royal Charter, which meant it was able to broadcast live sporting events for the first time and subsequently the first radio commentary of a football game was broadcast. That's right. For the first time in history, football fans were able to listen to a man with a beautifully plummy, received pronunciation accent describe a full football match from start to finish without the haunting spectre of a Robbie Savage-led angry phone-in afterwards.

And how do I know the very first radio sports commentator had a 'beautifully plummy, received pronunciation accent'? Well, portions of his oeuvre still exist in the BBC archives and, if you haven't heard them, his name was Captain Henry Blythe Thornhill Wakelam, which should probably tell you everything you need to know about his style and delivery. Again, Robbie Savage he was not.

It turns out Thornhill Wakelam was quite a character. A captain in the Army, he started out as a rugby player and actually delivered a rugby commentary for radio earlier in 1927, well before he commentated on football for the first time. He remained a dedicated rugby man for his entire life. He also commentated on a number of sports throughout his career and a highlight of his professional work was undoubtedly when accidentally setting fire to his notes during a tennis match at Wimbledon in the 1930s. Now, I have no idea how he managed to do that (I'm tempted to suggest ash falling from his pipe; it was the 1930s, after all) but apparently the great man carried on as if nothing had happened anyway and very few, if any, listeners noticed. The BBC was clearly not the health and safety minefield then that it is today.

In fact, radio commentary would have undoubtedly happened even earlier than 1927 had it not been for the newspaper industry. Guglielmo Marconi invented what he called the 'wireless telegraph' in 1895 and received a British patent for the technology in 1897 before development continued apace. Yacht race results were being reported by radio as early as 1898. However, the newspaper industry, terrified at the thought of dwindling circulation of their dailies in the face of new technology (sound familiar?), were able to lobby and block the adoption of radio commentary in football until a good twenty-nine years later.

The first game that Wakelam covered for the BBC and the keen-eared masses was a 1–1 draw between Arsenal and Sheffield United at Highbury, by the way. So it's comforting to know that it's not just in the last ten years that the Gunners have found a way to be underwhelming. But the past can occasionally seem a completely foreign land – Newcastle won the old First Division that year by five points from Huddersfield Town in second, something the Magpies have singularly failed to do since.

Of course, the big development post-radio was television. In 1926, a full three years before Captain Wakelam was doing his thing on the radio at Highbury, in a laboratory in a house in Soho, London, John Logie Baird was able to first demonstrate television to members of the Royal Institution. He would later be recognised in Britain as the father of the medium, something he would be rewarded for by being voted the forty-forth greatest Briton in a public poll conducted by the BBC in 2002, just two places above Boy George and a full eight below Sir Steve Redgrave. That's gratitude for you.

Seriously, take some time to appreciate that. The UK public in their infinite wisdom have decided that the man who essentially fathered an invention that has now extended to be a part of everyday life for around a billion people is only two notches on the ladder of success above the man who sang *Karma Chameleon*, and eight notches *below* a man that could row a boat quite fast. It beggars belief.

Luckily for Baird, he died in 1946, a full fifty-six years before the publishing of the list and so would never have to suffer the ignominy.

Anyway, I digress. It's fair to say television took off. There are just under a billion TV sets in the world as I write this, and that doesn't include other devices that are capable of broadcasting such as mobile phones, laptops and tablets. The very first football game to be broadcast on TV happened in 1937, and it was those north Londoners again, Arsenal, who were the beneficiaries. The BBC showed a specially arranged game between Arsenal and Arsenal Reserves on 16 September of that year, and the first international match (between

England and Scotland, who else?) followed soon afterwards.

The FA Cup final was broadcast for the first time in 1938, on 30 April, as Preston beat Huddersfield with a goal in the last minute of extra-time in a game that featured a certain Bill Shankly, a man who would later go on to influence the game as we now know it in more ways than one – not least in the shape of all those motivational quotes that now pepper internet forums and Facebook memes. But again, more on all of that later on.

Incidentally, that FA Cup final was presumably broadcast without any sort of presenter, commentator or punditry – at least I can't find evidence of any – so not only did the members of the public who were able to afford a television get to see a game for the first time, they didn't even have to get annoyed by Andy Townsend afterwards. Halcyon days, indeed.

In 1989, Tim Berners-Lee (ninety-ninth on the BBC's Greatest Britons list, thirteen places below Bono and twenty-two below Robbie Williams. Seriously, the INVENTOR OF THE INTERNET!) brought the World Wide Web, now known as the internet, to the fore. Fast-forward to 2016 and there are a staggering three billion regular users of his invention, which is now the largest source of information in the world, making it even harder to understand why none of my brilliant jokes on Twitter get any traction.

So, that potted history over a few pages brings us up to the modern day. Of course, the reason I've not gone into all these developments in huge detail is because there is so much to talk about in the present. Football has gone from a pastime conducted on a Saturday afternoon in your local area with like-minded individuals to an ever-present, ever-evolving twenty-four-hour pantomime set inside a huge circus, and the modern media has made it impossible for any of us to miss a single beat.

From twenty-four-hour rolling news channels all over the world to the internet, and from more than 150 live games shown each season just in the top-flight in England alone to countless radio phone-ins, YouTube channels and fan forums, we truly now live in the football age. It permeates every level of our discourse and consciousness; it's a wonder any of us get anything done. In fact, thinking about it, do we actually get anything done? Maybe that's why the economy's in the toilet and has been since 2008. It wasn't a financial crisis, it was football's ability to finally invade every single part of our collective lives and stop us concentrating on the important stuff.

We should probably start thinking about how to sort it out. The problem is, I'm way too busy watching backheeled goals from the Argentinian second division on Vine to dedicate any time to it at the moment.

It's probably possible to conclude that these days the media is almost as important as the game itself – one can hardly exist without the other. Football owes its very livelihood to the money it receives from TV networks and, at the last count, that amounted to just over £5 billion for the right to show the Premier League from 2016–19 in the UK alone. With those TV networks then subsequently beholden to the amount of subscriptions and viewers they can attract, both rely on the other for their very survival.

So first then, let's look at that age-old messenger of what the great Pelé called the Beautiful Game – television. And he should know all about TV; he's done about a million adverts, including one for erectile dysfunction pills. There's a sort of macabre symmetry in the fact that the greatest footballer of all time is also the corporate world's greatest shill. If that doesn't sum up the modern game (we love it, but we have to pay a lot for it, too) then I don't know what does.

Television

Television has come a long way since our mate John Logie Baird did his thing for the world way back in the twenties. I imagine he had pretty high hopes for the medium back then and, in absolute fairness, his invention (or at least his part in it) did genuinely change the world and people are generally more connected, informed and inspired than they ever were because of that little box in the corner of the room. And, just as he never lived to see the disrespect handed to him by the Great British public in 2002, thankfully he also didn't make it long enough to watch a Jim White 'Transfer Deadline Day' on Sky Sports News. And I, for one, am hugely grateful for that.

When it comes to football on television, though, there really is only one place to start, and while the game started to be covered regularly in the form of highlights as far back as 1955 and an ill-fated attempt to broadcast games live fell foul of Tottenham and Arsenal (yes, them again) refusing to allow permission for cameras to be present at their respective grounds in 1961, it was in 1964 that the landscape was to change for ever.

Match of the Day was first broadcast on 22 August that year and featured, unbelievably, yet another Arsenal game. This time they played Liverpool at Anfield in a game that finished 3–2 to the hosts and, although the amount of people that watched it was only around half the amount that were actually in the stadium that afternoon, a national institution was born. Save for a few years in the mid-2000s when ITV took the rights to top-flight highlights (and if you weren't 'lucky' enough to witness ITV's *The Premiership* first-hand, keep it that way – I've got four words for you: 'Andy Townsend's Tactics Truck'), it's been on the old gogglebox ever since. In fact, even when the BBC lost the rights to ITV for a few years, they were still able to keep *Match of the Day* on air for FA Cup games, and so really it's never been away.

Of course, along with all this came presenters, commentators and pundits, all of whom are a staple of the game in 2016. It's impossible to imagine a live game or highlights on TV without the human book-end that is the pundit or the conversational steward that is the commentator and his co-commentating friend. And before I lower the tone of the discourse by saying 'Yes, it is impossible to imagine watching a game without a commentator, but sometimes I'd love to give it a go', a more charitable way of approaching the subject of football media men (and they are invariably men, with a few notable exceptions) is to say that they are, at best, a 'mixed bag'.

Before we go into the different presenting personnel that make up the modern football broadcast, though, it's important that we acknowledge the sheer impact that *Match of the Day* has made on football and culture in the UK over the years. To be on air consistently for more than fifty years is some achievement and even in the modern day, where it's pretty much impossible to avoid the day's top-flight football results with a view to watching the highlights fresh on a Saturday night, it still plays an important role. *Match of the Day* in 2016 is like your favourite uncle – he loves football and he's always been there. Hopefully he always will be.

Commentators

Let's start with commentators. Some of the older readers among you may insist that the greatest football commentator of all was the late, great Kenneth Wolstenholme. Now, while I concede that 'Some people are on the pitch, they think it's all over . . . it is now!' has a very special place in the pantheon of commentary, not least because of the event it was a part of – the only time that England have ever, and probably will ever, win a World Cup – the title of greatest football commentator obviously belongs to Barry Davies. He had the perfect balance of complementing the action, never outstaying his welcome and also never attempting to make the occasion all about him in that self-aggrandising way that modern commentators are occasionally prone to. He was the perfect accompaniment to a football match, and it's a real shame that he no longer commentates on football.

There isn't the space or time to go into detail about some of Davies's finest moments on the microphone, but there are worse ways to spend an afternoon than firing up YouTube and listening to his work – the man could bring something to any occasion. I'd have him commentating on my weekly shop if I could. 'Just look at the way he shimmied down the bread aisle, past the cakes, before coming to a perfect stop at the checkout. Magnificent.' Seriously, the potential to enhance one's life with Barry Davies doing a sort of permanent voice-over is endless.

Sadly, it's fairly hard to think of a commentator these days with the panache of the great man. John Motson, the man Davies was essentially sidelined in favour of, should have been put out to pasture a while back and has long been a parody of the great broadcaster he was twenty-five years ago. The man deserves respect – he's been a part of the *Match of the Day* furniture since the seventies – but this is a slow, lingering retirement and not one that has been particularly edifying to witness. I still shudder at the conversation that occurred on BBC Radio 5 Live recently in which he was absolutely incredulous that the latest England kit had mauve sleeves. 'Mauve?! MAUVE?!' he exclaimed repeatedly until, I assume, the producer turned his microphone down and everyone could move on. As you read this, he'll be sat in a coffee shop somewhere, in his trademark sheepskin coat and glasses, poring over his notebooks, silently shaking his head and occasionally muttering 'Mauve?!' to himself over and over again.

Sky Sports' Martin Tyler is probably the closest we have to a living, breathing national institution still at the top of his broadcasting game, but part of me thinks he's too much of a company man to be the real deal. I prefer to think of commentators up in the gantry like mad old colonels in some far-flung exotic outpost, ostensibly playing by the rules but in reality doing things their way. Yeah, those part-timers in the safe, warm studio are all well and good, but can they add drama and circumstance to a big football game when sat in a windy and cold gantry, fifty-odd feet in the air? I think not. Leave that to the big boys.

So then, the best commentators are anti-heroes but I get the impression that, despite now being in his seventies, Tyler still has way too much respect for authority. The rules are sacrosanct to Tyler; you don't get to stay at Sky Sports for twenty-six years and counting by rocking the boat.

All that said, though, he's undoubtedly a safe pair of hands – it's hard to think of any error the man has made in all his years on Sky Sports – and he's also more than capable of the odd iconic commentary moment (another must in the skillset of the best in the genre), not least the Manchester City 'Agueroooooo!' moment when Roberto Mancini's team won the Premier League on the final day thanks to a last-gasp winner against Queens Park Rangers at the Etihad Stadium.

So, on balance, maybe Martin Tyler isn't the commentator we want, but the commentator we need. I imagine we'll all miss him when he's gone; maybe he's the Gilberto Silva of football commentary. I maintain, though, that the stage is set for a new, hungry, talented young gun to swoop in and make the next generation his own. But I'll tell you one thing, I'm absolutely certain it isn't Darren Fletcher.

Co-commentators

As a co-commentator you have one role – to add analysis and colour to the commentator's description of the game as it unfolds. Co-commentary is, I imagine, a role that is a lot harder than it looks; you have to provide something new and interesting each time an event within a game takes place. If you get it wrong you look like you're stating the obvious or just filling the silence, and if you get it really wrong you sound like you're not even watching the same game as the viewing public. If you get it really, really wrong, you're probably Michael Owen.

Ex-wonderkid striker and horse-botherer Owen has really taken on the mantle of the world's worst co-commentator with aplomb since Andy Townsend hung up his funny-shaped microphone (and took up a job on the radio, in which he is actually markedly better). That's some effort when we take into account that, technically, Robbie Savage is also a co-commentator. I remain unconvinced that Savage is anything other than an experiment gone awry; a Universal Soldier-type project but involving ex-footballers instead of hardened special forces operatives. The battlefield isn't the Vietnam War, it's the Premier League. It's almost as if BT Sport tried to secretly develop a weapon so potent it would finally end the Sky Sports hegemony, but it went so wrong that Robbie Savage was the result and now no one can stop him.

But anyway, back to Mickey Owen. It's almost as if, in the midst of straining every sinew to be the world's fastest, jinkiest mini-forward in his playing days, he forgot to take the time to learn how to speak as an adult. Let's just say poor old Michael was always assumed to be a less-than-interesting man before he decided to move into media, and we were all quick to get confirmation when he did finally make the transition.

And it's not as though he's actually even just boring on co-commentary when he furnishes us with his thoughts for BT Sport. It's more that he is boring and confusing (not to mention odd) in almost equal measure.

Let us please take this opportunity to assess what is, in this writer's view at least, his crowning contribution to televisual broadcasting in the twenty-first century. There have been many broadcasting faux pas uttered by Owen over the years, but this truly is a line that I challenge you to read without furrowing your brow, creasing up with laughter or a combination of the two.

It was around the start of 2014 and Owen was co-commentating for BT Sport when he uttered the immortal line about a forward attempting, unsuccessfully, to nip in on goal for a scoring chance:

'It was a good run, but it was a poor run, if you know what I mean.'

No Michael, we don't know what you mean. No one is ever going to know what you mean. I feel like all of us could live for a thousand lifetimes and never even get close to understanding what you mean by that. Now please leave us alone. We're all paying £19.99 a month for this.

Presenters

What do we want from a football presenter? Well, in short, a comforting presence, a safe pair of hands, someone non-intrusive who can steward us through all the best action as it transpires, and finally someone who asks the right questions from the assorted pundits on the opposite sofa.

Since Des Lynam, Gary Lineker has assumed the mantle of best in the business, on domestic television at least. Lineker gives off an impression that he knows much more than he lets on, and on the rare occasions he's been given the opportunity has shown himself to be an astute pundit, too.

There are other presenters who play the role with aplomb (David Jones, Ed Chamberlin et al) but, given the nature of their role – wallpaperish, sort of comforting yet instantly forgettable at the same time – it's difficult to accurately assess them and their contribution. They tend to be a sort of giant gleaming smile in a decent suit. As football fans, we don't really want to remember them anyway, we want to remember the football. Presenters are facilitators to the action, a sort of human delivery mechanism.

It would be remiss of me to let this section pass without a mention for erstwhile Sky Sports anchor Richard Keys. While obviously a talented and experienced presenter, the fire he had in his belly to be the world's most embarrassing uncle just refused to be extinguished and eventually won out in the war for his heart. With Andy Gray, a man who would win first, second and third in a 'world's most baked-potato-resembling human' awards, he was part of the world's most cringeworthy double act, a pair who, when they weren't making wildly inappropriate overtures to any cognitive life-form that vaguely resembled a woman, actually thought their contributions to football media were as important (if not more so) than the football itself. And again, that's a key point to remember when we're assessing presenters, pundits and commentators – they should never usurp or attempt to usurp the football itself.

Presenters of football programming should be seen, heard and afterwards almost instantly forgotten, something that anyone who's seen the cache of Keys and Gray 'behind the scenes' videos on the internet will find it singularly impossible to do.

Punditry

This is a thorny issue. Everyone has their favourite pundit, everyone has an idea of what they think makes a good pundit and every football fan thinks that 90 per cent of pundits are total and utter shit – possibly because they once said something mean about the team they happen to support or, in their playing days, relegated their team with a last-minute goal, injured their favourite player with a bad tackle, or kissed the badge of a rival team one too many times.

Safe to say, it's probably pretty hard to be a pundit. You generally don't get much time to say anything meaningful, and the sheer volume of games on TV makes it hard to be original when you're sat in on your 400th broadcast that year. That said, the fact that it feels so refreshing when a genuinely good pundit comes along probably means that the overall standard is quite poor. Nevertheless, they fall into quite distinct categories and I think here, in these pages, it's important to establish what they are.

Before we get into this, it's important to remember that some pundits will fall into more than one category, and this is in no way meant to serve as a definitive list. It's just an example of the basic types you can expect to find.

The Angry Ex-Pro

This is a man permanently on the edge. Any incident could set him off, whether it be a comment from a fellow pundit he disagrees with, an on-field incident (usually a player not tackling hard enough or 'taking responsibility') or a refereeing decision. The Angry Ex-Pro has unfinished business that he knows he can never rectify because he isn't a player any more. This also annoys him, so he tries to sate his base instincts by being a pundit and getting as close to the action as he can, all the while knowing deep-down that no tell-all autobiography or newspaper article is ever going to quench that thirst for confrontation.

Graeme Souness, Roy Keane.

The Nice Guy

To these chaps, football is meant to be a celebration. They like nothing better than reminiscing about the old days, chatting with Adrian Chiles about a ball boy falling over during the game and celebrating a meaningless England win in a friendly at home against inferior opposition. They're generally terrible when it comes to actual insight, but the viewer will usually forgive them because of their boundless enthusiasm. These men are human Labradors – they just like to be out of the house, and who can blame them? Football is invariably brilliant and they're lucky enough to have played the game for a living – something that will keep them happy for the rest of their natural lives.

Ian Wright, Paul Merson, Chris Kamara, Ray Wilkins.

The Outdated, Confused Old Guard

These guys remember when the game was a lot simpler and they weren't expected to keep up with new-fangled inventions and developments such as Prozone, Twitter, websites, statistics and foreign players coming over here and stealing our left-back berths. These aren't necessarily the oldest pundits, just the most entrenched, stubborn ones who refuse to move with the times. The absolute apex of this breed was when Mark Lawrenson responded to the news that a man-of-the-match award for an England game he was co-commentating on was decided by an online poll. You know, on the internet. His one-word response? 'Geeks.'

It was 2008, a good eight years after the dot-com bubble. Still, at least Lawro wasn't voted above Tim Berners-Lee in the Greatest Britons list.

These individuals are also occasionally referred to, by their peers, as 'Proper Football Men'.

Mark Lawrenson, Peter Reid, Harry Redknapp, Tim Sherwood, Alan Hansen.

The Out-of-Work Manager Looking For a Way Back Into the Game

Now, before you accuse me of making this category up just to include a mention of Alan Curbishley (who has inexplicably been out of a managerial role since 2008, despite being seen as a safe pair of hands up until that point. I'm starting to wonder if there is another reason for his continued absence), there are many examples of this particular pundit, and it's undoubtedly the most depressing category.

Essentially the out-of-work manager will spend his entire time on the pundits' sofa trying to shoehorn his credentials and track record into any and every conversation that comes up in a desperate attempt to issue what's known in tabloid language (more on that later) as a 'come-and-get-me plea', just in case a football club chairman is watching. For example:

Presenter: 'And a lovely finish by Sergio Aguero, there.'

Out-of-work manager: 'Yeah, it was. And it's strange to think that my West Ham side were the only team to keep him quiet in the 2012/13 season, a season in which we only conceded 37 goals, which is fewer than a goal a game. I think I've shown that if you need a manager who can keep things tight at the back, I'm your man. I've only been relegated once as a manager.'

Presenter: 'Er, thanks for that. Up after the break, it's Newcastle v Swansea.'

The man who took this to a whole new level, through no fault of his own, was Gus Poyet. He was sacked from his role as Brighton and Hove Albion manager live on BBC Three while covering a Confederations Cup match after a member of the production staff handed him a print-out of a club statement during the broadcast. Now that's the sort of real-time news that Sky Sports News would kill for.

Mick McCarthy, Peter Reid, Gus Poyet (once, in situ), Alan Pardew, Sam Allardyce and, of course, Alan Curbishley.

The New Breed

These are the new kids on the block, the One Direction of football punditry, the men who make members of all other categories quake in their loafers. These young men of the future not only contribute to Twitter, they actually understand it as well. They use the big TV screen that Ed Chamberlin stands next to with ease; they drag and drop lines, arrows and circular icons representing players all over the pitch without a second thought. They also wear nice new suits, don't look like they live in the back of their car, and occasionally offer genuine insight, too. Of course, they also find plenty of time to say really stupid things. I'm looking at you, Jamie Redknapp. But hey, no one's perfect.

And you can't tell me that, after Euro 2016, Gary Neville isn't dreaming all day and all night about returning to Ed Chamberlin's warm embrace. Go to him Gary.

Gary Neville, Jamie Redknapp, Jamie Carragher, Jermaine Jenas.

Pitchside/Post-Game Reporters

Before we move on, it's important to spare a thought or two for the hardy souls that spend the entirety of match days skulking around the stadium looking for an angle, an insight, a titbit of information that they can furnish the big boys in the studio with. Naturally, though, it rarely works out that way and pitchside reporters rarely offer anything beyond the blindingly obvious, because how could they?

If a player goes off injured – and I hate to be the one to break this to you – Andy Burton and Geoff Shreeves aren't medical professionals so they can't tell you how bad the injury is. What's more, if a manager makes a tactical substitution, he's unlikely to tell an ex-estate agent (Shreeves) or an objectionable man-child in a bad suit (Burton) why he's done it. Let's face it, he's probably got other things on his mind.

The role of pitchside reporter is essentially pointless, then. Still, at least they have the post-match interviews and press conference to look forward to, at which they have the opportunity to be patronised by football managers and players who are at best indifferent to them and at worst actively despise them. It's a funny old game, but not for them. These are the men in exile, the poor individuals on the fringes, the margins, the match-day hinterlands of the broadcast. There exists only one rung on the outsiders' ladder further down than the Pitchside/ Post-Game Reporter, and that's the poor men out in the regions who have to contribute to the subject that's been haunting this chapter since its very inception – Sky Sports News's Transfer Deadline Day.

Sky Sports News

Seeing as though, in the last few years, Sky Sports News has become this lumbering, all-encompassing carnival of nonsense, I thought it prudent to give it its own section. There is one main reason for this and that is the modern phenomenon known as Transfer Deadline Day.

For two days a year, one at the end of January and one later in the year, usually at the end of August, Sky Sports News has a day off from running interviews with second division cricketers and journeymen boxers on an endless loop in between adverts for personal injury protection, and provides live, non-stop coverage of the final day of the transfer window (the adverts for personal injury protection still exist on these days by the way, because not a day goes past when they don't feature on that channel).

Of course, Sky Sports News isn't put off by the fact that well in excess of 90 per cent of all activity on Transfer Deadline Day is boring, irrelevant and contains players (and sometimes even clubs) that no one's ever even heard of. They press on with the carnival regardless, milking it for all it's worth, right up to the deadline and beyond, like a sort of charity telethon in which absolutely no one benefits, with the exception of players' agents, obviously.

The ringmaster of this absolute circus is a Scotsman by the name of Jim White. Jim, who has the appearance of a suntanned bollock with a big grin drawn on it and tends to be absolutely caked in studio make-up, treats this broadcast as his own personal Christmas Day after a year in which he has been a very good boy indeed. He quite literally shouts and yelps his way through every single rumour, transfer and move whether it happens to be Cristiano Ronaldo heading to Paris St Germain for a record transfer fee, or Ryan Brunt moving from Bristol Rovers to York City on loan. It really is apocalyptic television in which every tiny incident is inflated to gigantic proportions in a bid to justify its own existence.

The supporting cast of Transfer Deadline Day tends to be several men, all between the ages of thirty and sixty, reporting from various locations around the country trying to get the big scoop on any moves that may have happened during the day. It's not immediately clear why they do it – I've yet to see someone break a story by standing out on the street in the general location of a football club, the chief reason being that most businesses tend to conduct their affairs, you know, *inside*.

What those reporters can expect to be met with during their ten-hour stints out in the cold is several men and children (women are almost always sensibly absent) gathering around them, making faces, shouting annoying slogans and generally making life hard for the godforsaken reporters who have drawn the Deadline Day short straw. The absolute nadir of this came at the end of the summer transfer window in 2014 when north-west reporter Alan Irwin was bringing news from outside Everton of a potential move for Tom Cleverley when an overzealous fan approached him from behind, brandished a large purple dildo and proceeded to thrust it into Irwin's exposed ear.

Ostensibly a funny incident, I nonetheless challenge anyone to watch it back on YouTube and not be deeply affected by the look in Irwin's eyes as the dildo danced around him in the filthy mitt of a godless loon that we, as a society, helped to create by collectively subscribing to this abject nonsense.

It was probably the moment that Transfer Deadline Day finally jumped the shark, and indeed Sky announced shortly afterwards that they would no longer be posting reporters in public outside the stadiums or training grounds of the UK's biggest football institutions, opting instead to position them within the safety of the clubs themselves, presumably after pleading to each club directly with an email containing the subject line 'Dildogate'.

Going back to Sky Sports News itself, when Robert Oppenheimer invented the nuclear bomb, on realising the power of his creation he famously quoted the Hindu manuscript Gita, commenting: 'Now I am become Death. The destroyer of worlds.' It's hard not to be put in mind of that quote when one thinks of the power Sky Sports' huge investment has given them over the game and then in turn think of White, in all his splendour, taking our old friend John Logie Baird's beloved invention, his life's work, and turning it into a vehicle for pure, unadulterated evil. Because when you're sat there after fourteen hours of Transfer Deadline Day, giddy from the sheer amount of senseless and needless information about League Two left-backs you've been subjected to, and still you're greeted by Jim White's unflinching, dead-eyed grin, it's easy to understand that, in the event of a nuclear winter, the only things to survive will undoubtedly be cockroaches and Sky Sports News on an endless loop reporting the latest on which stadiums have survived the apocalypse.

'But, Jim!' you'll scream back at the burnt-out but miraculously-still-working television. 'How on earth can there still be transfers to report? Everyone's been killed in a massive nuclear explosion!'

And Jim will just smile and then scream at you that he'll be back with more after this short advert break. For personal injury protection.

It's fair to say that overall, though, the coverage of the actual football itself has never been better, with scores of high-definition cameras at each game and endless replays of key incidents. It really has come a long way since those early days of *Match of the Day* and millions of football fans' experiences have been improved immeasurably as a result. We may be overloaded by needless information, but we also need never miss a big game again, wherever it is in the world. And that's a great thing. John Logie Baird would, hopefully, be astonished and delighted in equal measure. Best keep him away from Jim White, though.

Newspapers

As we mentioned at the start of this chapter, newspapers have essentially been there since the beginning and they continue to play a big part in the circus surrounding the game, even though their circulations continue to dwindle. That great bastion of truth and honour *The Sun* is the most popular daily newspaper in the UK, yet its sales have fallen consistently, every year, since 2004. The same is true of just about every other newspaper still in print, and all are looking to their online presence to make up the shortfall in revenue.

However, their influence on the game at large shouldn't be underestimated. While they obviously don't have any say at all in what happens on the pitch, off it they are great drivers of the narrative, they have the power to call the tune around what they would describe as the 'public mood' on a manager, team (at both national and club level) and still seem to have the power to pile such pressure on individuals within the game that they can arguably instigate sackings, resignations and transfers.

While, of course, the media moves at a much faster pace these days thanks to the internet, the connectivity of all the main protagonists within the sport and the public's insatiable appetite for real-time, up-to-the-minute information on their club, journalists have still found a way to adapt to the changing times by drip-feeding information via their own social media channels and online versions of their newspapers.

The contacts journalists develop and maintain within the game – owners, agents, players and managers – means they essentially become conduits for whatever message that contact needs to communicate. A player who wants a pay rise or a transfer can quickly, via his agent, start a story with the help of a journalist that can then build and build before he invariably achieves it. If, like me, you detest the summer-long transfer saga around whether a particular player is going to sign for a particular club, which tends to rumble on every single day in the mainstream press, it's important to understand that there are machinations going on behind the scenes between journalists, agents and sometimes the player himself to pursue an aim. The newspapers know that a constantly evolving story can help to sell papers, and if their journalist has the exclusive ear of the agent and player in question, no other newspaper is going to beat them to the punch.

Likewise, if a particularly influential journalist takes a dislike to a manager, he is able to drive a narrative on an almost daily basis and inflate any negative aspect of the manager's track record, results or management style simply with the aid of a headline writer, an irate player or two who happen to be out of the team and a willing public eager to consume any football story thrown at them.

A notable example of particularly the tabloid press's influence is the tale of Tottenham Hotspur and André Villas-Boas. In 2013, Villas-Boas, a charismatic, multi-lingual, urbane young coach was able to draw the ire of some of the more unsavoury parts of the tabloid newspaper media simply by being fairly exotic, cultured and a little aloof with his quotes. Fresh off the back of a Spurs season in which they achieved a record Premier League points haul, reached the quarter-finals of the Europa League and narrowly missed out on Champions League qualification, Villas-Boas turned down overtures from big clubs in continental Europe to pursue a second season in north London, a season that didn't turn out anything like he expected it to.

No one would suggest that there weren't problems with Villas-Boas's results in his second season, but with the benefit of hindsight it's possible to come to the conclusion that he was never really given a chance to succeed with the weight of a determined and biased tabloid press pack snapping at his ankles. Minor indiscretions were amplified, as were the complaints of sidelined players and backroom staff, and players that were being selected were arguably influenced by the mainstream tabloid press that they undoubtedly read on a daily basis, leading to a breakdown between the management and the playing personnel. Villas-Boas was under a constant barrage of pressure that made it increasingly hard for him to fulfil his responsibilities. Of course, the selling of Gareth Bale for a record fee and the subsequent influx of new players exacerbated the problems, but it was nonetheless the press that were able to call the tune.

Despite a start to 2013/14 that saw Spurs sat in a reasonable seventh position and boasting an undefeated record in the Europa League, heavy defeats to Manchester City and Liverpool meant the young Portuguese left, 'by mutual consent', way before Christmas and press pack favourite Tim Sherwood, who could have been part of the project as the press's man on the inside (he was working at the club in a coaching capacity at the time) was moved over to take his place. A sorry saga but a telling example of the sway and influence still possessed by a form of media that it is tempting to categorise as outdated and old-fashioned.

So, even in these straitened times in which fewer and fewer people are actually buying newspapers, it's important not to underestimate their influence. Their readers may be moving online in more and more numbers but, as long as the world of football is determined to use them as a vehicle in which to achieve their aims off the pitch if not on it, they're going to continue to play a huge part in how we form our opinions and consume our news, opinion and debate in the future.

As an aside, there also exists a language around football that is used exclusively by tabloid newspapers in the increasingly cartoonish way in which they insist on reporting the news. While the stories they report can obviously occasionally be at least semi-serious in nature, the language employed is anything but, and it's generally impossible to find this kind of parlance in any other aspect of life.

For instance, a transfer budget is rarely agreed by a chairman and given to a manager; in the tabloid world he is 'handed a war-chest'. Players are rarely injured when they can be 'crocked', and they never ask to leave a club, they 'demand a transfer', 'want out' or 'head for the exit door' after a 'bust-up'. Player caught having an extra-marital affair? That'll be a 'sordid romp', then.

Ah, the modern tabloid press pack. When they're not using their power for nefarious purposes they're continually using words and phrases that don't exist in the real world. Fleet Street's finest.

Radio

Radio, on the other hand, is far more benign for the most part. Relatively unchanged in terms of delivery, style and tone in recent years, the radio is the place to go for football when you have no access to a television or internet-connected device to watch a game, or simply want a round-up of the day's news in a manageable chunk. There is something fantastically romantic about listening to a football match on the radio, allowing the commentator to paint pictures that you, the listener, are then able to interpret in your mind's eye while driving along, or walking down the street with your headphones in. Some of the more florid radio commentators are truly gifted and able to bring something you can't see to life, and there are some masters of the medium out there who deserve every bit of credit that the well-known TV commentators receive. All that and more.

If football is a great, entertaining companion to everyday life, and tabloid newspapers are that gossipy friend that you don't really like that much any more but keep forgetting to phase out, then radio is a true pal.

But not all radio is benign, comforting and calming. In addition to news round-ups and coverage of games there is also the modern phenomenon of the phone-in show. Never has a style of programme varied so wildly depending on the host, but a radio phone-in is probably the only mainstream example of an entertainment show that can't be planned, can't be predicted and certainly can't always be controlled. At their worst they are unlistenable noise, but at their best they are utterly unmissable.

Clearly the relative quality of the shows week to week is dependent on the host and their skill at garnering and then handling callers as they come on, but the machinations behind the scenes as producers and assistant producers battle to pre-approve contributors in a fast-moving on-air environment can be akin to a war room during a key military operation.

It's tempting to wonder if the increased popularity of the radio phone-in is down to the decline in pub culture, as the smoking ban, higher alcohol prices and the continued closures of local pubs the length and breadth of the country further erode a former cornerstone of British culture. The less people head to the pub to rant and let off steam about their club, the more they seem to want to do it on the radio, the key difference being that on the radio there is a far bigger audience and most of them are actually listening.

That's an aside, though. The real highlight of a radio phone-in for me is when, despite the aforementioned studio team doing their utmost to screen the callers, a rogue, unstable fan slips through the net. There is no finer example of this than in 2009 when Colin, a Newport County fan, was able to give *606* host, Chelsea fan and professionally smug idiot Tim Lovejoy one of the most dextrous and dramatic series of put-downs in modern times.

That particular day, the *606* phone-in on 5 Live had started off like any other. And then Welshman Colin turned up with his heavy-breathing, incredulous tone and utter disdain for Lovejoy and a legend was born. Colin starts off with a strong gambit of: 'You're an absolute disgrace. You're so incredibly biased [towards Chelsea] and you've obviously been told by your producer to rein it in' before a bit of back and forth occurs in which Tim proclaims to be a 'well-known Chelsea fan', to which good old Colin responds, without missing a beat: 'Not to me you're not! I don't know you!' He then follows that up with: 'You are the most arrogant man I've ever heard on the radio.'

Now, to his credit, Tim at least understands when he's been out-manoeuvred and makes an attempt to cut Colin off and kill the call. The man on the line clearly has other ideas, however, and screams 'No, no, no! Don't you cut me off! You disgrace!' before getting a bit flustered and labouring on about the finer details of an incorrect penalty decision. He admittedly didn't end as strongly as he started, but the big man's work was done – poor old Tim was out of a job just a week later.

The salient point from me recounting this tale, though, is that it's the almost unique direct access between member of the public and presenter in a live environment that makes radio phone-ins so compelling. It's impossible to predict what's going to happen next, and that makes it such a worthy contributor to the wider conversation around the game. And if it gets the likes of Tim Lovejoy off the airwaves, long may it run.

Internet

The greatest thing about the advent and development of the internet is that it has given everyone a voice. Which is, coincidentally, also the worst thing about it. The internet exists as this big amalgamation of contra-dictions. Positives vie with negatives for breathing room, causing us to lament the fact that everyone spends far too much time in front of a computer screen these days yet forcing us to admit that we'd be absolutely lost without the convenience and information it furnishes our lives with.

The internet has almost completely revolutionised football in an even more drastic way than TV did before it. Outside of the fairly standard official club channels, which tend to be as boring as they are predictable (with the exception of Man City's official website and video content, which is actually very good – well done City!), there are: the endless streaming services that enable peo-ple that have neither the ability nor the desire to pay to watch their favourite team; the fan forums that assist football supporters in their quest to find like-minded individuals that support the same team as them; the very unofficial YouTube channels that offer tens of thousands of skills videos, vloggers' opinions, some club-specific, some not, and provide an alternative to traditional media. And then there is the huge glorified echo chamber that is social media.

Social Media

The fantastically entertaining emergence of footballers themselves appearing on social media and favouring us with their opinions holds big appeal. Some of these contributions are genuinely witty and insightful, yet some showcase a personality that probably warrants the moving of the author of them firmly over to the very fringes of our society; just because you're a footballer, that clearly doesn't automatically mean you can think like an adult. Those opinions, whatever their merit, are usually responded to by fans of various clubs offering various levels of abuse, from gentle banter to actual criminal offences, and so the carousel continues on. And, to their immense credit, the players are rarely put off by abusive fans online. It's almost as if they've spent every working Saturday of their life experiencing it in the flesh.

At its best, social media and the internet enables football players and clubs to cut out the middlemen in the traditional media and further empowers them to project their message without fear of spin, agenda-driving or downright manipulation – the at-times delicious irony being that most football players and clubs simply don't have the skills or experience to successfully communicate their message and are regularly just one step away from a constant and devastating PR disaster. From Yaya Touré complaining about his shooting stats on the latest iteration of the FIFA game to Jamie Vardy's now-infamous 'chat shit, get banged' Facebook post, the online landscape is littered with players who lack the dexterity on the internet that they show on the football field. Fans have quite simply never been closer to their heroes. And there really is nothing more terrifying in the modern game than that. For both parties.

We've seen relegated players 'accidentally' tweet pictures of sports cars sending their fans into meltdown, the publishing of private arguments between player and pundit threatening violence and a bid to 'sort this out once and for all', not to mention a club legend tearing into a current player, suggesting he's a money-grabber and calling him a 'slimebag'. And yes, all those examples revolved around erstwhile Aston Villa defender Joleon Lescott, but you take the point.

The fact that it's possible to reel off that many examples around just one player across a three-month period shows just how prevalent the warts-and-all access is on social media in 2016, and that's before even mentioning the one-man Twitter tornado that is Joey Barton.

Barton is the footballer that Twitter was invented for. In his short time on the micro-blogging service, he's found room to compare Barcelona and Brazil's Neymar to Justin Bieber ('brilliant on the old YouTube, cat's piss in reality' – that's the Neymar with thirteen major trophies, seventy-plus Brazil caps, forty-five-plus Brazil goals and a 2015 FIFPro World XI place), share his disdain for ex-England striker and current pundit Alan Shearer ('a selfish, boring man' – OK, that one is arguably fair enough) as well as *Match of the Day* presenter Gary Lineker ('an odious little toad'), all while maintaining a current playing career. He also does a pretty good line in comparing himself (favourably, naturally) to some of the world's best midfield players, despite having one Football League Championship trophy in his cabinet and a single England cap. Go get 'em, Joey.

Barton and other social media-active players of his ilk have brought the footballer chat out from the local pubs after the game into the twenty-first century via the internet. It's not that the message has necessarily changed, just that the medium has. Of course, plenty of footballers, both old and modern day, are fully content to keep their counsel and not offer up interviews or opinions to anyone, but we're hardly going to talk about them here now, are we?

YouTube

But YouTube is perhaps the biggest influencer in the way that those truly obsessed with football can engage with it on an almost twenty-four-hour basis online. These fall into a few distinct categories:

1. Ex-footballers making low-budget videos in a basement with other people that can't get a gig anywhere else, in a bid to offer 'alternative' football coverage that is essentially just an ersatz version of what is already on TV, and usually features Ray Parlour
2. The skills video specialists who didn't quite make it as pro footballers and so now spend their time endlessly volleying footballs on to crossbars and into bins before throwing outdated LA gang signs at the camera
3. Young, impressionable men outside football grounds conducting vox-pops in a really earnest fashion about how either angry (Arsenal) or deludedly positive (Liverpool) fans happen to be on any particular week. These vox-pops tend to be peppered with completely under-qualified individuals giving advice to the manager of the club they support in a completely unthoughtful way as if they know better than a man who has dedicated his life to the professional game. For example, there's Warren (one O level) standing outside Old Trafford giving tactical advice ('go back to a 4-4-2!') to Louis van Gaal (seven league titles,

one Champions League, one UEFA Cup, four domestic cups and forty-four years as either a player or a manager at a professional level)

4. Other young men/teenage boys playing the latest iteration of the FIFA video game and shouting about how annoying it is living with their parents when some of them are so wealthy from selling FIFA coins online they could probably live on their own island

It's not that I want to be frivolous or disrespectful about the YouTube community, it's just that I feel it may well be a joke that's now gone a touch too far, like when you thought how funny it would be to move your mate's car around the corner so he couldn't find it and then suddenly found yourself being the getaway driver for a bank robbery because you quite like Ryan Gosling in the film *Drive* and now you've been caught and, oh God, you're doing a ten stretch on B-Wing with some pretty unsavoury characters and you wish it would all just go away, quieten down and you could perhaps just get out of here and go for a kickaround with your mates. With absolutely NO cameras, and NO, YOU CAN'T PUT IT ON THE INTERNET FOR PEOPLE TO COMMENT. So that's YouTube to me, a 36-year-old man who would quite like a bit of peace and quiet.

And that, in a nutshell, is what football and media is in 2016, from Captain Thornhill Wakelam to Jim White and everything in between. The good captain could hardly have predicted it when he sat down to commentate on his first game, could he? It's graduated from a nascent, experimental, novel idea for a small section of sport lovers into an all-encompassing, twenty-four hours a day, 365 days a year behemoth that is completely symbiotic with the game itself, and it's only going to get bigger.

What does the future hold? GoPro cameras surgically inserted into every player's body in order to capture every moment of their lives ('press the red button now for live coverage of Daniël de Ridder's son's bar mitzvah!')? Commercial breaks at every stoppage in play? Daily Snapchat stories of a player's recovery from a leg break? Jim White personally negotiating every single transfer deal in English football? YouTube stars managing Premier League teams?

The possibilities are not only endless but terrifying too. Watch this space. I guarantee you at least one of those suggestions in that last paragraph happens at some point between now and 2020. You can't stop the endless march of progress.

What would Captain Thornhill Wakelam think? Well, first, he'd obviously be confused. But I think he'd also be quietly pleased that he'd started such a revolution. After he'd put his latest pipe-related fire out, obviously.

3. Managers

Pete Donaldson

Early football clubs were run by committee. Team selection and player acquisition were handled by a mob of important-looking men in three-piece suits in smoky boardrooms. This obviously meant that when the team stunk to high heaven, there was rarely one person to blame and a whole heap of finger-pointing. Thus, the role of team secretary was created; a nice fleshy focus for your ire, and one that only got more and more popular as we hurtled towards the twentieth century.

Major William Sudell was the first of these. He became chairman of Preston North End at the ripe old age of twenty-four, taking on management of the team the very next year. An outspoken proponent of professionalism at a time when football was a decidedly amateur concern, this professionalism didn't extend to his latter years, embezzling money from the cotton mill he managed to pay his players – a manoeuvre that would later be named 'the reverse Mike Ashley'.

Probably.

Three years in the clink, he then buggered off to Cape Town where he became a 'well-known sporting expert', which sounds like a eulogy you might give at the dullest man in the pub's funeral.

His crowning achievement was very much the league and FA Cup double in 1888 – the first year of the former; Preston won it with several matches to spare. The team included ten Scots, Sudell spending inordinate amounts of time trying to tempt the best players from north of the border, something that was easier to do since players were unpaid in Scotland. The formula for Irn-Bru was some thirteen years off, so there was basically nothing to keep them there.

The winner of the league title was to receive a tatty old flag, which quite clearly wasn't as much fun to put on one's head while dancing and singing, plus soaking up champagne with a flag and then wringing it into your colleague's mouth is a little contrived, so Sudell persuaded the FA to spend an almighty fifty guineas on a trophy. Brasso salutes you, Major.

Another prominent early manager was Ernest Mangnall at Manchester United. Forefather of the modern disciplinarian, he insisted on a rigorous schedule of physical fitness drills, maintaining that players should be allowed to play with the ball only once a week. And unlike the 2016 vintage Aston Villa, who looked like they regularly performed the same training routine, they managed to blitz their league. As a sidenote, if you ever see fit to type Ernest's name into Google, you'll be met with a thousand pictures of Ernest wearing a boater hat. Headwear goals.

So secretaries became managers and then managers became coaches everywhere except for England. But what is the difference between a manager and a coach?

God knows. I think it has something to do with access to executive bathrooms. I know El Tel was awarded the England 'head coach' role rather than manager as a result of that *Panorama* episode. Or maybe a member of the FA had made the mistake of buying their wife one of Tezza's 'Thingummywigs', which was a hat with integrated wig, invented by the great man, which allowed them to leave the house with their curlers in, onlookers none the wiser.

Watching the modern manager on the touchline, you'd be forgiven for thinking their main job is to murmur sweet nothings to their assistants behind a cupped hand – and you'd be right – that is definitely their main job. Loose lips sink ships. But they're also responsible for a small army of baby men, who can't even screw in a lightbulb; men who are probably unaware of the very concept, and think that their houses have pre-installed minute suns installed in the Artex.

From explaining to prospective players that Stoke town centre can compete with the very best cities in Europe for stocks of Grey Goose vodka and women with those mad lips that look like they've just eaten a peach made of bees, to calmly explaining to a Portuguese eighteen-year-old that the little magnetic circle on the tactics board is just a representation of him and that you didn't mean anything by it, honest – managers have got it tough, especially in the top leagues.

For every Pep there is an Egil Olsen; for every José there are ten Tony Adamses – an image that should see this book banned under the Obscene Publications Act of 1959.

The manager is the guy who's not only responsible for his team's fortunes on the field, he's a chap who's responsible for his player's very identity. Finding the right nickname is key. So, a player's joining your club and his name is Smith? Come in Smithy and have a sit down. Johannes Vennegoor of Hesselink? Johannes Vennegoor of Hesselinky better leg it round all those conesies.

Top managers beguile with the subtle art of sobriquet on a whim; nicknames are his business and business is invariably good. Unless you're Joe Kinnear and you've just called your star player Yohan Kebab.

What Do Managers Look Like?

It depends. The best managers are usually trim, with well-proportioned suits; pocket squares on special occasions. If the ball gets kicked near them the crowd get excited because they're probably not too many years away from their playing days, and they're probably still well good at keepy-uppies.

The mid-tier level of manager's main look is exhaustion – his eyes are glassy like an old dog's, his face pink like a baby rat. The game's moved on a bit, he doesn't understand the technology and he keeps forgetting the code for the office printer. He just wishes he could retire but he doesn't know what he'd do with himself. He'd probably have to talk to his wife, who just doesn't understand him as much as that training ground aluminium footballer the lads use to practise free-kicks. Love that guy.

The poorest managers at first sight could resemble the first group – trim, tanned and well-coiffed – but dig a little deeper, maybe go through their phone and they'll invariably own a digital subscription to Maxim and a camera roll full of low-rent memes with tits in them. Men whose circles of friends contain gents who speak only of cocaine and Regaine.

Managers are never black or women. Nobody seems to know why.

Mad Dogs and Englishmen

One of the most pervasive arguments in modern newspaper squawk is the relative merit of football clubs employing foreign managers. Endless ex-pros bleat on about how clubs aren't giving British managers a fair crack of the whip when it comes to the top jobs, and papers are invariably more than happy to go along with this argument, being staffed in the main by Tippex-white men hailing from Leeds or Norwich or Stafford or Chelmsford.

A statistical number-crunching exercise cobbled together in early 2016 by the writer Krishen Bhautoo looking at top-flight English football since 1992 exposes some really interesting stuff. Since the beginning of the Premier League, British managers have a win percentage of 34.1; foreign managers winning 47.1 per cent of matches.

Taking out those managers who have managed only a handful of games apiece (people like Pat Rice, Brooking and Giggs), of all the managers to exceed a 50 per cent win ratio, 68 per cent are shifty-looking blokes with funny names from overseas. Bear in mind that for the first ten or so years of the Premier League we barely had any foreign managers in the league, so if anything they're underachieving in this poll.

Nationality-wise – Chileans lead the pack with a hefty 2.17 points per game – and the Portuguese have

graced us with a chunky 2.09. Admittedly, we're talking about Pellegrini at Man City and Jose at Chelsea
who've both been able to sign the creamiest of the
crop, which skews our figures somewhat. By some
distance the most underperforming nation is Germany,
with just 1.06 points per game at time of writing.
Come on, Kloppo. In the main, these figures appear
to suggest (to your writer at least, who was in second
set in GCSE maths) that the bigger clubs who've consistently finished in the European spots are best served
by a foreign boss.

If you're a Barry Big Balls chairman with a taste for
the finer things in life, go for the bookish European
with confusing anecdotes peddled in his fifth language. If you're a perennial relegation-philanderer,
you might be better served with the bloke that
frequently holidays in places that end in 'os', the
resorts replete with ex-pat shops selling Yorkshire
Tea and two-day-old copies of the super soaraway
Sun.

Managerial Rivalries

There's nothing more unedifying than watching two
fifty-year-old men publicly going at it, like two young
lasses scrapping over a Zac Efron poster. That said,
though, I've always been a fan of a person falling up a
set of stairs, so bring it on, I say.

Ferguson v Wenger

'He's a novice and should keep his opinions to Japanese football'

— Alex Ferguson

That comment wasn't even barbed, it was all barb – and, as such, was Arsène Wenger's welcome to English football from one of the league's greats. And while we'll freely admit that once the lanky Frenchman heads off into the sunset with an Arsenal-branded carriage clock jangling about in his padded coat pocket Sir Alex and Mr Weng will no doubt share a glass of wine and a hearty chuckle about their intense rivalry in the hottest seats in club football, but when they were in their prime, these guys really got under each other's skin.

'They say he's an intelligent man, right? Speaks five languages? I've got a fifteen-year-old boy from the Ivory Coast who speaks five languages,' Ferguson, the more aggressive of the pair, exclaimed back in 1996.

Now I've spent hours trying to figure out who this Ivorian was or is, but my extensive connections in football have failed me (Google and a copy of *Championship Manager 97/98*.) Wilfried Zaha was like three in 1996, so maybe he saw John O'Shea wrapped in an Ireland flag upside down.

Did he even mean a football player? Maybe the boy in question was a tiny fifteen-year-old jockey at his stables. Either way, I'm worried about what happened to that young West African as he was never mentioned again. Alex, I presume your lawyers are reading this – the people deserve to know.

Wenger would maddeningly bleat on about how the fixture computers were set against the north London team and favoured the Manchester side, and refused to press the flesh with the pink-faced one for many years. Finally getting the upper hand and completing a season double over Sir Alex, the latter described Arsenal as over-physical 'scrappers'. 'Everyone thinks they have the prettiest wife at home,' was Arsène's retort, which somehow managed to ally misogyny with romanticism.

Pep v José

Presumably those of you who got this book for Christmas are reading this in the new year and, while the lorries take the vast proportion of copies of the FR book to the pulpers, we can sit back and reflect on the first Guardiola versus José half-season on these shores. I presume it's gone as spectacularly as expected.

Finally . . . English football has been graced by the most celebrated, continental-strength rivalry in football. Slight in stature, stylishly dressed, but both willing to give it some when it matters and frequently when it doesn't, Pep frequently brings the worst out in José, and vice-versa.

Some have said that when the Peter Crouch-loving Josep turned his back on Barcelona for the second time, he was more exhausted by the constant tinnitus-like hum of discontent from the other side of the Ebro (Ebre to Pep) about some perceived favouritism shown to the Catalan club – culminating in the Spaniard calling José the 'fucking boss of the press conference'. All very un-Guardiola like, to the casual observer.

Where this maddening lack of candour comes from is unclear. Guardiola was a Cruyff loyalist when Bobby Robson and José rocked up at La Masia. Mo felt it quite necessary at the time to establish a bond with the leader of the Catalan-Spanish faction in the dressing-room and the two were reportedly close at times. Where this new-found animosity comes from is unclear; but chances are it'll probably end with an eye gouge. Get a room, lads.

Sacchi v Capello

Fabio Capello was a celebrated international footballer; Arrigo Sacchi a man who could barely get into the side he managed at twenty-six, a side that propped up the ninth tier of Italian football. When parachuted into the Milan hot-seat in 1987 from Parma, who found themselves in *Serie C1* a season before, Sacchi had an even bigger job on his hands to convince fans of his worth.

When Sacchi's qualifications were first questioned in front of a microphone, he caught journalists off-guard with the wonderfully parsed: 'I never realised that in order to become a jockey you have to have been a horse first.' Surely the stunned silence and nervous laughter that followed that statement had more to do with the technicalities of a recursive horse riding a horse riding a horse riding a horse, an image that fired off synapses in the minds of football journalists not used to conjuring and handling such wanton whimsy.

Less celebrated mic-rocking was his insistence, at the age of sixty-eight, that there were 'too many black players' playing at youth level in Italy, proving once again that white men approaching seventy should retire their mouths and jam their pension books between lip and tooth sideways, as they've had the attention of the room for long enough.

Whereas Sacchi was a technician who favoured hard work, industry and organisation, Capello was a man keen on doing a bit of a Barry Fry – buying every forward-minded player in the league. At Milan he brought in George Weah and Bobby Baggio, as well as Paulo Futre and Paulo Di Canio. Capello already had Lentini, Savićević, Eranio, Donadoni and Marco bloody Simone. Surely he must be applauded for being able to keep that goal-drunk ego time bomb from exploding in everyone's chops.

Just as summer gives way to autumn, autumn to winter, so Sacchi replaced Capello at Milan and four years later found himself replaced by the legendary midfielder. The intense rivalry between the two men of the Milanese merry-go-round in recent years has cooled slightly, but before Fabio took the England job Arrigo couldn't help but describe his match preparation as 'evil'. Mwah ha ha.

Managerial Clothing – A Study

A season before Arsène Wenger's Arsenal team went on an obscene season-long run in which they remained unbeaten from the first kick to the last, a T-shirt was thrown at the Frenchman emblazoned with the rather unwieldy slogan 'Comical Wenger says we can go the whole season unbeaten'. A truly odd thing to have printed on your best Fruit Of The Loom, but honestly I think the person who balled that cotton monstrosity up was just pleading with Arsène to consider wearing something a little more seasonal – his almost weekly problems with wearing anything heavier than a cardigan had become legendary.

It was bad enough that he was spotted fighting with his zip in the Arsenal dugout. He managed to somehow top this some weeks later by being unable to find his coat pockets.

Like a drunk man blindly stabbing at a keyhole at 1 a.m., his face was an alloy of fury and confusion. Then came his baffling photo-shoot with *L'Equipe* – a pictorial descent into sartorial preposterousness. One picture had him leaning into a gentleman's club bar, staring into a glass of wine as if it was his only friend in the world. The next, sitting next to a fedora frowning at a smartphone, woollen trousers draped over gangly limbs – topping this off with a shot of him in a long coat on a short pier, leaving the viewer wondering if he was about to end it all.

So, though Arsène is very much high tide in Shittythread Bay when it comes to poor managerial fashion, I doubt any man of his stature could carry high fashion off. At no point in Wenger's life has he suited either sportswear or a single-breasted suit jacket. He's a man who resembles a television aerial jammed into a flesh suit at the best of times – starched arms, hinged tendrils waving this way and that – his clothing really does have little hope of tidying that up.

The problem with any football manager over the age of fifty is that their playing days are well behind them, and our memories aren't capacious enough to store images of how athletic and thrusting they once were.

Ex-pros only recently retired invariably have the physique but since they're only a few years out of the game (the game of being a footballer and wearing bad clothes) they're unfortunately unable to dress appropriately. Half-time punditry regularly looks like a TK Maxx has just fucked a branch of Maplin, with bits of computer screen, giant iPad and tech jostling for attention with men in shiny suits, monogrammed shirts and abhorrent scoop-fronted waistcoats.

Paul Tisdale, after enjoying a less than sparkling career in lower league football, decided that he needed to up the fabulousness as he began his career in management; experiments in the art of the cravat, jazzy blazer and flat cap soon followed.

The problem with rocking anything more than a club tracksuit is that, when you begin to get animated, you invariably find yourself in moments of elation three yards deep into a knee slide – the sort of thing that makes your dry cleaner shudder – see José, Paulo Di Canio et al.

Types of Football Manager

Managers can be grouped into several distinct geno-types, which is really useful when you're writing a book about football but less useful if you're a pigeon estate agent, because everyone hates being pigeonholed, even pigeons. Here are some of the Ramble's favourite bench-botherers . . .

The manager who smells of Lynx . . .

Pards

The Dunning-Kruger effect is a cognitive bias in which unskilled people suffer a delusion whereby they think they're more skilled than they actually are. Not understanding one's limitations is useful when you're pushing your body – not so great when you're pushing your mind.

Once the intoxicating fog of Alan Pardew's 'bought the T-shirt lads', uncle-on-a-stag-do banter dissipates like so much dressing-room Lynx Africa, the thrill ride that is the 'Pardiola slide' kicks in.

Those science boffins in their lab coats and spectacles will tell you that perpetual motion is impossible owing to the laws of thermodynamics being a real shit about things, but if there was some way of hooking up the Pardi-slide to a capacitor, I reckon we'd be in business.

His chicanery when a *Match of the Day* post-match mic is in view is legendary; this man on occasion has blamed his team's repeated poor performances on the Olympics, the Notting Hill Carnival, the Republic of Senegal and . . . science. That said, you can't say he isn't creative. He's practically Tony Hart. Same colour hair, anyway.

The manager who smells of Blue Stratos . . .

Phil Brown

What positive things can be said about Phil Brown that haven't been whispered by his reflection in the side of a freshly waxed Harley-Davidson? As orange as mummified bone, Phil really takes the Red Bull by the horns when it comes to rocking that 'Mum's new boyfriend' look, and his dedication to all things mid-life crises really does put other men of his vintage in the shade.

From the motorbikes and cigar-chomping, to the leaving of his pregnant mistress, to the wacky on-pitch team-talks and relegation scrap singalongs, Phil really does take the biscuit – and then demand a paternity test on it. He once compared rape to a speeding fine infraction, and if I were a betting man I'd get fairly short odds on him owning a bandana.

At least he didn't do a touchline bogle in an FA Cup final in which his team eventually lost, I guess.

The manager who can't bear to be away from football for like a second and whose entire identity hinges on the fortunes of an inflatable plastic orb . . .

José Mourinho

'Hey! Remember me guys? Yeah, I know I outstayed my welcome at Chelsea the second time, but I'd be more than happy to get involved. I'd put the cones out or something. Seriously, I miss the hushed adulation from greying men with varying degrees of heart disease when

I walk into a press conference. They got me a cake once for some reason. I live for that kinda stuff.'

Known to many as the Special One, known to Juan Mata as the spooky evil clown that haunts his dreams, this Portuguese prince gets the modern tabloid editor hotter than a 2020 World Cup stadium whenever it comes to a fucking dead tree with pints of ink.

'Who would play you in a film?' they ask.

'George Clooney!' he says.

Our editor chokes on his Itsu. 'Brilliant! Ask him some more mad shit. People are eating this up.'

'Can you give us a weird metaphor about a blanket, José, one we can print again and again, and then spaff out think-pieces about it for the next few weeks? Please?'

'Sure!' Mo exclaims.

'It's like having a blanket that's too small for the bed [injured footballer]. I cannot buy a bigger blanket [healthy footballer] because the supermarket [transfer market] is closed. But the blanket is made of cashmere [I dunno, I hate Juan Mata?].'

For José, the grass is very much greener on the other side of the fence. Not only is he fond of a Béla Guttmann-style move himself every couple of seasons, he abhors the very presence of his own youth academy. Fifteen years in management, at six clubs, has seen him give first team league opportunities to just twenty-three academy players.

Comparing his youth players at Chelsea to melons, he mused: 'Only when you open and taste the melon are you a hundred per cent sure the melon is good.'

The most celebrated of his youth league debutants was the middling Davide Santon at Inter, who is a player who lost his place in the Newcastle team to Paul Dummett. Maybe José's just really bad at opening melons.

Not that he's obsessed with buying in young talent. He's obsessed with buying in young talent and making sure they have tidy haircuts. 'I want to push the young players on my team to have a proper haircut. Not the Rastafarian or the others they have.' (Our editor squeals in delight and sees dollar signs dancing in his salmon sashimi.)

The manager who would calmly pull off your arms and legs and drown your mum just to win an argument during a football match . . .

Roy Keane

Four daughters. This man has four daughters. Four daughters who will never kiss another human tenderly. Will never be held with anything less than a bear hug.

I say this because I can't imagine a man or woman who would be brave enough to ask Roy for their hand in marriage, but in my head I'm imagining one of those Enforcement Droids from *RoboCop*, and even then

Keane would lure them down some stairs and begin cleaving its logic boards from its guts with his bare hands, as it stumbled forwards into the darkness.

A tough tackling, no-nonsense midfielder in his playing days, his Manchester United career came to an end after a 'let's go with the word spiky, shall we?' MUTV interview, where he called six of the United first team feckless and squabbled with Alex Ferguson about a racehorse. Football boots have indeed been hoofed at players for less.

Leaving behind two inflammatory books and a Keane-Ferguson rift as impressive as the Turkmenistani Door to Hell, Roy won promotion to the Premier League as manager at the first time of asking with Sunderland – his interview with *The Northern Echo* seemed to mainly consist of him denying the fact he'd been interviewed for the Sunderland role in the first place. In a suit.

'I went in and met the lads. It was all very casual. I had a suit on but I didn't feel like I was being interviewed. I had a suit on but it was all very casual and I didn't feel like I was being interviewed or being put under any pressure.'

The world gulped when he lost the Ipswich job in 2011, gulped again when his trusty dog Triggs passed away a year later – it looked for all the world that Keane was about to go proper bat-shit Super Saiyan and reveal his true form and Dr Manhattan the crap out of us, incinerating a planet or two. Instead he grew a gargantuan beard in under two months and joined Martin

O'Neill at the Republic of Ireland. He was at Euro 2016, either on the touchline or on ITV, earning a couple of quid. In a suit, no less.

'I appreciate the days are gone when you could go around assaulting people.'

Roy says he appreciates, but one would assume he doesn't fully understand the reasoning behind why that is.

The manager who would calmly pull off your Mum's arms and legs and drown your dad just to win an argument during a football match . . .

Nigel Pearson

Performing a miracle perhaps approaching the levels of appropriate miraculous-ness witnessed at the King Power Stadium in the 2015/16 season, Nigel managed to steer his Leicester team away from relegation in his second spell at the club by winning seven of his team's final nine games in the 2014/15 league season. Remarkable stuff indeed. Almost as remarkable as this little lot . . .

Mad stuff Nigel Pearson has done:
Called a journalist an ostrich
Produced a dreadful child
'Managed to get rid of' a pack of wild dogs in the
    Carpathian Mountains
'Throttled' an opposing manager's player while on his knees

Things I'm sure Nigel Pearson has done but won't admit:
Pulled apart a plasma screen television
Punched a fridge to death
Thrown bits of bear down a well
Sheared a sheep using only his hands

The manager who would gleefully yet calmly pull off your arms and legs and drown both your parents just for a bloody good laugh . . .

Louis van Gaal

Hours after the final match of the 2015/16 Premier League season was abandoned (fake bomb found in the loo – standard) Louis van Gaal hot-stepped it to Wing's, a five-star Chinese eatery and his favourite in Manchester. He was pictured wearing a sharp suit with a frankly obscene lining – a collage of tiny Manchester United greats. It was as if a real bomb had gone off in the club shop fridge magnet section as he'd been trying to defuse it.

It's clear, then, that LVG loves his MSG – and if I was going to pinpoint why exactly this manager is so . . . interesting, it'd be the sweet moment when that sole sodium molecule hits the glutamic acid and creates a big old party in his brain.

There's a commemorative plate that hangs in the same restaurant. It's inscribed by the Dutchman himself. It reads: 'Relationship is a matter of process but your

Chinese food was from the beginning fantastic.' This is him post-supper, off his face on crispy shredded beef and in full flow. He's addled by the stuff, clearly.

To say he knows how to perform a full-on *gegenpress* on the concept of being crazy would be undercooking it (something Wing's would never do). Mind you, with a win ratio of over 60 per cent over a twenty-three-year career, it'd be hard to deny him the right to get his testicles out every once in a while. Let them breathe, Louis mate.

Managers with mysterious ways . . .

Felix Magath

A six-time *Bundesliga* winner as player and coach, this psychotic high-lactose maniac once told his Stuttgart players to show up for training the day after a loss and when they got there, he ordered them to stand in a circle on the field. The temperature was but 1C that day, and he left them there for ninety whole minutes. The tenor of his argument was that their movement the day before had been poor. God knows how stiff they were come the next match.

Oh yeah, and the cheese thing. Brede Hangeland injured one of his many beautiful knees at Fulham, and Magath almighty's plan was to tell him to apply a block of cheese to the affected area. Magath was more than happy to admit to this rennet-based transgression, though stating for the record: 'This story has now been taken on and distorted by the media.' How you distort a story so bizarre in the first place is up for debate.

Managers for whom the game has possibly passed them by and who don't understand why everyone is fussing about them being a bit shit . . .

Roberto Martínez

Roberto Martínez once stated that he's not a data-focused manager, in an age when data dictates every last facet of our lives.

'When you see a player,' Martínez explained, 'you'll watch his warm-up, the way he speaks to the referee, the way he speaks to his team-mates after missing a chance, the way he celebrates a goal – the way his team-mates react when he scores . . . it's a gut instinct.'

To state how poorly this style of management has served him, in his final season at Everton, television presenter Richard Keys described him as 'mediocre'. Low praise from a low grader, indeed.

Managers who wear not only their hearts but their entire circulatory systems on their sleeves . . .

Kevin Keegan

Players need stability when it comes to managers. Calm. Fans need it, too. We impute so much of our club's misfortune into what particular words are screeched by the denizens of the technical area.

A supporter needs to be able to peer into our team's dugout and see a man in control of his faculties, his emotions. His team.

What fans probably don't need to witness is a man in a greying mullet collapsed across an advertising hoarding after lady-puncher Stan Collymore has just scored a late winner in what would indubitably be referred to as a 'sixteen-pointer'.

But with Keggy, isn't there something a bit charming in his inability to keep his shit together?

Voted the most memorable quote of the Premier League era, Kev's rant during the post-match interview on Sky Sports on 29 April 1996, his seminal 'I would love it' explosion on live television, at (the presumably at that time of night pyjama-ed) Alex Ferguson, sums up everything that's great about our salt and pepper messiah.

It had it all. It was unprofessional. It was unbecoming of a man who'd played at the highest level of the game. It had that wonderful greasy inertia of a proper unhinged freak-out – going from quietly irked school-teacher to raging impotent cuckold in seconds. More than that though, it was understandable and ever so human.

For crying out loud, it wasn't even delivered into the camera lens. I almost guarantee that feed from the Sky Sports studio was only going in one direction (into the studio) and that Keggy had no one to eyeball except a put-upon producer, clipboard in hand and pencil behind ear, wondering what he or she had done to warrant this torrent.

Here are some of my favourite things about the clip:

'We just wanna keep . . . our 'opes alive.'
Kev's voice wobbling as he pleads to the footballing gods.
    Heartbreaking.

'A lot of things have been said over the last few days, some of it almost slanderous . . . we've just gone on working, trying to pass the ball like we do in training.'
King Kev's only plan to psychologically outsmart the whip-smart Alex Ferguson is to go on passing the ball. You know, like they do in training.

'I think you've gotta send Alex Ferguson a tape of this game, haven't you? Isn't that what he asked for?'
Said put-upon producer turns to his or her superior. 'Do we need to contact the tape department? Is this request part of our contract with the Prem?'

He defends Nottingham Forest's honour by calling them 'Notts Forest' twice. Their fans HATE that.

Richard Keys, oscillating between trying to retain balance and stoking Keg's ire further: 'That's part and parcel of the psychological battle Kevin isn't it?'

Andy Gray's only offering being a murmur in the background: 'Noooo . . . I mean'. It's as much as the Scot could muster.

Kev's voice is almost at breaking point when he spits out: 'Honestly, I will love it if we beat them. Love it . . .' And then, with almost comic timing, it cuts back to the studio and revealed for the first time is Barry Venison, sat there the whole time, stony-faced and loudly dressed, late of Newcastle's parish and now playing his football in Turkey. He clearly doesn't know what's just happened.

We could probably recount tens of situations where KK's somehow come off second best, usually through little fault of his own: the layby attack, Johnny Giles punching him at Wembley, Billy Bremner punching him at Wembley, the world seemingly punching the man.

But let's be clear about one thing, Kevin Keegan is a dear; a man for whom football was perhaps too cruel a mistress. His inability to keep his head together when faced with a devious Scot or a misfiring England team was all too apparent. That said, he knew when to get out; he knew when to turn tail. For that, he's better than any manager who clung like a limpet to a big-money contract. He's all too human but I for one miss him

and his magenta suit jacket. A player who gave generations before me joy and then some, and gave me the
most exciting times watching my football team. I WILL
LOVE HIM.

The manager with some seriously itchy feet . . .

Béla Guttmann

Best remembered as the man who managed flippin'
everyone, for a bit – Béla took charge of no less than
twenty-six sides in his career, one for every letter of the
alphabet. Not his alphabet, mind – the Hungarians have
forty-four letters, the flashy sods.

His most fertile years were spent at clubs such as AC
Milan, São Paulo, FC Porto, Benfica and CA Peñarol.
The longest spell at any club was an almighty three
years in Lisbon. Truly, this was a guy cursed by the
pants-ants.

At constant loggerheads with his paymasters, he was
fired so many times he must have had an entire filing
cabinet dedicated to P45s. Losing a fair chunk of change
in the 1929 Wall Street Crash, in Romania he would
later insist on being paid in vegetables because of food
shortages. This was a man who knew how important
health, liberty and food on the table were.

Butting heads with such leading characters as Ferenc
Puskás and the entire AC Milan board, he was fired
from the latter while his team were sat atop the table,

stating for the assembled media: 'I have been sacked even though I am neither a criminal nor a homosexual. Goodbye.'

From then on, he would insist on having a clause in his contract preventing his employer firing him if his team were top of the table. Nothing about kissing lads or robbing them, mind.

Signing Eusébio in 1960, he reportedly learnt of the Black Pearl's availability and skill with a football while having his hair cut. Together, the two went on to win the European Cup in 1962 and Eusébio himself would go on to score a superhuman 638 goals in 614 matches. Truly, Béla had given the club something for the weekend.

After the '62 final, Béla went to the Benfica board and asked for a modest pay rise. Receiving short, Maradona-sized shrift, Béla allegedly cursed the club, declaring: 'Not in a hundred years from now will Benfica ever be European champion.' Benfica have gone on to lose all eight of their subsequent European finals. Eusébio even prayed at his grave in 1990 before the team took on Milan in Vienna, which didn't help a jot.

In 2014, when Benfica again got close to lifting the Europa League trophy (which resembles less a cup, more an artificial leg for a shire horse), head coach Jorge Jesus told the media: 'I'm not superstitious. I believe in people's value and the quality of their work.'

Good luck with that, Jorge.

* * *

The well-refreshed manager

We inhabit a time in which it's almost gauche to think of over-indulgence as anything but a filthy, secret shame. The same people who sit there and tap out a merry drumbeat on the F5 key in front of the football365.com forums day after day, addicted to the honey drip of twenty-four-hour rolling football news are the same who think that managers and players shouldn't be afforded their own vices. That somehow a scorched oesophagus is more damaging to a person's wellbeing than the crippling lack of social skills the football-obsessed keyboard warrior exhibits. I mean fundamentally it is but, if I were asked to choose, I'd rather hear a story about a man smashing down a yard of ale in front of a braying crowd of simpletons than Jürgen Klopp's pan-European win ratio, frankly.

Some of the most impressive men and women I've ever met have been outrageous boozehounds. Some of the worst, too, but they're not getting in this book. You hear that, Paul from school?

While not making light of football's inextricable, dark relationship with alcohol – a palsy we're hopefully seeing the back of, culturally, in the sport – there were a few managers who managed to make it work for them, at least early on in their managerial careers. And here are two boozy beauts . . .

Howard Kendall

Born in Ryton, an area of the North-East that was incorporated into Tyne and Wear in 1974 – presumably because the name sounds brilliant when Geordies say it – Kendall began his career at Preston North End, which every footballer seemed to do back then. The other thing they all did back then was look about forty-five. His appearance in the 1964 FA Cup final against West Ham made him the youngest player ever to feature at a Wembley cup decider – forty-five, he was.

Putting in more than 600 appearances as a player for Preston, Everton (twice, and his returning to Goodison was to be a recurring theme), Birmingham, Stoke and Blackburn, he then took charge of Blackburn and then Everton to gift the latter the closest thing to a dynasty they'd ever experience – Kendall remaining the last English manager to win a UEFA competition with an English club.

An infectious, jovial man, Kendall refused to step into Bobby Robson's shoes after the 1990 World Cup. He was shortlisted for the England role but was unwilling to take the reins, stating for the record that it was a lonely job and it wasn't for him. He was a truly social man.

Performing media liaison regularly in the public house, the *Sunday Express*'s James Mossop talked fondly of an interview that started in the ale house and ended in the club sauna, as Everton had a game that evening. On another occasion, during a stinking run of form, an exasperated Howard took his players for a Tuesday bonding session in Liverpool's Chinatown. Whistles were soaked to excess and, thanks in part to this regime of now weekly Great British booze-offs, the team forged a new-found camaraderie, and went on to collect quite a run of wins.

When the wins inevitably dried up, Howard collected the team together and stated that the boozy Tuesday meals simply had to stop. 'How do you feel about Wednesdays?' he asked.

Not that Slaven Bilić has particularly fond memories of the midweek Chinese meal. He once had to leave early and left his credit card to pay for his share. Kendall promptly oversaw the purchase of some rather capacious and above-all punchy magnums of champagne. That's probably what he was crying about at the last game at the Boleyn – his overdraft.

The first time Blackburn-era Kendall witnessed binman-turned-bincat Neville Southall was on Big Nev's father's insistence – they'd often find themselves drinking together in the same bar in Llandudno. As a favour he popped down to check the goalkeeper out. He'd wanted to sign him on the spot, but was told that

Blackburn had two professional goalies on the books. Howard would have to wait some years and pay some £150,000 to secure his services.

We'll no doubt go on to talk about Big Nev but just for the 700-plus times he pulled on the keeper's shirt, Kendall's legacy would have been secure. His time at Bilbao, under their restrictive transfer policy, and his playing days at Preston, Birmingham and Stoke just about pushes him over into legend status.

It's for his three managerial stints at Everton that he'll be most fondly remembered though, and when asked about the possibility of a statue bearing his likeness he reflected: 'Just make sure the statue looks like me. You know, with a bit more hair on my head and a bit more flesh on these old bones. And remember to place a wine glass in my right hand.'

Brian Clough

There's a reason why every town wants to lay claim to this confirmed madman. Everywhere he went, whatever he seemed to turn his hand to, he was maddeningly successful and maddeningly maddening.

Middlesbrough – a whopping great 197 goals in 213 appearances for the Boro.

Sunderland – 54 goals in 61 appearances.

Hartlepools United – he began his managerial career at the age of thirty, at a club that became 'Hartlepool' singular during his tenure. He was that impressive that one of the Hartlepools walked off its own pier.

Derby County – from Second Division also-rans to Division One winners. Astounding.

Brighton and Hove Albion . . . Leeds – errr . . . hey, look over there! There's a squirrel on that tree. Look at him go . . .

Nottingham Forest – NOTTINGHAM FOREST! Seriously Ranieri, you can stick your Premier League trophy jammed up with pizza dough up ya bot-bot. This achievement tops the lot.

At Forest, Clough and Taylor won the Division One trophy, collecting two European Cups for their trouble – and that's before we talk about the two League Cups they bagged. We probably don't have time.

As with legendary figures in the game, there's always a quote or two that sums up their temperament in a pithy couple of lines. We nod and chuckle away, we bark them at our friends down the boozer – all the while not really caring a jot about their veracity. As a result, most of Clough's musings are woefully wide of the mark. Here are a few of the more popular ones, in full. As you can see, they were a little more clunky before the nip and tuck . . .

To his new players at Leeds United:

'Throw all your medals in the bin. Then throw that bin in a bigger bin. Keep on throwing the bins into successively larger bins

until the bins are bigger than the biggest bin you can ever imagine. Then I'll step in and imagine an even bigger one. Now where was I? Oh yeah, I've done a drawing of a massive fucking bin.'

On his standing in the game:

'I wouldn't say I was the best manager in the business. But I was in the Four Tops. We defined the Motown sound.'

On long-ball football:

'If God had wanted us to play football in the clouds, he'd have put grass up there, and he did want us to, and that's why he did it, and that's why we play football in the clouds.'

Pretty weird, huh?

Managerial hobbies

Let's face it, most managers have very little imagination when it comes to finding things to do outside of football. Extra-marital affairs and golf. That's the lot of your run-of-the-mill manager. But these two go the extra mile:

Fabio Cannavaro

One of the finest defenders of his generation if not of all time, Cannavaro is a paragon of good taste when it

comes to most aspects of his life, apart from that time
he was filmed getting injected with phosphocreatines
in a moody hotel room on the eve of a cup final. Each
to his own, I guess.

Fabio's great love is pizza, like every other free-
thinking Neapolitan, and he's got a special Cannavaro
family recipe for the bready treat. 'It's all in the mozzarella,' he says, which is the sort of line that can only
be delivered with a wink and a turn on the heel back
into the kitchen – leaving you to speculate as to what
disgusting way he could have possibly meant that.
What's 'all' in the mozzarella, Fabio? What 'all of' have
you put 'in' the mozzarella, Fabio?

If you'd like to make *pizza alla Cannavaro*, here's the
recipe directly from the horse's mouth, the horse fresh
from the Tianjin Quanjian dugout . . ..

- Never put your cheese on uncooked pizza dough. Add
  it half-way through baking so that it stays softer.
- Dissolve the yeast in warm water. Flour the pastry
  board and add all the other ingredients.
- Knead the mixture for a long time and once it's the
  right consistency roll the dough into balls and leave
  them to rise in a warm place for an hour.
- Roll out the dough and add tomato, oil, a pinch of
  salt and a basil leaf in the centre.
- Cook for 5-7 min at 190C.
- Add the mozzarella and cook for a further 5-7 min.

- Ejaculate into the mozzarella and serve.

I bloody knew it.

Martin O'Neill

Manager by day, cold-case detective by night, Martin O'Neill's love of criminology was ignited by the conviction and subsequent execution of James Hanratty in the 1960s (isn't that always the way?). He was a regular spectator at Peter Sutcliffe's trial and he took in much of the Rose West trial from the public gallery, too.

His wife Geraldine once stated for the record, rather unhelpfully if he ever finds himself in the dock: 'I have been to so many murder scenes with Martin that I sometimes think that one of these days I will be murdered in one of these places myself.'

Now managing Ireland with his trusty attack dog Roy Keane, Martin has got his hands full with Mr Angry McPunchbeard, but if he had his way we all know what the curly haired O'Neill would be up to. He'd be getting his teeth into some of the worst crimes imaginable, poring over case files for days on end and leaping a full metre into the air once he'd solved them all.

Proper Columbo stuff. As long as he didn't try to utter anything more pithy than 'my wife loves your books' during the witness interviews. Heaven knows,

he's the one Irishman in the world that's not necessarily blessed with the gift of the gab – only this year
he referred to Keane and himself as suspected 'queers'
and told the Irish wives and girlfriends that they'd
only be allowed in the team hotel if they were
good-looking.

That said, I could definitely see him taking off a pair
of shades, wistfully looking off into the distance as his
colleagues in uniform bundle the culprit into a police car.

Football Management Video Games

As far back as I care to remember, I've been a fan of
the football management genre. From the off-field
formation-wrangling side of the Amiga classic, *Sensible
World of Soccer*, to the glorious watercolour majesty of
the little-known PC title *On The Ball*, I've always had
a lot of time (literally) for games that gave me the
opportunity to chance my arm, elbow and wrists at a
spot of dugout skulduggery. Not a Christmas went by
without me immediately installing Football Manager
on my dad's PC and then having a gargantuan argument about me installing Football Manager on my dad's
PC. We all have coping mechanisms when it comes to
annual family gatherings. This was very much my
father's and mine.

Maybe it's because I'd always elect to play as underachieving Newcastle United or Hartlepool, or because

I'm very much like Alan Pardew and can't arrest a slide – my season usually began with a cautious, methodical analysis of my new charges, followed by three months where I'd find myself out of options and out of my mind with anger, rooted to the bottom of the table and issuing club fines to all and sundry.

Most of the allure of the modern managerial simulator comes down to the ability to scout a player and then unceremoniously stick him in your team, willing this abstract collection of bytes to perform miracles for your lads.

Many an organ has run a witless listicle or two about cult players who underwhelmed in their club careers but shone in the virtual domain of Football Manager – players like Teddy Lucic and Taribo West. If it's good enough for them, it's good enough for my chapter. Here is my hot tip for those of you reading this book of the future back in 2006 . . .

In *Football Manager 2007* (post 'Football Manager' and 'Championship Manager' going their separate ways) a young Brazilian by the name of Claudio ruled the Premiership six-yard boxes in my Newcastle side, finishing off many a move that (a by then truly ancient) Robert Lee had started. My God, Claudio, my beautiful goal-scoring boy, was brilliant.

Though we never managed to finish a season any higher than ninth – mirroring what was around the corner for the Toon – our man was averaging a respectable eighteen goals per campaign.

But what about the Claudio in actual, real-life, fleshy football? Well, apart from falsifying his birth date and being suspended for a year (bantz) he doesn't appear to have scored any goals in the professional top flight. Sounds like a Newcastle purchase to me.

You'd always know that you'd been playing for way too long when you reached 2025 and regenerated players started to kick in, with randomly generated names appearing – Sol Shearer and Gary Gudjohnsen being favourites. As of 2016, Football Manager is a sprawling, insanely complicated game, with several different levels of density on offer, ranging from the length of season you could knock out in a couple of hours on a long train journey, to a season you'd only be able to see off if you'd just been sent down for manslaughter. So multilayered and wide-ranging are the experiences today, new features are planned three years in advance.

I was once the voice of the 'Football Manager adverts thanks to the head of Sports Interactive, Miles Jacobson, who is now an OBE (I think it was for services to 'making objectionable men not go outside'). I replaced Finchy from talkSPORT and *The Office* in the role. He then, in turn, replaced me a year later. Fair dos. He's thrown a kettle over a pub. What have I done?

So I, regrettably, can't keep a voiceover job for more than a year. Imagine how hard it is being a manager, where every instinctive knee slide (José), testicle sniff (Löw) and scream of 'Saido!' (Pulis) is analysed over and over again? Being a manager in a video game is supremely difficult. Why do we think that doing the job in real life is going to be any easier? There are very few souls who manage to get it right even most of the time. I for one salute them with a hand covered in virtual chalk.

4. Fans

Jim Campbell

People who don't like football have no idea what they're missing. They think they do but they don't. They'll often take pride in not liking it, wearing a look that suggests they think they should be heralded as free-thinking mavericks when they reveal that actually they don't care about twenty-two millionaires kicking a ball around, as if they're Stewart Lee, when in fact they're Stuart Lee, your cousin's new IT consultant boyfriend who you're sat next to at a wedding. Fair enough, though, Stu. Nobody has to like anything. Even so, you don't know what you're missing.

Most of us start off as kids. In terms of following football, that is. We all start off as kids, apart from FIFA executives. Most of them seem to have been born despicable old men. Maybe even hatched. Anyway, most fans are indoctrinated by a parent, or support their local team because they live in a one-club town. Others pick a team when they discover football at school and yet more get into it because they had a grandparent, uncle or dog who lived in Manchester, Liverpool or Barcelona – every school had one – depending on who's winning at the time. Whatever your choice and however you make it, it's with you forever, like a cool-looking scar or cold sores.

Football is brilliant when you're young. There's a pre-existing culture to explore and it's one of the few things where being a child isn't a hindrance to engaging with that culture. It's played by adults, partially for adults, but also for you. Not much else is like that and, as a kid, you have your own corners of the game, traditions that have been passed on through the years and are now exclusively yours when you and your friends are in the park. Things like playing headers and volleys, pretending to be your favourite players and 'next goal wins' coming into play because the score is 46–42, it's getting dark and everyone wants their dinner. These things are universal. It doesn't really matter who came up with them because everyone did them. In a way these traditions make it folksy, except that there are no harmonicas and nobody can grow a beard yet, though there is sometimes cider.

That's a hazy, nostalgic view but it's also easy to forget what school is really like. If you're into football you stake your reputation on your team. Lose on Saturday and Monday is an inescapable hell. Through no fault of your own you're an absolute laughing stock. This never changes. However successful your club may be, heartbreak, disappointment and humiliation are absolutely guaranteed. Why do we put ourselves through it? On the face of it doing so makes no sense. It would be easier to not support a specific club and just enjoy the sport as a whole. You can love music without only 'supporting' Bob Marley, so why is it different with football? The answer is that it wouldn't mean anything if you didn't. You do get those weirdos who like football yet don't support a team. Watch out for them. They're trying to blend in and are certainly lizards. For it to matter you have to invest in it. You have to really care about what happens to your team. To do that you have to allow them to represent you, to put your credibility at stake. That's how it becomes important, when it stops being just a game. Your good name is riding on these clowns!

There is, of course, a tribal element to it: the sense of belonging to a group and losing your identity in a crowd of like-minded people who represent the same thing as you; the rivalry with people who are fundamentally similar to you but competing for the same prize. Those looking in often seem baffled by this but we all know that we're not always exactly the same. Certain groups of fans do have their own unique characteristics, to the point where it's easy to come up with descriptive collective nouns for them, like a Brioche of

Arsenal, a Fare of Chelsea or a Yesterday of Liverpool. We're all the same but we're all different, like people in general.

Loving football is also about so much more than what actually happens on the pitch. The sheer breadth of it is its charm. It's an entire world in which to escape, one every bit as storied and fantastical as Middle Earth, Narnia or the Marvel Universe and filled with as many heroes and villains, as long as you know where to look. You can lose yourself in it in the same way you can a gripping book, or a great movie, or a horse race if you're Michael Owen as he hates all movies, only having seen eight, one of which is *Cool Runnings*. Lizard.

It's exactly that kind of incongruity that's so appealing. Yes, Owen's solo goal against Argentina in the 1998 World Cup was a great moment, but the thought of him sat in a cinema, absolutely hating the heart-warming underdog story of the first ever Jamaican bobsleigh team to the point where it's really weird is, in its own way, just as good. Football is a million things at once and not one aspect of it represents the whole more than any other. You either get it or you don't and if you don't you're missing out on so much more than a sport . . .

Culture

While Stuart from the wedding would state that football culture is an oxymoron, then tell you what an oxymoron is, even though you know, Stuart from the wedding is a bellend. It may be steeped in tradition but the culture of football evolves constantly, much like anything that evolves, as Stuart would also point out. The image of the football fan itself is gradually changing. Once, however unfairly, the stereotype was of the shirtless, bulldog-tattooed, bright pink thug making drunken, unintelligible noise, teetering atop a bar while their team were on TV. While a certain laddishness will likely always be attached to the broad image of the football fan, that is far from the full picture. Recent times have seen an increased visibility of the football nerd, or 'football hipster' as people who would generally also fit that description like to sneer. As with any kind of escapism, football is a brilliant thing to be a little bit obsessive and nerdy about.

The increasing globalisation of football means that aspects from one culture start to take hold in others. We're already seeing a form of this in England with the increasing presence of banners and home-made signs. Banners can be a great way to add to the atmosphere of a game when done right, as with any splash of colour. An even cursory glance at any Boca Juniors crowd shows a maelstrom of banners, flags and ticker tape, all combining to create the feeling of a carnival that you simply do not get in Watford. In Italy in particular, gigantic yet detailed banners have long been displayed to express support for the home team or question the chastity of opposing fans' and players' mothers.

In a way they're years ahead of us. In a way. Perhaps it won't be long before we're all throwing Vespas around. That might sound like mild xenophobia but famously this actually did happen in a match between Internazionale and Atalanta in 2001. Inter fans stole a scooter from an Atalanta fan, somehow managed to get it into the stadium, attempted to set it on fire, then when that didn't work settled for trying to throw it on to the pitch, which also didn't work. Luckily nobody was hurt as it simply flew into an empty stand. Good luck explaining that to your insurance company.

The home-made signs seem to owe more to wrestling than football if the quality is anything to go by. There has been a noticeable upswing in their presence over the past few years and it's tempting to think this is the fault of the instant gratification culture we're now engulfed by. It would appear that some people feel their opinion is so important that it must be seen and acknowledged everywhere, that the very idea that their displeasure won't be known is a grave wrong that must immediately be put right so that their club know to do exactly what they want all the time. Perhaps Twitter and the comments sections of websites have effectively turned them into real world trolls who are compelled to take their angry, impotent tweets everywhere with them on two badly taped together pieces of cardboard. Block.

Some fans even seem hell-bent on building their own brand around their support. There's something slightly tragic about a person who bases their entire identity on football, or anything for that matter. Do that and you're basically Disco Stu from *The Simpsons*.

Famous individual fans are nothing new, though in the past they really had to put the work in to stand out. Colombia's Birdman is one of the most famous fans in the history of football. Making his 'debut' at Italia '90 he has become an iconic part of both Colombia's national team and the World Cup itself. When his team scored an injury-time equaliser against West Germany in Italy he was being held aloft by ropes and the fans holding them were so delirious they forgot about him and let go. Luckily one had tied the rope around his waist so he lived to fly/fall another day. Michael Keaton is said to be in line to take up the mantle once he retires so that people can go: 'Oh my God, that's so meta.'

In England there is the famous John Westwood, the guy at Portsmouth who rings a bell throughout every game and has turned himself into a kind of living mascot. His full name is John Anthony Portsmouth Football Club Westwood, he has sixty Portsmouth tattoos and even has PFC engraved on to his teeth, comfortably making him Portsmouth's second most flamboyant fan . . .

Both of these fans have been accused of attention-seeking but claim that in reality they're expressing the love they feel for their teams. One famous fan who can make no such claim is Jimmy Jump. During Euro 2004

Jaume Marquet i Cot, to give him his real name, ran on to the pitch, threw a Barcelona flag at Luis Figo then jumped into the net, creating the bizarre impression that he'd scored a goal with himself. 'What an idiot' thought everyone, Figo especially, but then he just kept coming back. He has popped up at various Champions League games, was there again at Euro 2008 and has 'jumped' on matches throughout Europe. In 2010 he got incredibly close to placing a *barretina*, a traditional Catalan hat, on the World Cup shortly before the final, only to slip over as security ran towards him. He has also appeared at rugby, basketball and tennis matches, jumped into the pool at a water polo game, ran through the starting grid of the Spanish Grand Prix, joined the dancers on stage for Spain's performance of their 2010 Eurovision Song Contest entry, uninvited obviously, and has even popped up in a Hungarian weather forecast. There comes a point where you just have to take your traditional Catalan hat off to the man; he is really, really good at this.

The increasing popularity of football in the USA is giving us the unusual chance to see a fan culture develop. It feels like a bright-eyed, optimistic teenager, loving having some outsider, underdog status compared to the other established sports but quickly growing in strength and confidence. At the 2014 World Cup fans of USMNT – which is what Americans call America but is actually the US Men's National Team – charmed everybody with their vibrant and committed support, impressing as much as their team. With so many match highlights and so much information readily available on the internet it's no wonder that football has started to take off there. If you are an American reading this book: Hello. Sorry that English people always mock you for saying 'soccer'. It's actually an abbreviation of 'association', as in association football and is an English word. So we gave you a word, claimed it was yours and now attack you for it. Burn! Spring break! Sorry about that!

While the Premier League is popular, Major League Soccer has an increasingly fervent group of supporters. MLS expansion means that new cities are getting clubs and, with a high immigrant population, a love for football is often already in place. Nowhere has this ready-made support been more apparent than in Philadelphia, whose Philadelphia Union supporters group, Sons of Ben, or SoBs – they know what they've done there – pre-date the actual team by three years. They were founded on the 301st anniversary of Benjamin Franklin's birthday, beginning when rumours of a Philadelphia MLS team began to circulate. They were formed in the hope of aiding the chances of this becoming reality and lobbied so hard that they effectively willed their team into being, with their first game taking place in 2010. They were even known to appear at New York Red Bulls games chanting about their then non-existent team. Starting with just a few people but now numbering in the thousands, they even have their own section of the stadium. To sit there you need to be a member and buy a special season ticket. They're as ingrained in the culture of the club as it's possible to be. Once it was confirmed that Philadelphia Union would indeed come into being they developed a philanthropic side, raising money for and helping out with various causes in the city of Chester, home of their Talen Energy Stadium. This continues today. It's hard to imagine the Chelsea Headhunters or West Ham's Inner City Firm rocking up to a soup kitchen, unless they wanted to warm up before kicking each other's heads in.

MLS also has one of the most unique mascots in world football, Portland Timbers' Timber Joey, real name Joey Webber. He's unusual as a mascot in that he's an actual person, rather than the gigantic felt nightmares we're used to. Not that ours aren't inherently unusual, we're just so used to them we forget how weird they are. Arsenal's Gunnersaurus is a huge dinosaur who fires T-shirts out of a cannon, wears a watch around his neck, rendering it useless to him as he's the only person who can't see it and for some reason joins in with what should be contemplative minute's silences. Not that I don't love you, mate.

Timber Joey is just a guy with a big grin and a chainsaw, which is still less creepy than some of ours. Every time the Timbers score he cuts a piece of wood from a massive pitchside log, it's passed around the ground so that the fans can touch it and is then presented to the goal-scorer at the end. This may seem like a charmingly innocent and new interpretation of fan culture but Timber Joey is carrying on a tradition that began in the late 1970s, when a man named Jim Serrill brought a chainsaw to a game when the Timbers were competing in the original US league, NASL. For some reason they were OK with this and it evolved into the log-cutting tradition Joey still upholds.

New fan bases are a huge source of potential revenue for clubs and we're now seeing an annual fight for dominance in the USA, the Far East and the Middle East, with teams targeting entire countries in an attempt to turn them into Premier League cargo cults. They're even competing on social media, fighting for global dominance on every front. Can Manchester City, for example, really expect fans in, say, Indonesia to become fully fledged supporters because the club's timely, snackable social media content creates a bond between them? Apparently so.

Right now, the Premier League TV deal dwarfs anything that has come before it because of its worldwide popularity but can it last? China, one of the most important global markets, are spending big on strengthening their own league, with Hebei China Fortune's Ezequiel Lavezzi being the world's highest-paid player at the time of writing. Lavezzi is a good player but, even so, that shows how serious they are. China's football-loving president Xi Jinping has stated that he aims to make China into the world's biggest sporting economy by 2025 and, while most Chinese fans support a Premier League team, it's easier to change your allegiance when your club are on the other side of the world in a place you've never been to. Perhaps one day they'll emerge as a truly dominant force in global football and we'll all be supporting Guangzhou Evergrande, Shanghai Greenland Shenhua and Liaoning Whowin FC.

Match Day

In the current age there are so many ways to experience live football. It used to be that your options were to buy a ticket to the game, climb a nearby tree or listen to it on the radio. Now, you still have all of those options – accessible trees permitting – but you can also see it through a huge amount of channels and live streams on your TVs, tablets and smart fridges. You could fly a drone into the stadium and watch the camera feed on your VR headset if you were skilled and weird enough.

However many options we have, though, nothing will ever compare to being there. There's nothing quite like the feeling you have before a match in your home stadium. The collective anticipation, the sense of unity, the smell of the grass if you're sat close enough to the pitch. It's addictive and it's understandable that it means so much to so many people. Witnessing your team score a goal to take the lead and the mass primal scream therapy that follows is something that never gets old. You know you're not part of the team – I, for one, gave up on that dream ages ago – but when you're in the stadium, during the game, you feel like part of the club. When they're losing you feel like you personally have to do something about it, cheering the players on to give them a lift being about all you can do. When they win it feels like a personal achievement, like you and everyone else in the stadium did their part. It would be priceless if it didn't very much adhere to an inflated pricing structure.

The match day experience in general has, of course, changed a lot over the years. Now we have all-seat stadiums, corporate boxes and tourists watching the games through their phones as they film them, which I've personally witnessed on more than one occasion. Watch the game you maniac! It's right in front of you. The camera crew in the ground have got this covered. Their cameras are far better equipped to capture the game than your phone and there are loads of them, though how do you even have a phone with the battery life to record a full match? That's without people doing a multitude of other non-football-related activities on their devices. This is a new and very annoying practice.

I'm tempted to follow the dad trope of saying that back in our day we had to make our own entertainment . . . which was really, really easy because there was a professional football match taking place right in front of us. We just looked at that.

All this said, accessories are nothing new. There was a time when people entertained themselves with massive wooden rattles. They were a serious piece of weaponry, too, verging on the medieval. The idea of taking a rotating piece of wood into a packed terrace and swinging it around your head seems unfathomable in our age of health and safety regulations and not swinging massive bits of wood around your head. Fans must have got smacked in the face all the time. People didn't complain in the past, though. They'd have remained stoic as stiff upper lips became fat upper lips. Rattles were banned in the 1970s, though, as people started using them as weapons on purpose.

Those of us who've grown up with the Premier League are often told about how much better the football experience was in the past. Apparently the muddy pitches were a good thing. The players would drink with the fans in pubs after the game, or before it depending on the player, and that was also good. Fans never, ever left early, ever, and that was better than now, too. This seems suspicious to me. It's hard to believe that throughout the entire 1970s there wasn't even one burly man, frustrated at watching a turgid 0–0, who didn't nip off a little bit early to beat the traffic. You just wouldn't have seen him leave because when you walk out of a terrace it doesn't leave a highly visible empty plastic seat behind. It's unsurprising that people view their own youth through rose-tinted spectacles. These experiences are often treasured and memorable – for one thing, an early experience of football provided many of us with a formative education in the great British pastime of unnecessary swearing – but come on. Pipe down, the past, you silly old prick.

That isn't to deny that some things used to be better, like the cost. The most expensive Premier League ticket in the 2015/16 season was £97, at Arsenal. Fifty years ago the same ticket would have cost only half a d and two-thirds of a thrupenny shillingbob. In today's money that's about the cost of a tub of Brylcreem. That's a rough estimate as old money is hard to work out. Many people are priced out of attending games and, where football was once rooted in the community, it now comes from the media, beamed into our homes rather than readily available out in the real world. It's difficult to comprehend the size of the Premier League's popularity now. Manchester United estimate that they have more than 100 million fans in China. There are only 64 million people in Britain. Chinese Man United fans could declare war on us, invade and feasibly win. Maybe we don't appreciate the pressure those players are under. For God's sake keep them happy.

Such wide coverage means that those watching in the stadium are in a minority. For those who can't make it to the stadium there is always the pub, which can provide you with equally formative experiences but comes with its own pros and cons. It can be a brilliantly vibrant place in which to bond with your mates or it can be a sordid, lonely hovel in which loads of gobby, drunk strangers laugh at your misfortune. There is a lot of etiquette to learn about watching football in pubs and there are lots of easy mistakes to make, all of which I have made. Younger readers may still be figuring them out so here are some tips:

- Do your research. If the pub is called The George or anything equally vague this could spell trouble. You know where you are with The Fox and Avocado, or indeed The Lamb and Bastard. Not so much The George. The name gives too little away. It could be a gastropub that serves Tizer and Drambuie in a light bulb or the kind of place that's so tough you wouldn't dare take your drink back to the bar if it had a jellyfish in it. If either of those things are a problem for you, a tiny bit of planning will help you avoid them.
- Have a plan, even a vague one. If the game is an early kick-off and your friends have other plans you may end up in a situation where you're alone and drunk in the afternoon. While there is everything to be said

for the spontaneity of youth allowing you to go out and meet your soul mate, start a band or discover the meaning of life, in this situation there is nothing to be said for a slowly creeping 6 p.m. hangover that descends just as it becomes clear that everyone else is too busy or sober to see you. You will choose this time to have a really long think about the important things in your life while you're unequipped to do anything about them and reach only terrible conclusions. So I've heard.

- If you like dogs find a dog pub for tournament football. Why? If a game goes to penalties everyone will go crazy when their team score. Excited by this, any dogs who are present will also go crazy, giving the impression that they support your team. I've seen this and it's the best.

Traditions

Football fans love tradition. In a sense our clubs *are* tradition as by their nature they connect us to the past. They existed long before us, they were there when we were kids and they're here for us now, like strangely invincible grandparents who charge us for their company and go on mysterious tours of the Far East every summer. In the same way they connect us to the future. We'll try to indoctrinate our children into supporting them, thus carrying on the line of support. They'll also be there after we're gone, unless some incomprehensibly minted egomaniac comes along and runs them into the ground in the pursuit of the reflected glory that apparently comes with processing title-winning invoices.

Some traditions are so ingrained that you forget they're traditions at all. Take scarves. They may have a practical use but at some point some genius optimised them as a way to essentially display clan colours, too. The sight of them being held aloft as the Kop belts out 'You'll Never Walk Alone' at Anfield is one that's almost as stirring as the song itself. Having them in a stand displays more of a team's colours, which displays more support to the players, a visual reinforcement that everyone is on the same side. It can even be dangerous to wear them near a big group of rival fans, lest they take your display of colour as a slight on their team, as if you're a lairy peacock inviting a fight. Even our knitwear has to have a competitive edge.

The natural evolution of this was, of course, the replica kit, which came about in 1974 when a man called Bert Patrick realised that his company, Admiral, could make a fortune from making England's kit, displaying Admiral's logo on it for advertising, and selling replica kits. Wearing the same kit as the team is a strange phenomenon, especially among adults, kind of like going to see *The Dark Knight* dressed as Batman, though it too clearly has tribal connotations. It's slightly different when you're a kid, as you're more innocent and just want to have the things you love on display. I had an Arsenal goalkeeper's top when I was younger and would naively walk around nineties Essex with 'Seaman' printed on my back, confused as to why all the bigger kids were laughing.

Norms in football are generally accepted without much questioning and nowhere is this truer than the football chant. Some are based on songs in the charts at the time, some come from traditional standards. What makes some stick and others fade is hard to quantify. At any given match you might hear a version of 'Sloop John B', a folk song about sailors having a terrible time getting drunk in various ports that was popularised by the Beach Boys and has inexplicably become a football staple. Phil Brown even crooned it to the Hull City crowd as his team narrowly avoided relegation on the final day of the 2008/09 season. A chant of which the origins are easier to trace is that of the White Stripes' 'Seven Nation Army'. It's probably the most successful of recent additions in that it is so commonly heard. In 2003 fans of Belgium's Club Brugge heard it being played in a Milanese bar before a Champions League match with AC Milan and sang along. Brugge recorded a surprise 1–0 win and the fans sang the song in full voice. From then on they started playing it in their stadium. Then, when Roma came to town in the UEFA Cup in 2006, they liked it so much they took it back home. The popularity of it spread and it became synonymous with Italy's triumph in the 2006 World Cup. Jack White of the band has said of this: 'I am honoured that the Italians have adopted this song as their own . . . Nothing is more beautiful than when people embrace a melody and allow it to enter the pantheon of folk music. As a songwriter it is something impossible to plan . . . I love that most people who are chanting it have no idea where it came from. That is folk music.'

It is certainly true that it's impossible to plan this, as *The Football Ramble*'s repeatedly fruitless attempts to get the England band to learn the *Jurassic Park* theme so fans can chant 'Come on Eng-er-land!' along with it have shown.

In the context of football the most basic things can become ritualistic and traditional, like food. It wouldn't be the same without the guilty pleasure of an over-priced pie or hot dog at half-time, though the object of these guilty pleasures differs everywhere. In Bosnia the football snack of choice is the interesting combination of salted grapes and pumpkin seeds. In Cyprus they sell doughnuts and call them sticky bombes, which is brilliant but creates a dilemma as doughnuts is already a good name. In Argentina they sell something called *pizza de cancha*, which is pizza that has no cheese on it. What? Eh? How does that improve it? That's like a 'burger' that's just sauce and relish in a bun, or a completely dry pie, or a *pizza* with *no cheese*! On the other end of the scale Germany is great for the British football fan as you can throw yourself into the local culture by simply drinking loads of beer and eating sausages. We aren't really in a position to judge anyone anyway. We still sell Bovril. If you don't know what Bovril is, it's a gloopy meat drink that's classed as beef tea. That tells you everything you need to know. Beef. Tea. Even the food is changing, though, with National League side Forest Green Rovers admirably being the first club to make their food entirely vegan. It's enough to make your dad choke on his cow broth.

The veneration of tradition is never more visible than when those fat cats at City Hall try to change something. People hate change. The debate about goal-line technology rattled on for years, with traditionalists arguing that it would remove a crucial human element from the game. Since being introduced it's worked without a hitch but there are further calls to apply it to penalty decisions and offside calls, with the same arguments against it not unreasonably ringing out. The concern is of how far it will go. Video replays are often inconclusive and some rules are open to interpretation anyway, so require a degree of faith in the referee.

In an increasingly automated world it could be that one day human referees are phased out all together.

There are many potential pitfalls with this. Technology doesn't always work, and what does any reasonable person do in this situation? They smack it, obviously. You can't just chin a robot referee to reset it if it's called you offside for taking a throw in. It'll send you off, or rise up and turn on those who created it, destroying all humankind. From a fan's perspective it's also pointless to swear at a robot ref. The whole endeavour would make you starkly aware of the futility of it all and that's the last thing any of us needs.

With football we like to feel we're part of something bigger than ourselves, so we indulge in all kinds of odd rituals and traditions, though thankfully the whole human sacrifice thing has now been knocked on the head, so to speak. Carrying on traditions reinforces our clubs' identities. Most are straightforward but with others one often doesn't have to take too much of a step back before they look a bit weird. Take Preston North End and Blackburn Rovers. If either club are relegated then fans of both line the streets as a coffin, draped in the relegated club's colours, is paraded through the equidistant village of Bamber Bridge and buried. This is to signify a bad season being put to rest. It's then dug up again when the relegated side gains promotion. It has a curiously English kind of creepiness to it, like *The Wicker Man* but so creepy it doesn't even need a massive wicker man to burn a policeman in.

Many of these traditions stem from superstition. Whether it's wearing lucky socks to a match, trying to sit in the same spot in the pub for every game or attempting to sneeze during every penalty in a shoot-out because you did it once and your team scored, something about football makes otherwise rational people believe, or at least do, some pretty odd things.

It's not just fans who indulge in it either. After all, club officials and players are fans, too, and they're the ones supposedly being influenced by these things. In the north-west of Spain, a region broadly known for its superstition, Deportivo La Coruña throw garlic cloves around their pitch before matches to ward off evil spirits. Hilariously, Real Madrid failed to beat them at Estadio Riazor for nineteen years, between 1991 and 2010, suggesting that they are at the very least descended from vampires. In Brazil, Botafogo once had a mascot named Biriba, a stray dog who ran on to the pitch while they were attacking during a match in the 1948 season. In the resulting chaos they scored and president Carlito Rocha adopted him and brought him to every game. He was paid the same bonuses as the players – though what he did with the money is anyone's guess – and Rocha would sometimes release him on to the pitch to break up opposition attacks. A shrewd move. No self-respecting referee is going to book a dog, however unsportsdog-like their conduct. Before one match Biriba cocked his leg on a Botafogo player and, unfortunately for him, they went on to be victorious. Rocha would try to make Biriba do this to the same player before every game and they went on to win the league. The lesson is that football is so enchanting it makes people who are otherwise capable enough to become presidents of successful sporting institutions believe in the powers of magical dog piss.

Superstitions among players are, of course, common. Johan Cruyff would slap Ajax goalkeeper Gert Bals in the stomach before every game, which must have been confusing for Bals. Did that make his stomach good or bad? Their team-mate Gerrie Mühren would wear winger Sjaak Swart's pants in every European Cup game. The logic beggars belief. Give yourself the credit. Ajax didn't win three consecutive European Cups by appealing to the God of Pants and Slaps. Of what value is a European Cup to such a deity? Former Italy striker Filippo Inzaghi had a different approach. He would eat a box of rusks before each game, making sure to leave two because: 'That way the stars will stay aligned in my favour.' I don't know either, but no wonder he barely ever ran. He must have started every match reeling from a sugar crash.

Maybe it's the spontaneous nature of sport and the tremendous amount of variables involved that make people believe it can be influenced by fate or any force outside that which is happening on the pitch. Even now, in the age of data, superstitions are commonplace. Perhaps Opta are missing a trick by not trying to quantify the effects of belly slaps, rusks and garlic on football.

Rivalries

The worst thing about football barely even needs to be mentioned. You know what it is already. It's those pathetic, deluded, pungent, cretinous little cry-baby philistine pillocks who support Whoever Your Rival Club Is. Mugs. Sometimes you'll meet one via a mutual friend and when your teams are revealed there's a weird moment between you, a simultaneous sizing up. Will they be one that's 'typical' or all right, despite their obvious deficiencies? Terrible as these creatures are, they need to be there. Every great story needs a villain after all.

Many factors go into rivalries: geography; success, both current and historical; league position; a long run of one team beating the other; whatever may be riding on the outcome and countless others. The more of these elements that combine, the higher the intensity, like in the kind of scientific analogy that you might find in a better book.

Geography is obviously the most common cause of a rivalry. Nothing is more of an affront to the proud reputation of your area than people who also live in it.

Dundee and Dundee United are the most extreme example of this. They have the closest grounds in the world, just 300 yards apart, yet won't share a stadium to save money. That's one in the eye for Scottish stereotypes. The rivalry is surprisingly amicable, though, to the point where fans even formed a joint hooligan firm to combat larger, visiting hordes. It's so close to being civil, yet so far because of all the punching. In Lisbon, Benfica and Sporting's grounds are only a mile apart yet they display an almost quaint civility. Sporting call their neighbours 'The Lamps' because they play in the Stadium of Light, while Benfica call Sporting fans 'The Lizards' because of their green and white kit. Celtic and Rangers it isn't.

Geography is sometimes irrelevant, though. Manchester United and Manchester City can't bear each other, Manchester United and Liverpool are fierce rivals, Liverpool and Everton have a heated competition, but Manchester City and either Merseyside club, and Manchester United and Everton don't really care about each other. That's quite hard to explain to an outsider.

As is to be expected, the most heated rivalries are sporting, those where the teams are most evenly matched on the pitch. Take *El Clásico*. Barcelona and Real Madrid are arguably the world's two biggest clubs. They are from the two biggest cities in Spain, one associated with Spanish nationalism, one a symbol of Catalan nationalism, each representing differing political ideologies. Everything about them is opposed. When Luis Figo made the dastardly move of signing for Madrid from Barcelona he became a hate figure for ever, with one fan even throwing a pig's head at him during a game. Poor Figo. He's always getting stuff chucked at him. Someone even kicked a football out of a telly at him in that hair dye advert he did.

El Clásico is probably the biggest fixture in sport. It's become a hugely marketed mega-event and what makes it so good is that it rarely disappoints. How do you top *El Clásico*? With *Superclásico*, that's how!

Superclásico is the name of the hotly contested Buenos Aires derby between Boca Juniors and River Plate. The clubs boast more than 70 per cent of Argentinian football fans between them and the derby is known globally for an intensity that borders on the hysterical. Both clubs were originally based in La Boca, a working-class dock-yard area, before River relocated to the more affluent north of the city in 1925. The rivalry has often been painted as one of class, with Boca representing the working classes and River actively embracing their image of the haves to Boca's have-nots, calling themselves *Los Millonarios*, or The Millionaires. This is, of course, a pretty abstract concept as like any teams both have supporters from different backgrounds but River fans revel in it. They call Boca 'little pigs', 'manure collectors' and 'the cabaret', a brilliantly snooty swipe at their players' reputation for individualism. They also have a gigantic, helium-filled pig in Boca colours that they hover in front of them from the stands. Boca simply call them 'chickens', in reference to River's supposedly gutless performances.

The intensity is such that both stadiums are known to physically bounce during the derby. Carlos Tevez was once sent off for doing a chicken dance when he scored, the referee claiming that he was inciting violence, while River's Matías Almeyda also received the same charge for kissing the River badge in front of Boca's fans. There's a convincing argument that the whole fixture is one giant incitement to violence and at times it has gone too far. A 2015 *Copa Libertadores* clash between the two was abandoned when Boca fans fired pepper spray into the faces of four River players, leading to Boca's suspension from the tournament; a little more extreme than an inflatable pig. Such is the status of the game that summer friendlies are played for the spectacle – and a crucial revenue stream – and it is even being taken around the world. Hopefully casual fans will be a little calmer. If you end up getting a ticket, leave your chemical weapons at home.

We all know about the big Premier League rivalries, the Old Firm derby, the Milan derby, *El Clásico* and the *Superclásico* and, while they're all fascinating, some of the lesser-known rivalries in world football are worth exploring, too. Some are a lot more intense than their obscurity would suggest . . .

Uruguayan club football isn't something that receives a lot of international coverage despite the achievements, star players and proud history of the national team. The Montevideo derby, however, is one of the craziest in football. It is the oldest outside Britain and is contested between Peñarol and Nacional, who between them have dominated their domestic league and won eight *Copa Libertadores*. The competition between them is furious. In 1902 and 1903 Nacional went unbeaten throughout both seasons. Not to be outdone Peñarol won the title in 1905 by winning every game and not conceding a single goal. If that seems like an incredibly well-executed kind of pettiness, there's every chance it was. Pettiness defines it. In 1941 Nacional beat Peñarol 6–0, the highest margin of victory in the history of the fixture. The second teams also played that day, with Nacional winning 4–0. This became known as *'El Di Del 10–0'*, or 'the Day of 10–0'. Nacional fans still crow about it today and, in retaliation, Peñarol supporters sing about their 7–3 win in 1911. Today.

The pettiness was such that, in 1949, 2–0 and two men down at the break, Nacional simply refused to play the second half. Legend has it that they climbed out of the dressing-room window in protest at the referee. Peñarol fans weren't convinced, dubbing it *'Clásico de la Fuga'*, or 'the Derby Where They Ran Away'. They compete at *everything*. In 2011 Peñarol broke the world record for the longest flag at a football match, at 309 metres. Two years later Nacional smashed that with a 600-metre effort, which they must have spent the entirety of those two years making. The atmosphere often transfers on to the pitch and multiple red cards are commonplace, with twenty players eventually sent off after a game descended into chaos in 1990. It's unsurprising given the atmosphere it is played in, but in 2000 it was so bad that nine players spent a month in jail.

In sporting terms India is best known for cricket rather than football but when East Bengal and Mohun Bagan meet in the Kolkata derby they can draw crowds bigger than many cricket matches, the record being 131,000 at the Salt Lake Stadium. India are at 162 in the FIFA rankings at the time of writing and the game is incongruously massive for a nation not known for football. While it has been marred by crowd trouble in the past there are a few interesting traditions among fans that must surely be unique in the sport. To taunt each other, fans drop their pants and wave their penises around – willycoptering, to give this practice its correct name – and the fans of the losing side go hungry. If they win, the East Bengal fans eat hilsa fish, whereas if Mohun Bagan take the spoils they dine on king prawns. Roy Keane would go ballistic, though you can say that about most things.

Football never feels like it means more than when you're playing your biggest rivals. It is a nerve-shredding, mentally exhausting experience, even when you're winning, because the high levels of pressure often make it unpredictable. If you're putting your reputation on the line in general whenever your team play, you're doing it doubly so against that lot. A win on derby day is one of the most satisfying feelings in football. You won *and* you made them lose. Perfect. Of course, there does come a time when such rivalries can be put to one side . . .

Your Country

One of the joys of being a fan is that you get two teams. One you choose, one you don't. For the majority of fans their early memories are of international tournaments, in England those generally ending in glorious defeat or disappointing exits, depending on your age. It sort of doesn't matter, though, as there's something utterly magical about the summer tournaments. Suddenly everyone supports the same team, football is on all the time and you can even appreciate players from your rival clubs because suddenly they're on your side. Even better is someone from your team chipping in for your country. It can also provide a welcome break if things aren't going your way; when your club disappoint, you always have your country; when your country let you down, there's always your club.

If you're lucky your team will play just well enough to make you think, hope, maybe even believe for a little while that maybe, if Denmark did it, if Greece did it, if England have already done it, then maybe you might have a chance. You probably won't, but those moments are precious and only come along once every two years. There are lots of ways to rationalise a tournament exit: there's always next time; the domestic season starts again soon; and anyway, it's only a game. It's not *really* important, right?

So yes, football is just a game but, put simply, it's more than that if you want it to be. Yes, it's ultimately unimportant but the important things in life are often scary or boring. Tax is important. Bouncy castles are not. Bouncy castles are way more enjoyable. What's wrong with appreciating that? To be fair, bouncy castle appreciators rarely, if ever, chant drunkenly and aggressively about their castle at people who don't care on public transport but if they did it wouldn't be the fault of the bouncy castles themselves. To suggest so would be absurd. Roy Keane would go ballistic.

Sport is unique in that it's spontaneous entertainment. Movies could learn from this. Imagine if you went to see the latest James Bond film knowing that, in different screenings, you'd get different endings. Maybe he saves the day again, maybe this time he really does get his balls lasered off. If you enjoy something enough to care about it, it matters. That's a luxury that we have in the developed world and to not appreciate it would be absolutely criminal. Deep down Stuart from the wedding knows this because he's exactly the type of person who will say football fans are all sad before spending hours on the internet arguing about the latest episode of *Doctor Who*.

So what are people missing? A whole culture. The elite level skill and athleticism on display at the top. The addictive rush of a match-day crowd that can't be replicated elsewhere – a unique biological experience, a whole *feeling* some people will never know. The strange, nerdy little quirks of this giant, absurd, real-life soap opera, aspects you can understand only with the insider knowledge you have as a fan. There's Nigerian side Police Machine denying match-fixing after winning a play-off game 67–0. There's the simple joy of a strange name, be that Bahaman team Insurance Management Bears, Belgian defender Mark de Man or former Cardiff City player Jazzi Barnum-Bobb, a man who sounds like a cockney grandad on ketamine trying to describe a young person's haircut. There's Sergio Ramos getting sent off again, there's '*Diamond Lights*', there's so much, and the more seriously football takes itself the more appealing all this incongruity becomes. So next time somebody is smug about not liking football or seems to look down on you because you do, remember: we know something they don't know, and to paraphrase Millwall: you don't like it, we don't care.

5. Refereeing

Luke Aaron Moore

Football would be nothing without admin. It's painful to admit it but really, every single mazy run, through-ball, tackle, goal and trophy win is underpinned by a bunch of men (and it is almost always men) in suits in a boardroom somewhere making decisions and administering the sport we all love so much, and, most importantly for this chapter, another bunch of men on the pitch itself making sure everyone behaves themselves. In football, as in life, officials are needed everywhere. Otherwise, how does hell sound? In a handcart. Because that's where we'd be.

As Jim mentioned at the start of the book, football started as a sort of collection of disparate sports, pastimes and hobbies that slowly but surely all gravitated towards each other in the same way that Earth was formed from a giant disc-shaped cloud of dust and material, eventually clumping together to form asteroids and then, finally and gloriously for the purposes of us being able to write and read this chapter, the Earth. The rest is obviously history.

Several billion years after the Earth was indeed formed, the inception and formalisation of the Football Association helped to standardise the game around the world. This meant that, if England weren't able to be the world leaders in anything that happened on the pitch very often – save for a period at the end of the nineteenth century, when no one other than them and Scotland were even playing the game properly, and a heady summer in 1966 – they were at least able to make sure everyone was doing as they were told as per the documents that a bunch of men (again, it's always men) drew up one afternoon above the Freemasons' Tavern in London in 1863.

As Jim also said, the beautifully named Ebenezer Cobb Morley and his pals were probably drunk back in '63 and, if they were, they should have made more of an effort to load the dice in favour of England. At least then we could have had more of a chance on the pitch itself in the 150 or so years that followed, because what's currently being adhered to seems a bit too fair and balanced for my taste and, if the tabloid newspapers are to be believed, almost specifically designed to scupper England in major tournaments.

But that's a digression we can't presently afford. So, back to business. At that point there were only fourteen laws passed by Morley and his mates, and they didn't include such staples of the modern game as corners, goal-kicks or even penalties. For example, it wasn't until 1891 that the penalty was introduced as a punishment for a foul because, and I absolutely love this, at the time it was thought that no gentleman would ever lower himself to deliberately foul an opponent. Yeah, as you can probably imagine, that didn't last too long. In 1891 they had to swallow their pride, accept that none of them was really a gentleman in the truest sense and introduce the penalty kick, as suggested as a rule change by an Irishman, William McCrum, in 1890.

McCrum, clearly no stranger to drama, didn't propose it be called a 'penalty kick', though. That came much later. McCrum, in what would prove to be a chilling portent for any English football fan unlucky enough to witness their team at an international tournament exactly 100 years later, settled on the rather more atmospheric moniker, 'the Kick of Death'. Yes, really. The Kick of Death.

It was noted by McCrum's great-grandson in an article for *The Observer* in 2004 that he was, in his capacity as a goalkeeper, getting more and more concerned at the increasing competitiveness and excessive tackling that was going on and so thought of a rule change to curb it. How marvellous it would have been to be involved in football at a time when, if you didn't like something, you could suggest a law change and it would actually be considered. There's also something very poetic about a goalkeeper inventing the concept of the penalty – how many times since has the man between the sticks been the hero for his team by saving one? Although largely forgotten by the game now sadly, McCrum has left a legacy for his fellow goalkeepers that's lasted 100 years and counting. Good for him.

The main reason 1891 is an important year for the purposes of this chapter, though, is because it was also the year that the first referees began to appear in the modern game. Previously, players would decide contentious decisions among themselves and the amateur nature of the game meant that every participant was assumed to be the model of honesty and gentlemanly conduct. Corinthian Football Club, a proud and amateur footballing institution that helped popularise the game worldwide with its overseas tours, famously refused to even contemplate the idea of accepting a penalty kick, and one of their most prominent players, C.B. Fry, remarked on McCrum's new suggestion by saying it was 'a standing insult to sportsmen to have to play under a rule which assumes that players intend to tip, hack and push opponents and to behave like cads of the first kidney'. Mr Fry was clearly quite the resister of progress.

At that point, on the rare occasions that something relating to the laws couldn't be decided upon, it was referred to two off-pitch umpires for the final say. But in 1891 that all changed and an on-pitch referee was introduced, with the two umpires becoming what we now know as assistant referees. For the first time an official referee, who didn't have to listen to any sort of appeals from players when making decisions, was now a part of the game.

New laws were added here and there in the following years and in the 1930s Stanley Rous, an Englishman who would go on to be FIFA president in 1961, decided to update the language from Victorian English and tidy up and order the laws that had been added to and amended over the previous fifty years. Stanley, a former referee, did such a good job that they wouldn't be looked at again properly until 1997. See, if nothing else, we're good at this admin business, us Brits.

As of 2016, the FIFA Laws of the Game run to 144 pages, but they're all still based around those fourteen original laws from more than a century ago.

So that's a quick rundown on how the game has been officiated on the pitch since its inception. Now let's take a more general look at refereeing and officiating – an aspect of the game that's become more and more important as the coverage and scrutiny of football has increased. And I promise this isn't all a huge and elaborate ruse to give me an excuse to talk about how much I love watching Premier League referee Mike Dean in action. Because I do, you know. I really, really do. The man is box office. More on him in a bit.

Referees

Despite me mentioning that today's rules are based on those original nineteenth-century laws, it should be obvious to everyone that refereeing in this day and age is a million miles away from those nascent gentlemen quietly and classily overseeing games between amateur players with moustaches in grainy sepia.

Nowadays, the granular detail in which every big game is analysed includes refereeing decisions as well, and the role has never been tougher. Far too often referees are used as scapegoats to cover up a manager's or team's shortcomings. There are too many managers at all levels of the game who are all too ready to hide behind a questionable refereeing decision or a perceived injustice meted out by an official rather than turn that focus inwards and concentrate on what they or their team could have done better. As we'll see in the remainder of this chapter, refereeing is not only hard to get right, it's also essential for the smooth running of the game we all love.

Of course, refereeing at the top level has been professionalised for some time now, and that select group at the top of the Premier League tree have to be almost astonishingly good to keep up with players who can be half their age and twice as quick, as well as having the authority to keep discipline, ensure the safety of the players and also make decisions in the blink of an eye, all while millions of people watch on.

While we all like to demonise and admonish referees for decisions that go against our team, I think if we're being totally honest it's such a hard job in the modern day it borders on the impossible. Players get faster and trickier, the money and therefore the pressure associated with the game gets higher and more suffocating, and the analysis is ever more detailed. Being a referee is like babysitting twenty-two unruly children, all of whom get paid millions more a year than you and so tend to have an inflated opinion of their own contribution to the world. Unlike babysitting, you have to do so in front of several million of their most loyal followers, inside a thick, smothering atmosphere where everything is magnified to the finest detail, usually by scores of cameras providing an angle on every incident. And when it's all done, a load more loudmouths run the rule over exactly how many times you were wrong. Utterly thankless.

Yet despite this referees still, according to Premier League figures from 2013/14, get around 95 per cent of decisions right (a figure that rises to 98.4 per cent in the penalty area. William McCrum would be proud) and an almost miraculous 99 per cent of offside calls right, too. And yes, it's tempting to think that the Premier League *would* say that, but when you stop to think about the sheer amount of decisions that are made, it seems pretty accurate to me. So, never mind hero-worshiping the player who pulls on the shirt of your club and scores a last-minute winner – these men and women with the whistles are every inch the superstar, too.

Being A Referee Is Hard

So, just how hard is it to be a referee? Well, we obviously can't replicate the conditions or the intensity of a big game or even a training game between professional players to find out but, as I mentioned earlier, they have to be fit, agile and athletic to have any chance at all of keeping up with the modern-day player. As a result of this, the select group of top referees train almost as hard as the young men they are expected to officiate, despite many of them being quite a lot older (Phil Dowd, Mark Halsey and Chris Foy have all taken charge of Premier League games when north of fifty years of age), and that's before we even get to the presence of mind they need to have to make clear, cool-headed decisions when the pressure is on or fatigue sets in towards the end of a game.

But if we can't replicate the decision-making process, can we at least get an idea of how difficult it is to pass the regular fitness test, something that top referees have to demonstrate at a basic level before being assessed on their game performance? It turns out that we can, to an extent. I found the FIFA Fitness Test for Referees and Assistant Referees online and then had it verified by an official at the Premier League. It consists of the following:

- 6 x 40m sprints, each to be completed in under 6.2sec, with 90sec recovery time in between. If prospective referees fail once, they are awarded one more sprint. If they fail more than once, the test is failed.
- Laps of a 200m athletic track, sprinting 150m inside 30sec before completing the last 50m in 35sec as recovery. This test must be completed ten times and prospective referees are not permitted to fall behind or go ahead of the allotted timed sections.

The tests are to be performed twice a month.

As a man who has criticised not just refereeing in the past on *The Football Ramble*, but the fitness levels of certain referees operating in the upper echelons of the game, I thought it was only fair that I walked a mile or so in their shoes to give myself a greater understanding of what it's like. To help me, and to provide a further set of data, I enlisted my fellow presenter Marcus.

A bit of detail to help you build up a mental picture: I am a reasonably fit 36-year-old man. I run three to four times a week over what could be termed 'middle distance'. I ran the ten-mile Great South Run in 2013 in what I would call a perfectly respectable time of 1hr 24min 58sec, and I am younger than most Premier League officials. Fair enough, I'm carrying a bit of timber – at 6ft 3in, I come in at about 15 stone – and when it comes to running I'm a bit of a slow-and-steady plodder, but who isn't at our age, eh? Besides, carrying a bit never stopped Phil Dowd, or Alan Wiley. In fact, if I was to compare myself to a referee in terms of physique it would probably be a taller, hairier Alan Wiley. I'll leave that a while to sink in.

At first glance I was less worried about the track laps, which seemed a bit like a slightly adapted bleep test. The sprints, though, looked pretty tough.

Marcus, on the other hand, is slightly younger than me, probably more naturally athletic and has played football to a reasonable standard. I would describe his physique as 'Carlos Tevez-esque': shortish, but broad, barrel-chested and tenacious. He is also very quick for a 33-year-old man over short distances. I rated him as having a better chance of making the grade than me. His refereeing doppelganger, to see these unnecessary comparisons through to their final conclusion, would probably be a slightly shorter Kevin Friend.

And so it came to pass that one late spring afternoon Marcus and I drove to our nearest set of football pitches armed with some training kit and a few cones to mark out distances (we didn't have access to a speed gun, a stopwatch would have to do) and attempted to become, in fitness terms at least, FIFA referees.

It should be said at this stage that I also extended this invitation to both Jim and Pete, the other two presenters on the show, but they both respectfully declined to be involved. I say 'respectfully'. Jim said he 'massively didn't want to do it' and Pete said that his 'legs hurt' and he has his own portion of this book to write thank you very much and could I please stop bothering him.

For the record, let it also be said in these pages that, in the following few paragraphs, when you judge Marcus and I for what happened in this attempt, please do bear in mind that neither Jim (thirty-four, gangly, hates exercise) nor Pete (thirty-five, tiny man, no body strength, weak-minded and willed) would have had a prayer of making it anyway and it would have been a huge waste of time for them to even attempt it. Marcus and I were secretly delighted they weren't involved, the little slugs.

Right, back to Marcus and me, in a park. The first thing to say is that it was pissing down. We trudged over to a huge patch of grass and put our football boots on (extra grip; I was going to need all the help I could get).

There was a two-man consensus that we should attempt the sprints first. I got the impression that Marcus, as a naturally quick man, was actually looking forward to this part of the test. As someone whose pace could be described as 'glacial', I wasn't.

We meticulously measured out the 40 metres, both commented that it looked like way too far and we must have got it wrong. So we measured it out again. It was correct.

After an all-too-brief warm-up, Marcus was to go first and he stood at the start point next to the first set of markers and started stretching out.

'Ready?' I shouted. 'Yep,' came the reply.

I counted him down from five. He exploded from the line and ran through the makeshift gate at the opposite end. He actually made it look pretty easy. 5.92sec. Well within the 6.2sec target time.

'I was probably going at about 80 per cent then,' he said, in a tone that came a little bit close to showing off for my liking. He used the 90 seconds he had to make his way back to the starting gate, and prepared himself for his second run.

During the next five he had to complete there is no doubt that fatigue played a part, but as the rain stopped and the wind started to die down he made it fairly easily – 5.55sec, 5.8sec, 5.73sec, 5.68sec and finally another 5.55sec.

I was up next. I was actually pretty nervous. Having spent a decent portion of my broadcasting career slating referees I was now fairly certain I was going to be proved a hell of a lot slower than them. Still, at least there weren't that many people around.

On my first sprint I pushed as hard as I could and clocked in at 6.11sec – narrowly inside the standard needed. The problem was that I was running as near to 100 per cent as my pathetically weak legs would carry me. Initially the recovery time wasn't a problem. By the time I had to start my second run I had caught my breath, but I didn't start very well and I registered 6.25sec – outside the target time, which meant I'd now fallen foul of my one permitted failure and would have to nail the next five in a row. I picked up a touch in the next two: 6.01sec (that one was with a serendipitous tailwind and I couldn't have been more grateful) and 6.19sec.

When it was time to go for my sixth, but effectively fifth, sprint I didn't have much left in the tank and I was still blowing. In what was possibly the slowest sprint an able-bodied man has ever performed in Dulwich Park, south London, I clocked a pathetic 6.48sec. I was (and am) technically not fast enough to be a top-level referee.

So how fast have you got to be, in real terms? What do those times actually represent? Well, I'm not the fastest runner by any means but Marcus is pretty nippy, and I wonder how many more of those he had left in the tank by the end of the exercise.

When one takes into account that top-level refs probably have to make those types of sprints well in excess of twenty times a game, with no way of telling how much rest one is going to get in between them, it's a pretty impressive display of not just speed but fitness and recovery, too.

The second part of the assignment involved us marking out a huge rectangle 150 metres in length and 50 metres wide as our makeshift running track. Once we'd done that we set out running the first 150m inside the 30sec time limit. After we had evened out how fast we would need to move to make it, my first instinct was: 'Wow, this is a decent clip.' It also soon became apparent that the recovery time (50m to the next marker in just 35sec) would soon feel almost non-existent. One lap alone was enough to get us both seriously blowing – ten was . . . beyond us.

I managed two laps, Marcus bravely soldiered on for five before calling it a day. At one point after catching his breath Marcus turned to me and chuckled incredulously: 'How on earth is a fifty-year-old man doing that?' I could only shake my head because I was still too knackered to speak. My legs were still sore a good three days later, largely due to the explosive nature of the sprint test.

As youngish, active men, neither of us were anywhere near fit enough to come close to the standard needed. I shudder to think what we'll be like when we hit Chris

Foy's age, especially when we later read that, for the 2016/17 season, the tests were to get even harder. Massive respect due.

Refereeing Top Five

Now we've established, in humiliating fashion, just how hard it is to be one of these superhuman officials in the middle of the pitch, it's probably prudent for me to bring you a list of my top five most notable referees, those men in the middle who have repeatedly caught my eye for differing reasons. Every football fan has a problem with one referee, or more, because of decisions they've made when officiating one of their team's games but, as we've already established, it's bloody hard being a referee so let's put that to one side for now and take a moment to look at these men whose contribution to the game is all-too-often forgotten.

There's only one place to start. The man who, according to one newspaper at the end of the 2015/16 season, was the subject of more tweets than all the other Premier League referees put together . . .

Mike Dean, aka the End of Level Boss, aka King Ref, aka the Nicolas Cage of Referees

Forget what you might hear about Howard Webb refereeing the 2010 World Cup final, or Mark Clattenburg being given the 2016 Champions League final in the same year as the FA Cup final AND the European Championship final – there is only one truly box-office referee working in the game today and that man's name is Michael Dean.

Whereas every other referee in the game appears to enjoy refereeing football as an extension of their own authoritarian personality – think police officers, prison wardens, politicians (by the way, you have to wonder about the cerebral make-up of individuals who actively decide they want to spend all their time telling other people what to do) – Deany is a pure, unadulterated performer.

For the purposes of this, try to think of a football match as a West End musical. Mike Dean is, without question, the principal performer. He interprets his role with gusto, undoubtedly warming up his disciplining voice in the referee's room before the game with a series of scales, stretching out with a barre in front of a portable mirror he's brought along with him. In another universe, Mike Dean is a RADA graduate.

If any of this has passed you by up until now, next time you catch a game being officiated by the great man, just watch him. Tear yourself away from the actual football for just one game to watch Dean in all his glory – his accentuated hand movements to deny a fallen striker a penalty; his fantastic no-look caution, when he flashes the yellow card as high as he can while purposely looking in the opposite direction just to exaggerate his disdain for the infringement; and his magnificent head-shake while grimacing sympathetically at the player he's about to penalise, as if to say: 'What do you want me to do? What choice have you given me, pal?', all the while secretly delighted he's got yet more screen time.

I'd be fairly confident that Dean hardly even likes football. At heart he's simply a man who loves an audience. I'd be in no way surprised if at some point in his adolescence he worked out that he could perform in front of an unimaginably large crowd on a weekly basis if he just rigorously worked on his fitness and studied the laws of football. There's a lot to admire in that.

It's impossible for Mike Dean to be intimidated by any big-earning superstar on a football pitch because, as far as he's concerned, *he* is the only superstar in football, and that's fantastic. If you need further proof just how little anything else outside of the refereeing process matters to the great man, then go online and check out how many times he actually celebrates advantages he's played that have led to goals. He actually celebrates – I've seen him do it at least twice. A referee, a man whose career is essentially over if any rumour about him being in any way biased were to be in the least bit substantiated, celebrating goals, on the pitch, in front of tens of thousands of people. If you can't admire the sheer not-give-a-fuckery of that, then I pity you.

Everything about Mike Dean is magnificent and I'll not hear anything to the contrary. As football fans we are all merely supporting actors in the play of Mike Dean's life and I am hugely happy about that. Long may he run.

If I'm dishing out an equivalent Hollywood actor to Mike, it's Nicolas Cage. Nicolas Cage in anything. Overacting is *not* a problem here, it's an asset.

Phil Dowd, aka The Great Debater, aka Captain Disdain

There's one main reason why Phil Dowd gets a mention here, and it's not that he was very impressively still a Premier League referee at the age of 52 before injury led to his retirement in 2016. As a man who is still now trying to get his breath back after one of those fitness tests, believe me I know how remarkable that is.

Dowdy is in this list of notable referees because he was a man who, in spite of being on the end of what I assume were several tellings off from his superiors and instructions to stop being so confrontational, genuinely appeared to enjoy having full-on stand-up rows with football players in the middle of football games. The aloof, move-away-from-me-my-decision-is-final style of refereeing was something Phil had no interest in. He liked confrontation, he appeared to actively pursue it, and he wasn't intimidated by any player he ever met.

I lost count of the times I saw him cut off a player trying to remonstrate with him by interjecting with a 'No, no, no!' and a shake of the head. It was a joy to watch. And although Mike Dean will always be the king of the no-look yellow card, Dowd provided a career highlight of his own in October 2014 by sending off Chelsea's Branislav Ivanović in the most nonchalant way I've ever seen. Ivanović, already on a yellow, was adjudged to have fouled Angel Di María in the left channel and Dowd was straight over there like a bullet from a gun (those fitness test sprints no doubt playing their part. Recovery time? Non-existent). He showed another yellow and then the red in such quick succession that poor old Branislav barely had time to register what was happening. To compound his misery, Phil refused to even look in the general direction of the Serb, such was his disdain. It was a masterful display of authority from a man who was born for the role. By that stage in the game (it was in stoppage time) Ivanović knew better than to say anything lest he be cut down to size by yet another witty broadside from the master. Take your medicine Branislav. Mr Dowd is deaf to your witless complaining.

And yes, I know he had a bit of 'fun' with Robbie Keane during a Spurs game once, but that was ages ago and way before Dowdy became way too old for this shit. If I had to compare him to a character from a Hollywood film I'm going for Danny Glover's in *Lethal Weapon*. 'And who's playing the Mel Gibson role?' I hear you ask. That's easy. Every footballer ever.

Mark Clattenburg, aka the Preener, aka the Cristiano Ronaldo of Refs, aka Let's Be Mates

'Clatts' is a funny old fish to analyse. Not immediately a man who looks like he relishes the authority or the responsibility that comes with doing his job, he seems to be the type that likes to fit in, hence the gelled hair, the preening style and the constant 'banter' with the players. By the way, don't make the mistake of conflating this player interaction with a Dowd-esque authority of sharp wit and derision. Clatts almost certainly wants to be one of the lads.

By way of analogy, in my experience of a number of terrible dead-end jobs, a line manager almost invariably fits into two distinct categories: they either want to boss you around whenever they can, or they want to be your mate. Clatts is the matey type, without question.

How else could we possibly explain the Craig Bellamy and Adam Lallana incidents or the ersatz footballer tattoos? Let me put it this way, if you cast your eye across the Wikipedia pages of several of the top referees I've mentioned here, they almost all have a 'Controversy' section. Usually, those sections consist merely of a list of high-profile mistakes made by fallible human beings doing a job in ridiculously difficult circumstances. But not Mark Clattenburg's.

His is made up of those same type of mistakes, too, but also the type of controversies you'd expect from a man who very much wants to be part of the football furniture, a sort of 'let me in, I'm one of you' type of desperation in which he appears to want to endear himself to certain footballers by 'bantering' with them about other players he assumes are unpopular. Hence him allegedly asking the Man City bench 'how they put up' with Craig Bellamy all week, and remarking that Adam Lallana had 'changed' since he started being picked for England.

Take a tip from the old masters, Mark. The only words Phil Dowd has for players are laced with heavy sarcasm, and I'm fairly sure Mike Dean doesn't even know any of their names.

So Clattenburg is Johnny Depp. He's sort of popular, and he's done some high-profile stuff (refereeing three big finals in 2016, that was his *Pirates of the Caribbean* trilogy, and no, I'm not even recognising the fourth and fifth instalments) but the more this carries on the more you start to wonder if he's just a bit needy and weird. Besides, all that hair product must be a killer when the rain starts pouring down. At least Depp can wear a shit hat.

Howard Webb, aka Born To Do It, aka the Good Guy

If Mike Dean was born to perform, then Howard Webb was born to referee. Although he was, and now is again since retiring from the game, a police officer by trade, Webb was always an enjoyable watch.

If Deany does his thing by just blowing everyone away with his charisma and Dowdy just oozed contempt, then Webb used his physical presence and Yorkshire personality to keep things ticking over nicely. His thigh muscles were a rival to any player's, his height and breadth colossal. His shiny bald head adding a sort of tough-guy type dimension to his work, Webb was at home on any stage. I liked him, and I even thought he did a good job in the 2010 World Cup final, despite the Netherlands' blatant attempts to turn it into a bloodbath. The big man had little choice than to take the game into the trenches that night, and he did it with gusto. His notebook had steam coming off of it by the time it came to blow the final whistle, but a man like Webb does what he has to do. Someone has to keep the scrotes in line, and if those pencil-pushers down at City Hall don't like it, they can have his badge (notebook) and gun (vanishing free-kick spray).

Since retirement, rumours persist that in addition to his work on BT Sport punditing, Webb is equally at home in the crowd at Rotherham United, where you can find him patiently and happily fielding questions from fellow fans about decisions, the laws of the game and explaining controversial incidents. A measure of the man.

Big Howard was Clint Eastwood – a man for the big occasion who took absolutely no nonsense whatsoever. If he had to trek through the desert on a horse with no name to find you and book you for a cynical foul to stop a counter-attack, you can bet a fistful of dollars he'd do so.

Pierluigi Collina, aka the Greatest, aka the Man It's Impossible To Do This Section Without

There are readers of a certain vintage who silently mouth the words 'Pierluigi Collina' just as soon as the word 'referee' is mentioned, like a football-themed word association test. Although retired from the game since 2005, Collina was the best there ever was, and he now heads up the referees department at UEFA.

He elevated officiating a football match to an art form, and was voted the best referee in the world for six years in a row by the International Federation of Football History and Statistics from 1998 to 2003. It's probably near to impossible for a referee to transcend his trade, but Collina came as close as anyone to doing so.

One of the few referees untainted by the *Calciopoli* scandal in Italy, he was also unrivalled on the pitch. He has a bit of a penchant for hoovering up big wads of cash since retirement, taking on endorsements all over the place and also controversially assuming a lucrative role as head of referees for the Football Federation of Ukraine despite rarely visiting the country and not really having any ties there. But hey, no one's perfect and there's enough money swilling around football's trough for everyone to get their snout wet. Go for it Pierluigi, that's what I say. I'm fairly certain he even got his bald dome on the front of a FIFA video game once, and there can't be many (if any) other referees that have done that. Lofty stuff.

The answer to your next question is Marlon Brando. The greatest (and also bald and gluttonously rich, as was Brando in his later years).

Other Officials

Of course, the men in black can't do everything themselves. They need an assistant or three to keep everything from descending into bloody chaos both off the pitch and on. As Jamie Redknapp would say, your Dowds and your Deans and your Clattenburgs are good, but they're not literally superheroes, are they Ruud? Here's a rundown of the other personalities that keep every match day ticking along.

Assistant Referees

Assistant referees, back when they were called linesmen, used to be the absolute whipping boys of the crowd. I can remember fans at Fratton Park, when I used to watch Portsmouth back in the nineties, following them up and down the touchline and screaming obscenities at them all game and then screaming further obscenities when they made a mistake, chiefly because they'd had a selection of drunken psychopaths screaming at them from two yards away for the past eighty minutes and could barely think, let alone concentrate on a marginal offside call. The stewards would do nothing at all. It was almost perverse, like a public humiliation that the victim had actually volunteered for.

Thankfully, things have moved on a touch since those days, and assistants have a far wider remit beyond waving their flag for an offside or throw-in. They're also expected to be even faster than referees; I thought those six sprints in under 6.2sec was hard – well, for assistant referees it's 6sec flat. Those offside calls (reminder, they get 99 per cent of them right) don't make themselves you know.

I feel like assistant referees get a bad reputation among football fans because there's a certain amount of telling-tales-out-of-school element to their role. It's a superhuman effort not to deride them when they call a referee over to grass on a player, and then they do that thing where they put their hand over their mouth so no one can lip-read them and the whole thing just looks like a secret society that absolutely no one wants to be a member of. As I'll come on to shortly, it's important we all respect officials and the job they have to do, but there just *has* to be a better way of communicating that stuff. To their further detriment they occasionally get piled into when a full-back slides in on a winger and it all spills over the touchline. For some reason, rather than fall gracefully, the assistant's first instinct invariably is to protect their flag by not letting go of it. What follows is a hilariously inept fall to the ground, making them look even more silly.

In the words of the great Barry Davies, they will not learn.

Fourth Official

It's hard to think of a better representation of purgatory-as-job than being a fourth official. Standing right at the coalface, between the managers' technical areas, they take care of the admin of substitutions, added-time announcements and liaising with referees and their assistants when necessary, but their real role is to try to explain away every single decision to either one irate manager or the other and, in turn, stop them tearing each other's head off. It would take remuneration on the level of a member of FIFA's Executive Committee for me to even consider the role.

One thing I would criticise them for, though, is the frankly bizarre interpretation of the added-minutes law. It never seems to be even in the same ballpark as the correct amount of time. But then, if everyone else just calmed down a bit and let them get on with it maybe their calculations would be a bit more accurate. And what's more, based on my experience, if the games were even longer because of that, referees would probably drop down dead with exhaustion.

Additional Assistant Referees

For a selection of European games, the International Football Assocation Board (which establishes the laws of the game and is recognised by FIFA) decided to implement the use of additional assistant referees to stand behind the goal-line and advise the referee of any infringements that they had a better view of. To enable them to fulfil this role, they were given a magic wand-type device with which to attract the referee's attention – something that they did, to my knowledge, fairly irregularly but occasionally nonetheless.

For some reason, most football pundits and commentators singularly failed to understand that they were there to help a referee, and that any extra officiating that ensured that correct decisions had a better chance of being made was generally what's known as a 'good thing'. They instead whinged on about it like they were put there to annoy them personally and then spent each and every game deriding and undermining them. I have never witnessed such a sustained assault on anything or anyone from the punditerati (not a word, but should be) than when these extra officials were brought into the fray.

And as our old pal Pierluigi Collina said in his capacity as UEFA's head of referees: 'Two extra pairs of eyes focusing on the penalty areas are of valuable assistance to the referee, and strengthen the refereeing team in confidence and numbers, while allowing the game to flow.'

Which is fair enough, especially when, if you're a pundit, you're partly to blame for the pressure and scrutiny referees are under in the first place and you're so arrogant that you think every single thing in the world is out to piss you off personally, including extra officials to make a referee's job easier. I'll tell you what we could do with – extra pundits to make the existing pundits' job easier. Then maybe they'll shut the fuck up about it.

The Future of Officiating

While we've ascertained that officiating is getting harder and harder it's interesting to have a think about what the future of the game looks like in this area. And instantly, what springs to mind is the subject that is discussed more than anything else – the creeping clamour for the introduction of real-time video technology.

At first glance, it appears to be a no-brainer. The money at stake and therefore the pressure and importance of each game at the top level has never been bigger. So if a video referee can assist and help in real time, why shouldn't they?

Well, and at the risk of chucking my shoe into the lace-making machine of football, I don't think it's as simple as that. That argument fails to acknowledge not only the secret of football's success but also makes the mistake of viewing the introduction of video technology as a panacea that will not only wipe out all refereeing mistakes, but also put an end to controversial decisions full stop.

Football is the most popular sport on the planet. And it's not even close. FIFA have estimated that more than 250 million people regularly play football and around 1.3 *billion* have 'stated an interest' in the game. The combined audience for the 2010 World Cup was a little more than 26 billion. These are staggering numbers, and numbers that are based around one thing: simplicity.

Football is the most popular sport in the world because there are no barriers to participation. A football can be fashioned out of just about anything – rolled up socks, plastic bags tied together and balled up, an old tennis ball – you name it, it can be a football. The environment can serve as your goal – there's a reason 'jumpers for goalposts' is now a tired old cliché.

It is vital that the sport as we watch it remains as close to that aesthetic as we can feasibly achieve. That doesn't mean football at the professional level shouldn't be maintained, improved, officiated and properly regulated but it does mean that the people running the sport have a duty to ensure it doesn't disappear into a black hole of its own conceit. It is and will always remain a sport – and sport doesn't and shouldn't exist as a set of binary decisions boiled down to 'mistake/not a mistake', or elevated above its station, and it certainly shouldn't do that because of the amounts of money involved.

And if you don't think money is behind the clamour, then why have we all been perfectly happy to pootle along enjoying the drama, narrative and controversy as a fully-fledged part of the sport we all love for the best part of 100 years until now? And don't tell me it's because the technology previously didn't exist. I've not heard a single person say 'Oh the technology is so good now, we should definitely use it' because football is, at its heart, a simple game.

The reason money is the motivating factor is because the sums involved bring with them their own pressure – investors (sponsors, gamblers etc) want to ensure they don't lose out because of a mistake. Yet players make mistakes on the field all the time, it's accepted as part of the game. If we think football has become more important over the years, it's because we've been told that's the case. But when was it decided that football is so important that referees have to get absolutely everything right 100 per cent of the time? Why now? My contention is that it's because football now believes its own hype. The simplicity is in danger of being lost and video technology's introduction into refereeing decisions is the first vehicle in getting us to that sanitised and perfect destination.

Well, football should be careful what it wishes for. The money awash in the game is intrinsically linked with its popularity, which in turn is based on its simplicity and the ease with which people can play it and watch it and understand it. The less the game on television resembles the game played in the local park, the greater the chance of the connection being lost, and the greater the chance that football loses something it takes for granted every single day – its popularity.

'But why wouldn't we try to get every single decision right if we have the means to do so?' you may ask. For one thing, real-time video technology isn't a panacea anyway, despite the continual implication that it will serve as one. Decisions taken by officials are often based on contextual interpretations of the laws at the time, and that will rarely be aided by a replay. For instance, if an attacking player is sprinting into the penalty area with the ball at his feet and there is a tangle of legs right on the edge of the eighteen-yard box, we've seen every type of decision given in the past – dive, free-kick, penalty, play on. No video replay in the world, whatever the angle or definition, is going to definitively solve that problem by deciding what the correct decision is or was.

Other sports, including American football and rugby, use the technology and they regularly fail to come to a satisfactory conclusion that pleases all parties. The column inches dedicated to one controversial decision alone – a catch incompletion ratified by a video replay in Super Bowl 50 back in February 2016 – were eye-watering. Many will tell you that, despite the availability of video replays from all angles, the wrong decision was nevertheless made. And in the emotionally charged arena of sporting competition that shouldn't come as a surprise to anyone. NFL's rules can be described as badly defined in some areas, but the officiating of football regularly comes down to a referee's *interpretation* of an incident.

The future of the game as far as officiating goes is, I feel, not the red herring that is video technology, but the greater power of a referee (or assistant/fourth official for that matter) to be able to implement the laws as they are without fear of recrimination or haranguing on the pitch by players or off the pitch by the media. A raising of consciousness is needed in which referees are respected more – and, of course, they can play a role in that themselves by not being so regularly preposterous in the ways I've described earlier in the chapter.

Would officiating of the game be improved if players didn't surround the referee or tell him to 'fuck off' when a decision went against their team? Almost certainly. But the laws exist for the referee to do something about that anyway, they just need to implement them more readily and evenly safe in the knowledge that they'll be supported universally when they do so. But equally, would officiating of the game be improved if Mike Dean and Phil Dowd were a bit more like Howard Webb or Pierluigi Collina and didn't treat players with so much disdain and aloofness/arrogance? Absolutely.

Refereeing is something that we – referees, players, managers, fans, the media – all need to take collective responsibility for. It's not simply a case of calling for 'better referees' or chucking a load of technology in their face and hoping it'll solve the problem and we don't lose sponsors. Because if we do that blindly, at best we'll further compound the problem by over-complicating it, and at worst we'll alienate future fans by making it harder for them to fall in love with the sport in the same way we did, because it'll simply bear no resemblance to the game they play themselves.

Refereeing in future generations needs to be far more about accepting and acknowledging that those officials perform an important and necessary role that we literally can't do without, and the sooner we recognise their role as legitimate and important (something I don't think we've properly done as a football community yet) and then respect them as the full-time professional athletes they are, the better. The move by the Premier League, FA and English Football League to give referees more power to take action against 'unacceptable conduct' from the 2016/17 season is a welcome step in this direction, but we'll wait and see what transpires long-term in the implementation of it. Currently, it's the tip of a very large iceberg.

But referees themselves need to take responsibility also. As sad as it would be to have to say goodbye to the comedy antics of Messrs Dean, Clattenburg and Dowd, ultimately it would be for the best. And it's what Ebenezer Cobb Morley and his chums would have wanted, too, I'm sure.

6. Players

Pete Donaldson

People don't get *trials* for football clubs any more. Pretty soon we'll be in a situation where you'll look around your local pub and there will be pretty much no one on hand to gob off about how close they were to playing for Celtic, or Northampton, or Portsmouth. Nowadays football players are grown in underground cryo-labs and then put into development programmes, pumped full of synthetic footballer gel and then, when they reach nineteen and they've somehow been unable to secure their club a ton in image rights, they're ground into a fine paste and fed to the club pigs.

Seriously, though, it hasn't always been this way. Footballers used to be like us. Broken, fallible, heart-on-the-sleeve humans who just so happened to have a decent left foot on them. They didn't need to commit to a life of riches and fame at the age of five, they were free to live a little. Maybe learn a trade on the side. Play a little non-league and get discovered while working as a sparky on a housing estate. Although I appreciate the sacrifices and devotion to the craft of the modern footballer, they have about as much in common with me as a Michelin starred chef. A NASA engineer. Wonder Woman.

Because of this, meeting your idol is invariably like sniffing a bottle of week-old milk. You know it's on the turn, you know you'll be wholly disappointed with the experience, but for some ridiculous reason you want to make sure.

Nowadays the modern footballer is a well-drilled PR mini-mogul. They give toothy smiles to every potato-faced youngster they encounter, knowing any slip-up could lose them thousands if not millions of social media followers. They conduct every conversation with their manager behind a cupped hand, knowing there are thousands of cameras filling up millions of SD cards, each taking in every conceivable trajectory, positioned in every conceivable place; and that's before we get to the scourge of the camera phone.

Before all this, players could get away with a lot. I have limited experience of any funny business first hand, though I did once meet Robert Lee and I had to ask him if it was true that he and John Beresford had once stolen a limo. (They hadn't. It was Robert Lee and

Warren Barton.) So with that in mind, here are three underwhelming anecdotes about the first three times I met a pro.

Brian Honour

The first professional footballer I ever met was Brian Honour, your honour. A diminutive Poolie hero who never left the North-East, taking in a couple of years at Darlington, Peterlee and Spennymoor, Brian spent the lion's share of his career shoring up the un-shorable midfield of Hartlepool United, a team whose raison d'etre at that time appeared to be holding up the rest of the Football League.

A lifelong friend of Peter Beardsley and his miner (and presumably at one point minor) brothers, this cueball maestro stepped off the X5 from Horden on 9 February 1985, a Darlington kitbag over his shoulder (an insolent decision at best) beginning a 319-game career in the first team at Victoria Park, performing his own industrious excavations at what was once a limestone quarry.

Playing his first five games while still signing on in Peterlee, the Brian that managed to curry favour with my fourteen-year-old palette was a rangy playmaker who once, legend had it, scored directly from a corner. Sidenote: Hartlepool is a coastal town and does a great line in gale-force wind.

The day I met him I was at his Saturday morning football training camp at Dyke House School, the secondary school where the naughty lads went. Thanks to a knee injury and a career that was closer to the end than the beginning, he'd put together his very own soccer school. For seven quid you'd get three hours on the sandy all-weather pitch at the school, overseen by some less-than-keen YTS lads from the football club, and entry to a home Pools match that afternoon.

Brian had made a rare appearance at his club one Saturday morning. In a crinkly club tracksuit he stood at the head of the room, leaning on a freshly painted wall and drinking a cuppa from a caramel plastic cup. Every ruddy-cheeked youngster present found themselves drinking in the sight of a genuine footballing deity.

Even though words were never traded between the two of us, one thing that has always stayed with me were his legs (all right, two things). Very much the business end of a footballer, these pins had pinged balls through to provincial heroes such as Paul Baker and Joe Allon, and whipped some devastating dead-balls in from the Rink End.

Without wanting to sound as if this was my sexual awakening (Michelle Gayle's performance of 'Sweetness' on Top of the Pops had already seen to that some months earlier), our hero's legs were magnificent and perplexing and astonishing all at the same time on that day.

Definition, definitely – calves like roast chickens – and below the troubled knees that eventually saw off his career, the shins appeared to want to hide themselves almost apologetically in the twin shadows of his quads. 'Nothing to see here,' they appeared to say. 'This is just dull, insensate bone.'

'Go north,' they whispered. 'Check out that beefy muscle.'

Scott Sellars

Brian's Hartlepool United testimonial allowed me my first glimpse of the first professional footballer I would actually glad-hand – utility player and careless driver Scott Sellars.

In 1995, Brian's knees decided to call it a day and the club (presumably aided by el Pedro Beardsley, el amigo) managed to set up a pre-season run-out against Kevin Keegan's Newcastle United. Making their debuts were superstars David Ginola and Les Ferdinand – the sight of Sir Les Ferdinand leaping the entire height of a full Sir Les Ferdinand was something I'd never seen a human do before, deadening a ball against his unofficially knighted chest. Come full-time, as many of my young peers would gleefully stream on to the less-than-hallowed Victoria Park turf, I knew exactly who I wanted to get an autograph from.

Sellars had arrived from Leeds some months before he scored against Sunderland, taking Newcastle up to the Premier League. Such an epic start to his Toon career wasn't the reason why he was one of my favourite players. I'm a very shallow pool.

Truth be told, I just liked his slightly wonky face. He looked like a PE teacher, or an equally unassuming bloke who worked in Rumbelows who played a bit at the weekends. I think even he was surprised that this speccy little dweebazoid made a beeline for him rather than Beardo, or Gauloises-smoking David. Even the late, great Pavel Srnicek got more attention than Scotty.

Rumble in the Burn Valley Jungle – Michael Brown

'The Burn Valley' is a patch of green space in Hartlepool that, according to the Borough Council website, is now known as 'Burn Valley Gardens' thanks to a characteristically egregious decision by someone with a stiffy for pageantry.

Known to everyone else as 'the place Tesco employees used to have to go to collect shopping trolleys that had been chucked in the canal', the Burn gave oiks like us an entire full-size football pitch replete with mod cons such as white lines and a set of square posts a full six inches thick – wide and steely enough to avoid bending when heavier children swung from the crossbar.

Not that we could ever get twenty-two kids together for a full match – this was years before WhatsApp or BlackBerry Messenger. A full-scale London-style youth riot would never have gotten off the ground in Hartlepool.

More often than not our games would involve kicking a ball against the walls of old doors that would encircle the allotments – a round or two of 'knockout doubles' or 'cuppies' or whatever you odd southerners used to call it. On the North-South divide that stand-up comedians from Bury love to write jokes about, a friend's cousin once came up from London to visit and genuinely thought the allotments were a bloody shantytown. It's grim up North, especially for the old men who are forced to live out their days in sheds with snuff and pornography. Not a bad way to go, on reflection.

One June Sunday, after an informative sermon about Jesus and his bumchums at Boys Brigade, we were in full flow, practising our Klinsmann dives in the Burn Valley mud. It was at this point a much older boy and his friends asked if they could join in.

The lad who'd asked the question turned out to be Manchester City midfielder Michael Brown, a man who would go on to boot seven shades of Zabaleta out of the opponents of Portsmouth, Spurs and Fulham. Michael's home-town sabbatical was clearly not complete without a session in the park with his mates, rinsing a set of fourteen-year-olds at knockouts, or

Wembley doubles, or however you cockney mafioso instigate a soccer match with elocutionary perfection through your beautiful, unbroken teeth, in your palace grounds.

Anyway, this guy was very good at football. Like really, really good. He was playing for Manchester City in the First Division for crying out loud. I hate to sound like an internet clickbait article, but what happened next astounded us.

Someone from my group shouted: 'Is that Trevor Sinclair?'

Sure enough, emerging from the woods on a mountain bike was Trevor Sinclair. Except it clearly wasn't Trevor Sinclair – it was a black guy with tight dreads, who, from a distance and through racist, glaucoma-ridden lenses might possibly have resembled the QPR air-cyclist.

You'll have to excuse the youthful, brackish bouquet of bigotry from my comrade's query here. Something that might go some way to explaining his lack of contact with anyone of colour was the fact that the first black person he'd ever seen in the flesh had been a year earlier at thirteen, and even that was the javelin thrower Tessa Sanderson, who'd come to our school for an awards evening. I mean, one professional footballer had just turned up; why not two?

That said, I doubt Trevor Sinclair had ever pottered about town one-handed on an Argos Rocky Mountain, much less waved a ball-peen hammer about with his other hand, which is what he was doing on that Sunday morning.

His ire (and hammer) were directed not at us, nor Michael on that day, but Brown's friend, who we later dubbed 'Super Mario' because of his very un-nineties moustache. We weren't privy to the whole conversation conducted at hammer-point, but our man on his metal steed kept on repeating things like 'you can't do that to a woman' and 'give her the money back'. Michael stepped in and used his considerable showbiz status to calm hammer man, and soon enough he was on his way.

Super Mario, exhausted by the encounter, bounded laboriously away towards the Burn Valley beck. Or ghyll, or stream, or whatever word you southerners see fit to trouble your lips with when describing a ravine filled with grim water that people kick dog dirt in.

The one thing we learnt that day is that it must be weird being Michael Brown the footballer if that was an example of a day off.

* * *

The Dean Windass Hall of Fame Five-a-Side Team

The career of the footballer is short and complex. They may very well be the personification of so many people's hopes and dreams, yet they're sadly bereft of the emotional skillset to deal with either adoration or hatred, due in part to being thrown into a locker room full of emotionally malformed babymen at sixteen, some even earlier.

It's no small wonder nobody has anything to say for themselves. Their whole existence, the way the world perceives them hinges on what happens during a kicka-round on a bit of grass for an hour or so on a Saturday. We all think we could do it, sure – but the simple truth is that just watching a game of football is tense. Imagine how nerve-janglingly awful it must be to actually be in one.

The Football Ramble show over the years has featured some of the greatest players who for some mad reason or another managed to overcome this debilitating start in life and become a force for good in the game, either on the pitch or off it.

We called it the Dean Windass Hall of Fame after Dean's well-dug-out volley in the Championship play-off final in 2008, at the age of thirty-nine. We interviewed him once on the show and, true to form, he wasn't all that impressed by that honour. Or the interview. Or anything, really. I mean, I do think you've got to go some way to impress the man who squeezed John Finnigan 'Begin-Again's testicles so hard he swung a fist at Dean and got himself sent off. I've certainly not got the plums to try.

Anyway, every week we'd induct a new player into our special cave for special players – from Pelé to, well,

Mark Hateley, to TV shows we grew up watching like *Fantasy Football League* and Croatia's performance in 1998, we'd spend a lovely nostalgic ten minutes filleting their Wikipedia page.

So, then, it seems like a nice time to revisit some of the more interesting players who skipped through those virtual doors – and put together one of the more interesting five-a-side teams, with subs.

GK – Lev Yashin

> 'What kind of a goalkeeper is the one who is not tormented by the goal he has allowed? He must be tormented! And if he is calm, that means the end. No matter what he had in the past, he has no future'
>
> – Lev Yashin

If you ever need convincing of the power of Lenin's Likbez campaign to rid Soviet Russia of illiteracy, you need look no further than any quote from any Slavic celebrity born after 1917. Everyone sounds like a damn poet.

This colossal Moscovite was born the month his country's NEP died, being scouted for Dynamo Moscow after leaving the factory for the army. His first match for Dynamo Moscow was a forgettable one; conceding straight from an opposing goal-kick. To say Lev was determined to come back stronger would have been somewhat of an understatement.

Spending a season or two on the bench after his calamitous first match, he kept goal for the Dynamo ice hockey team in his spare time. In 1953 this same team won the USSR Cup. By 1954 he was on the verge of being selected for the USSR on ice, and some months later he was back in goal not only for FC Dynamo Moscow, but his national team.

Lev Yashin saved no fewer than 150 penalties during his career. Sir Tom Finney deliberately took one with his weaker foot to try to confuse him. Every fair-play-loving soul is dead against the cynical dive in the box, but genuinely I reckon all football needs is more keepers like Lev. Why even bother going down in the box if you're not going to be favourite to score from the spot? Another startling stat – a 'start' if you will – is that he kept 270 clean sheets during his time in bins. A filth grenade of a fact.

He was infamous for tearing his defence a new one – if you thought Peter Schmeichel was a shouter, this guy kinda invented the bloody mouth. His match preparation included a shot of strong liquor, so maybe a lot of what he bellowed at his defenders involved them being his beshtest friend, and that they should set up a business the very next day.

His wife Valentina would constantly tell him not to roar at his team-mates so much as it was unbecoming. I imagine she got her shouty share in 1971, when he retired.

Keepers in the forties and fifties were expected to inhabit their six-yard box and no more. Lev, on the other glove, would hurtle forwards and narrow angles, start attacks with a quick bowl to a full-back. He was also one of the very first to utilise the punch. I think I speak for everyone when I say it's probably a good thing that he never lived to see the famous David James flap.

His imperious performances in the World Cups from 1958 to 1970 – the former competition being the first to be broadcast internationally – were notable not only for Lev's decision-making and shot-stopping. His dress sense also made headlines. Dressed in black from head to toe, he was called at various times 'the Black Panther' and the 'Black Spider', because of his cat-like reflexes and seemingly limitless limbs.

I'm all for respecting history but I'm sure they could have been a little more creative – why not the Three 'O'clock Shadow? Or the Crude Oil Crusher? Or the Ninja Star? These newspapers really weren't concerned about gaining hits and going viral back then.

The only goalkeeper in history to have received the Ballon d'Or during his career, he was awarded the highest honour his country would bestow, the Order of Lenin, four years later. In 1962, mere months before he claimed the Ballon and its friend the d'Or, *L'Equipe* had le-quipped that his considerable powers were failing him after letting in a couple of soft goals in a World Cup match against Colombia. He'd only had two separate bouts of on-field concussion during the campaign, for crying out loud. What a joker!

'The peerless goalkeeper of the century'

– Eusebio

DF – Gaetano Scirea

Known to many as the man who kept Franco Baresi out of the Italy team – which was no small feat – he was one of the finest liberos the game has ever seen. Without Scirea we wouldn't have Paolo Maldini, and without him defenders could have continued to ply their trade in indelicate hatchet-and-hoof merchantry for a lot longer.

Nowadays we take it for granted that our defenders can play with the ball at their feet, but back in the seventies and eighties the European centre-back was very much a fan of finding themselves in doubt and then proceeding to kick it out. Starting his career at Atalanta in 1970, the less than statuesque Gaetano, at 5ft 10in, was a quiet, calm and above all level-headed player who got on with his job with a minimum of fuss and bluster. His manager in the Atalanta youth set-up even imposed a bonus system in which he got a little more money in games where he earned himself a yellow card.

Brave 'Gay' Scirea's (strangely enough my nickname at school, too) reading of the game was second to none.

He was an operator who would frequently begin attacks from deep inside his own half and managed to command the respect of his team at a whisper. Trapattoni once called him 'a leader in a monk's habit'.

Linking up with the psychopath's psychopath that was Claudio (anything but) Gentile at Juve in '74, it's fair to say the size of the legacy he created there was as ample as the chasm between his good cop to Claudio's bad. As a result, he soon took up his place in the Italy squad in possibly the greatest international backline in history. Sexy Cabrini, monobrowed Bergomi and Franco bloody Baresi made attackers want to give up their jobs and take up something easier – like bomb disposal. If, by some sorcery, you'd manage to beat that blockade, Dino Zoff was there to give you a terse lesson in pride before a fall.

Scirea's reading of the game is still impressive even to this day, and is required watching for any defender not gifted with an ounce of pace. He's one of only five players in European football history to have won all international trophies for football clubs recognised by UEFA and FIFA.

In a match between his Juve team and Fiorentina, a fight broke out. Scirea broke it up by calmly pointing to the stands and offering the dictum: 'Your wives are watching.' So calm was his hotel room on away trips, it was dubbed 'Switzerland'. Other players would pop in to get some shut-eye. Marco Tardelli was a regular visitor.

I like to think they planned their goal in the '82 World Cup final in a big double bed, Bert and Ernie style.

Winner of no fewer than seven league titles, two Italian cups and more European titles than the Grimaldi royal family, he saw out his final years as a diligent and hard-working scout for the Old Lady of Turin. He died, aged 36, on 3 September 1989 on a trip to Poland to watch Górnik Zabrze for arguably an unnecessary second time (Juve were playing them in the UEFA Cup) a truck colliding head-on with his car, which was carrying four tanks of petrol on board. Such an uncharacteristically loud end for a quiet man.

The Gaetano Scirea award is given to those players in *Serie A* who embody the values and sportsmanship of the great man, and the south stand in both the Juventus and Delle Alpi stadiums are and were named after Gaetano. To say the back line in our DWHOF fives team is in good hands would perhaps be understating it somewhat. But that's what that man was. Understated.

MF – Dejan Petković

A man who's got a pretty good shout when it comes to being the most famous European ever to make the move to South America, though admittedly 'Pet' doesn't have much competition in this respect. I can think of only Adolf Eichmann who made that trip and he was definitely what you might call an acquired taste.

'Pet' hung up his boots in 2011 and was made an honorary consul of Serbia in Brazil, which presumably means he now has to process pet visas and locate lost passports. It's fair to say that in between debilitating injuries, he tore it up down there for many, many years. Starting his career at FK Radnički Niš, he became, in 1988, the youngest player ever to play in the Yugoslav First League at sixteen years and fifteen days. He quickly established himself as a creative playmaker with what a television pundit might call 'an astounding first touch and bags of vision'. They'd probably go on to say that he was a 'great kid with bags of potential', too.

A few moves later, finding himself unable to break into Capello's Real side that boasted a sickening forward line of Raúl, Mijatović, Šuker and Seedorf, a board member from floundering Brazilian club Vitória rocked up with a pair of business-class tickets to Espírito Santo and some old yap about the player making his name and getting a lucrative move back to Europe.

Believing he'd be in a situation to challenge for the title in Brazil, something that definitely wasn't the case as Vitória were eighteenth, the world's seemingly most trusting man made the move after the board member insisted that it was now or never – the Pope was visiting and the entire country shut down for weeks when the head of the Catholic Church was there. Of course, this was a load of old flannel. Pet's bullshit detector probably shares space in his shed with a load of magic beans.

His career in Brazil was admittedly punctuated by injuries and attempts to get big-money moves abroad – but seemingly every time he got away he was pulled back again, a Brazilian bungee if you will. From Vitória he moved to Venezia, returning to take up a place at Flamengo; from Vasco da Gama to a five million dollar contract in China for Shanghai Shenhua. He was back within a season to score eighteen goals from midfield the following year.

In 2005 he headed for the Middle East but was soon back in Brazil, this time for Fluminense, making the team of the season once again and scoring their thousandth goal in *Brasileirão* history. After a couple of underwhelming years in Goiás and Belo Horizonte, Flamengo took him back at the age of thirty-six – some say this was to help reduce some of the debt the team still owed Petković. Members of the board resigned over his return and the manager was sacked.

Destroying his critics in characteristic style, he managed to shake off the many injuries he was forcing himself to play through and he helped his team pick up their first *Brasileirão* title in seventeen years. Forgotten by Yugoslavia and ignored by the Serbian national team set-up, he became only the third foreign player to have his feet cast in the Maracanã Walk of Fame.

FW – Cristiano Ronaldo

Cristiano was never formally inducted into the Dean Windass Hall of Fame, as pretty much everything that could ever be said about this player has already been said, then those words analysed and re-analysed – then argued over in front of his considerable Opta stats, then made into a meme, then tweeted to Cristiano and his sister.

Named after Ronald Reagan for some mad reason, Ronaldo plays sport at an unfortunate time. Where the twenty-four-hour news orc has to be fed, he's the gift that keeps on giving (huffy interviews to salivating journalists) and his obvious chagrin at the love the people have for his Argentinian rival is intoxicating. In any other era this man would be a god, in this one however he's forced to sit to the right of Barca's Lionel Messi, a deity who recognises neither Newton's laws of motion nor the powers of the Spanish tax authorities.

FW – Ronaldo Luís Nazário de Lima

NFL star Marshawn Lynch: 'That's when it just clicked in my mind that if you just run through somebody's face, a lot of people aren't going to be able to take that over and over and over and over and over and over and over and over and over and over and over and over and over and over and over and over again. They're just not gonna want that.'

Interviewer: 'Think there's a deeper metaphor there?'
Lynch: 'Run through a motherfucker's face. Then you
don't have to worry about them no more.'

A man who's exceedingly hard to write anything on. Fact-checking any piece takes roughly three times as long as it should do as the writer is invariably sucked into watching highlights videos of the great man. I think I speak for all *The Football Ramble* presenters (apologetically male and heterosexual, to varying degrees) when I say that late-night screenings of *Il Fenomeno* highlight videos go toe-to-toe with pornography in frequency. For Christ's sake, they *are* pornography.

Ronaldhino said of his colleague (and I hope for everything that's right with the world, friend): '[Ronaldo] is the most complete striker there has ever been.' Zlatan went with: 'There will never, in my view, be a better player than him.'

This player had everything. Speed, guile, decision-making, impetuous feet and, above all, an explosive power that would make any defender drop his guts, which they frequently did, probably literally. This man truly ran through a motherfucker's face.

Two World Cups, two *Pichichis*, two Ballon d'Ors – every honour seemed to be the second he'd received, such were his considerable footballing chops.

It's galling that two of the most celebrated footballers of the past thirty years have had to share one name. Though that fact presumably irks the younger Ronaldo more than anyone can possibly imagine, so lovers of football and lovers of vain men getting upset are both suitably sated. Is there anything Mr De Lima can't do?

From his early years in Belo Horizonte to his time in the Netherlands, from Barcelona to Milan to São Paulo, Ronaldo was a hunter. Wherever he went, the ball found the net.

A goal-scoring paragon, Ronaldo's masterpiece – his *Scream* wrapped in a Sistine Chapel wrapped in a *Last Supper* wrapped in a *Mona Lisa* – must surely be the goal scored on 11 October 1996 against the then *La Liga* team SD Compostela. And on that day he truly turned that team into compost.

Picking up the ball inside his own half, the sort of thing you'd see only players with true hunger do back then, he manages to evade and power through a shirt-pull and an untidy foot down the back of the shin, outpace another two defenders with sheer unabashed acceleration and break into the eighteen-yard box, cutting inside, shifting his weight and giving himself room to shoot around the penalty spot.

Analysing the footage, one defender – Javier Bellido, a man who was once known as 'the wall of San Lazaro' – *appears* to *attempt* to put a foot in but, in all honesty, what actually happens is he gives off the air of a man who's only contribution to proceedings is a conceiving of a notion of a thought that in some alternate universe a chap who looks like Javier Bellido perhaps half-blocks that whipcrack shot into the bottom left-hand corner of the goal. In reality he just stands there, arms out and mouth open, like any of us would have.

Ten seconds, and the world's greatest striker. All it took. The apogee of pace, grace and power. Bobby Robson in the dugout shaking his head.

'Pelé Returns' said the newspaper *Diario AS*. Nike bought up the rights to show that historic goal in their celebrated 'Imagine you asked God to be the best player in the world, and he listened to you' advert. His opposition that day who also featured in that clip – William, Bellido, Passi, Pessoa, Perez, Juncal and Chiba – filed a lawsuit to try to gain some financial recompense for the use of their images. The court found against the players (the goalkeeper Fernando Peralta being notable by his absence in the suit – he probably didn't want reminding), arguing that the images of the players were 'purely instrumental and accessory', which does sum up that goal better than any flowery think-piece on the matter. A direct quote from the Supreme Court, in Plaza de la Villa de Paris (in Madrid): 'The reproduction of the images in no way affects their personal or professional dignity.'

Like fuck it didn't.

Ronaldo Luís Nazário de Lima can now be seen at a casino near you.

What Do Footballers Look Like?

Footballers used to come in all shapes and sizes. Now, with a rigorous gym regime and a vogue for those six-packs that resemble a dimpled beer tankard, our modern bladder-thumpers look like Tom of Finland cartoons but with fewer moustaches. Possibly more outlandish clothing, though.

In the eighties Danish Smørrebrød-wolfer Jan Mølby was capped by his country thirty-odd times while sporting a physique for which the Liverpool shirt emblazoned with 'Candy' couldn't have been more fitting – and more fitted.

'He's fat, he's round, he scores at every ground' Micky Quinn may never have held his moobs to ransom within the confines of an England shirt but a one-in-two goal record doesn't lie. Hell, even Mido had some semblance of a career – if not semblance of foresight. His plan of shedding the pounds by moving to Middlesbrough, the home of the béchamel-lathered chicken parmo, wasn't the greatest.

Truly, I miss the days of the big 'ol' chubbalub. For crying out loud, replica shirts shouldn't even be *called* replica shirts any more, as garments worn by those in the stands are several sizes bigger than ones on the pitch, with a way more generous cut. Us mere mortals all need a little more junk in the (Volkswagen Beetle-rear) trunk. One ruler for the pros, another for the breast of us.

But if the present-day player can't possibly hope to rock it with the big boys if they're the size of an actual big buoy, then what exactly *are* they eating at mealtimes that we're not?

It's the pasta, stupid. Well, pasta and those obscene bright green isotonic gel packs they frube into their mouths come the fiftieth minute on the touchline. The ones that contain the sort of marrow you'd expect to find inside the bones of an extra-terrestrial.

Whereas dugout-botherers such as Joachim Löw are forced to forage about for sustenance on their own person (be it left or right nostril), every calorie of a footballer's diet is managed and micromanaged and then turned into a nice big bar graph for some dull reason known only to nutritionists.

So when a player becomes a little cavalier about what he chucks down his gullet, their extra timber sticks out like a sore timber thumb. Come international breaks, when players like Hatem Ben Arfa get a weekend at home, they're only too happy to chow down on plate-fuls of Dad's *makroudh*, turning up for training come Tuesday several pounds overweight.

Millionaire footballer Wayne Rooney, who in another life would have probably been a pretty good physical fit for working security in a branch of Boots, once complained that he frequently has to force plates of pasta down on a Saturday morning to make an early kick-off. It's the sort of protestation that sticks in the craw since we live in a world where young men and women are told that carbs are very much the enemy, and if we shove anything denser than kale shavings down our kites, we're at risk of not bagging ourselves a Harry Styles or an Ariana Grande, who I'm informed is that one who looks like a child-cat.

In all seriousness, mind, Arsenal's head nutritionist James Collins, who worked with England at the 2014 World Cup, reckons that players' appetites dictate that it can't *always* be pasta and chicken. Post-match sashimi, for example, has been a big hit with both players and clubs in recent years.

Carbohydrates don't always have to come from spaghetti and rice as footballers can get terrifically bored of these. South Americans get a lot of their carb load in with amaranth grain to mix things up. The common name for this is 'pigweed'. Conversely, a cereal grain calling itself 'farro' gets the Italians and French salivating and then some. I'm told it tastes a little bit like posh barley.

Note to self: Pitch unlovable Yorkshire-based detectives show to ITV called Farrow and Pigweed.

From what our man in the nutritional know says, his main job *appears* to be finding peculiar ways to trick footballers into eating the same thing, loads of times.

'Different plays on eggs at breakfast – combined in wraps or with different kinds of bread.'

Listen to him! Hide the egg. He's just playing hide the bloody egg. The man's an albumen arsehole.

High-protein desserts are important, usually appearing at the dinner table 'in the form of flapjacks or high-protein mousses,' states James. High-protein mousses! Delicious! Really takes you back to being in short trousers, doesn't it? The jangly, merry tune of the local protein mousse man in his trusty protein mousse van as it turned into your street. 'Please Dad,' you'd shout. 'The protein mousse man is outside. Please give us a penny or two so we can buy one of his magnificent nutritional mousses!' And then the family moussing could begin.

There are exceptions, obviously. If you're bored enough to type the words 'why do footballers love . . .' into Google, autocomplete offers you but two offers of consummation – tattoos and Nando's.

Nando's is a Portuguese restaurant with South African roots. It's not quite fast food, it's not quite a full restaurant experience, but the youngsters can't get enough of that sweaty, hot-sauce asininity.

It's said that fiery chicken Nando's has resonated with youngsters of Caribbean and West Indian descent, who grew up eating their mother's and grandmother's jerk chicken, a theory that might have its merits – except this doesn't explain why footballers are so very smitten as they've constantly been accused of being wholly unsentimental and having no respect for their elders. Could it be that the man on the street has it wrong and they shouldn't be given soldier's wages and so on?

Brussels bairn Adnan Januzaj famously took a date, some seven years his elder, for a bit of spicy rice (which didn't impress). One tabloid kiss-and-tell later and we've got Andros Townsend and Raheem Sterling throwing out some Nando's love in his defence on the back page of the *Daily Mirror*.

If a British footballer was ever sent to death row for some egregious felony while playing in the MLS in, say, Utah (a state that last year, for some screwball reason, reintroduced the firing squad) undoubtedly his last meal would be some form of Portuguese chicken washed down with a bright blue Gatorade.

Speaking of liquid refreshment, this invariably involves lavish measures of energy drinks come three o'clock on a Saturday afternoon – the half-time cuppa now sadly the reserve of the slightly older campaigner. Ramble Jim once described drinking one of those colourful caffeine drinks as like drinking a tattoo. Spot on for me, Clive.

Whereas young Europeans like their liquids colourful and angry, South American footballers are rarely seen not dutifully cradling a hot mate gourd as they step off the team bus. It's an acrid and rather difficult drink, for which leaves of the yerba plant are steeped in hot water and sucked through a silver straw. Steam goals.

Crucially, footballers nowadays shirk the important boozing responsibilities their forefathers carried on their fat shoulders – the pace of the modern game dictates that the concept of training-day dehydration is very much a non-starter. Once the season's over, however, it's off to the nearest Mediterranean yacht with a carton of cigarettes and an airport-sized bottle of Patrón.

One of my favourite examples of an inebriated modern footie player is very much the sight of the greatest footballer who ever lived, Leo Messi, pissed out of his mind on the top of that bus in 2009, trying to grab a Gerard Piqué-sized Chupa Chups from a colleague. History will note that he never did get that lolly, and I like to think that haunts him just as regularly as his World Cup and *Copa América* disappointments do.

Rio Ferdinand once delivered an impassioned speech to his England colleagues about the importance of teetotalism during major tournaments. I can't help but think that he locked eyes with Andy Carroll as he said that, punctuating it with a y-axis Jaffa Cake snaffle as Andy burped blue MD 20/20 into his cupped hand.

There are exceptions to the rule, sure. Claudio Ranieri took his Leicester City team, after a succession of clean sheets, to Peter's Pizzeria in Leicester. They were expected to earn their dinner though – being led into the kitchen and taught how to bake their own pizzas under their manager's watchful eye. The sight of Danny Simpson throttling a big neck of dough really was something. Maybe he'd done it before.

Who Are The Worst Footballers?

John Fashanu. The worst footballers are John Fashanu. Let's take a look at his life's work . . .

1) He paid his brother Justin £75,000 not to come out of the closet, blamed him for the death of his mother, and said stuff like this: 'My daughter was very close to her uncle and it has taken a long time for her to understand that Justin wasn't really gay, he just wanted attention.'

2) He introduced Stan Collymore to Ulrika Jonsson. 'Ully's a great girl. I just wish she'd find Mr Right . . . I'll put my hand up; I was the bastard who introduced her to Stan Collymore. I was going out of town so I rang up Yorkie, Ugo and Bozzie and said: 'Listen guys, there's a big *Gladiators* party and the girls want some good-looking guys to go down and have a good time.' Of course, they took big Stan along and the rest is history.

3) When recounting a training-ground fight with Lawrie Sanchez to a reporter from *FourFourTwo*, he made it clear that his fighting hero was the man who lay on the floor and kicked Muhammad Ali in the knees.

   'And for [Sanchez] this was the walk of death because we were walking round the back of the bushes and I was gonna pummel him. I was thinking, what style should I use on him? Sanch was thinking, am I gonna get battered? Or maybe he was thinking, I'm gonna batter Fash. It was like something out of a film: two people who don't like each other, and now they're going to fight.

'Anyway, Sanch gave me a shot and, give him credit, it wasn't a bad shot. But I thought, don't hit Sanch, don't mark his face, and my mind went back to when Muhammad Ali fought against the martial artist in New York, and the martial artist just kicked the back of his legs until it broke the tissues in his calves and he submitted.

'So I thought I'd teach Sanch a lesson and gave a sweep of the legs, but Sanch has calves like most people have thighs and he didn't move. So I gave him another couple, but Sanch came back at me. So I thought, I'm gonna take this guy out, and I hit him with one of the best shots I'd been training with – BAM! Take that, Sanch! – right in the solar plexus, a shot that would supposedly knock a horse down. And still he stood there. Then Terry Burton came over to break us up.'

4) Armed with a dossier provided by the Church of Scientology, John Fashanu accused anti-scientologist poster boy Bob Minton of stealing $5 billion from the Nigerian government, then suddenly apologised. 'I can say it again and again, that there was nothing

like debt buy-back or any billions stacked away in any account anywhere.'

5) During a lunch with some British journalists during the African Cup of Nations in 1992 in Dakar, when the bill of £2 a head came, he insisted on taking 20p from the cash on the table because his dish had been cheaper by that amount.

6) Post-Gabon air disaster, Fash gave the Zambians the impression he'd managed to draft in celebrated manager Ian Porterfield to help the country reconstruct their national team as an act of goodwill. Porterfield would later reveal that Fashanu took a cut of his money, enfeebling him financially to such a degree that he was forced to quit.

7) He hosted the Nigerian version of *Deal or No Deal*. He's Noel bloody Edmonds for crying out loud.

What Do Premier League Players Do When They Get To 31?

They invariably look for one last payday before taking up residence on a pundit's sofa somewhere on Malaysian telly. Sometimes it's at home with an underachieving team with deep pockets. Sometimes they head to the tax havens of France, occasionally it's Turkey or the Middle East – but the smart, and let's face it big, money right now is very much Sven's China, as it will forever be known.

Latent Western arrogance has us scoff behind our sports supplements at the idea of China becoming the next great footballing powerhouse, over say the US and their occasionally vaunted Major League Soccer, but give it fifteen or so years and I believe we'd best be getting up close and personal with all that wacky tonal Pinyin.

China, in its various guises, has been around a heck of a lot longer than most other politically unified regions. They know full well when they're experiencing boom rather than bust – and there are very few countries in the world that could have survived the ritual slaughter of more than forty million of its inhabitants by a head of state in recent memory and still retain some soupcon of national pride and identity.

Politically and financially, England is distracted. On the world stage, we should by rights be pulling up our collective trousers and picking up that big hot pie we dropped some hundred years ago when we drunkenly divided up the Arab world with what looking like a giant haughty Spirograph.

But of course, we're not. Our leaders are indulging in a tried and tested bout of jelly-wrestling power-grabbing fuckery in a paddling pool on Parliament Square while their country pleads for sanity. The US and continental Europe are in the bleachers laughing and pointing, ignoring their own problems at home, all the while China slides about its South Sea like a graceful pond skater, pausing only to create another artificial island or two as Japan and Taiwan nervously leaf through the rules of international engagement.

But this is not a section about the grindingly inevitable Easternisation of the entire civilised world (my 2011 copy of Microsoft Word audaciously trying to autocorrect that word to 'Westernisation' as if the former isn't a painfully legitimate noun). It's a light read about where footballing careers go to die. I'm just saying that you'd best believe that when financial clout, the delicious fog of corruption and national pride combine like three Captain Planet rings, you'd best believe something seismic and kooky usually happens. The only two issues that will surely prevent China hoovering up some of our greatest players in the next ten years is the aforementioned corruption (not that football has ever been averse to a bit of that) and the fact that players travel so very badly. Flaubert's celebrated 'travel makes one modest' quote should really have ended 'unless you've got the ego of a footballer with the life skills of a toddler'.

Players: The Post-Match

All in all, it's always going to be unfair to project all our hopes, dreams and frustrations on to such young men who've enjoyed such financial riches at the expense of experiential affluence. What are we expecting them to say once the final whistle has blown? What human truths are we expecting them to help us disseminate in under ninety minutes, plus time added on? They've concentrated their efforts on such superhuman physical exertion and submitted the very laws of gravity to such trenchancy that when they get home they're physically and mentally unable to screw in their own light bulbs or pay their own taxes without a player liaison officer on hand. Why do we expect them to be anything but inhuman robot-men, spitting out platitude after platitude – heaven knows they've been burned one too many times by a word-twisting tabloid hack.

I'd love to see a talented, intelligent, honest player who felt comfortable in his own skin, enough at least to tell us how he's really feeling in front of the *Match of the Day* cameras. Take us on that journey with them and their buddies in the dressing-room – paint pictures with metaphor and aphorism and put a little magic back into our lives. Then I remember how much of an insufferable, inscrutable dickhead I was in my twenties.

Peers (and listeners) assure me I've brought that level of performance into my thirties with some distinction. Like CR7 in many ways, then.

7. Club Football

Jim Campbell

The Premier League is undoubtedly the most popular league in the world right now. We all knew it was big abroad but we knew that about *Top Gear*, *The Teletubbies* and Prince Philip. We otherwise didn't give it much thought, perhaps because it's hard to understand how the rest of the world relates to something we ourselves consider to be so fundamentally English. It's a bit like finding out that Quavers are a globally renowned delicacy. That said, as a nation we are really good at crisps. In fact, Gary Lineker, one of our finest ever footballers, has been advertising crisps for twenty-one years, four years longer than he played football. Makes you think. Mostly about crisps, but as I said, we are good at them.

It feels to me like the sheer scale of its reach has crept up on us and there's much about English football's hugeness that seems incongruous in a global context. Hull

City won promotion to the Premier League through the 2015/16 season Championship play-offs and, at the time of writing, are sponsored by Yorkshire-based theme park Flamingo Land. Should this deal continue while they're in the Premier League, and I'm sure it won't but allow me to dream, Flamingo Land will find itself with exposure in 643 million homes in 212 territories around the world. I've never been to Flamingo Land but I'm going to assume that this is a scale of advertising they don't need. There's also the chance that it will give a lot of fans from overseas a quite strange idea of what Hull is actually like, as if it's some tropical paradise inhabited by exotic, free-roaming avian life. Again, I've never been to Hull but I'm fairly confident that it isn't. If any tourists do get confused enough to visit, at least there's a theme park to cater for their needs, and so we come full circle. Maybe the long-term plan is to use this to turn the city of Hull into a financial superpower. I, for one, hope this symbiotic partnership continues and flourishes.

Part of the success of the Premier League comes from its ability to market itself, much of which involves simply shouting about it being The Best League in the World at every opportunity. That's not to completely discredit the quality of the league. In terms of entertainment there is definitely an argument that it is indeed The Best League in the World, while there is also a counter argument that this is a biased, Anglocentric stance. I will now weigh up both points of view and have this argument with myself, in the interest of balance – and because Marcus, Luke and Pete won't answer the phone after 2am any more, the cowards.

The Best

As I write this Leicester City are Premier League champions. *Leicester City*. If you're reading this book far into the future – perhaps by ingesting it in pill form, you lazy weirdo – you may well marvel at the strangeness of this time, full of unlikely champions and over-reaching flamingo-themed amusement parks. Yes, it's probably an anomaly and some people point to Leicester's relatively low points total in 2015/16 as proof that the league lacks quality but they must be utterly devoid of joy. Leicester won the league! It might not be normal for a team who narrowly avoided relegation in one season to go on and win the title the next but the league is certainly becoming increasingly competitive. Leicester's win means the Premier League has now had four different winners in four consecutive seasons for the first time since its inception. This, of course, doesn't count records from the old First Division but even including them it isn't all that common. In that time Spain has had two winners, while Germany, Italy and France have all had just one.

It used to be the case that the Premier League would be contested by Manchester United and one other but the cash injections at Chelsea and Manchester City have meant that this has not been the case for a while. Recent years have also seen notable title bids from both Liverpool and Spurs and only the most committed curmudgeon would argue that it is currently predictable. I don't think even Mark Lawrenson would say that and he hates football.

This competition is what makes it so entertaining. Something else we regularly hear about 'this league' is that 'anyone can beat anyone' and, though it's become a bit of a cliché, it is largely true. The teams at the top of the table do regularly drop points to teams way below them and it suggests either a lack of quality at the top or that the general quality is relatively evenly matched. Whatever your view, what's great about it is that it gives us all a chance to regularly laugh at the big boys. The aforementioned establishment of Chelsea and Man City as major players means that there are now more big teams and the nature of that means that most of them have to fail. That's just maths. *Schadenfreude*-based maths. The Premier League is the capital of footballing *schadenfreude*. It's the home of lumbering giants like Liverpool, staggering around in a daze, mumbling about the past in a demented fugue state as if they think they're still living in it, while Man United nervously laugh at them, growing concerned that they'll soon be doing exactly the same thing. Then there are the nouveau riche of Chelsea and Man City still managing to cock everything up despite effectively operating with the advantage of a real-life Football Manager cheat. There's Arsenal regularly snatching between second and fourth from the jaws of a supposed title bid by going on a calamitous run at the first hint of pressure. There's Tottenham finding a way to Spurs it up, whatever 'it' may be that season. Everyone can find a way to make themselves look like a bunch of idiots so when your team are playing like a donkey derby in a hurricane you know that it won't be long before someone else drops a teste and takes the heat off. That's to be applauded.

Another thing to appreciate is that we are no longer European football's odd half-sibling, kept out of sight on our rainy little island so that we don't make everyone else feel uncomfortable with our weird teeth. England can now attract top players, who can afford top dentists, and this wasn't always the case. Exotic foreign signings were once rare and while that did make it extra special when a player you knew from the World Cup arrived, the melting pot we have now has made the domestic game more diverse than it's ever been. Yes, this is largely due to money but that's OK. It's not as if they have to play with wedges of cash on them, though there is something appealing about the idea of Emmanuel Adebayor plodding around with a block of banknotes strapped to his torso, money stuffed into his shorts and socks, cash flying every time he kicks the ball, followed by a desperate scramble to pick it up and stuff it back down his pants. He'd cover more ground.

This talent isn't restricted to the players as some of the world's top managers ply their trade here, too. All the big hitters want a wedge of our delicious cash pie, to the point where Champions League winner Rafa Benítez is happy to manage North-East punchline Newcastle United in the Championship. We have Pep Guardiola, the most sought-after manager in world football, sought largely by his arch nemesis José Mourinho, relentlessly tracking him around Europe like a T-1000 programmed to be especially arrogant. There's Antonio Conte, Jürgen Klopp, rising stars Mauricio Pochettino, Ronald Koeman and Slaven Bilić, the wise old head of Arsène Wenger.

These men are often as entertaining as their teams and the best thing is that they have no choice but to mix it with Sam Allardyce, Tony Pulis and Pards. Mark Hughes doesn't care what you've won; you're going to shake his hand and you're going to shake it properly or he'll make a face and question your standing as a man in the post-match interview. These contrasting styles are reflected in the general playing style of the league, with the more technical teams forced to adapt to stubborn men who've gleefully built entire careers out of pissing them off. Sometimes it works for the old guard, sometimes it doesn't, but it's this exact clash of philosophies and styles that gives the Premier League the blend of continental flair and determined athletic grit that makes it so popular.

Not So Best

It should figure that The Best League in the World would feature the best teams in the world, and that if those teams entered into a competition where they played against the best teams from other leagues they'd always win it. As you may know, two of these competitions do exist and, of late, Premier League teams haven't done so well. Chelsea won the Champions League in 2012, then the Europa League in 2013, and Liverpool were beaten finalists in the 2016 Europa League so it isn't exactly a crisis but overall English teams have struggled to cope with the dominance of Real Madrid, Barcelona and Bayern Munich in particular. If it were truly the best league around then surely our teams, stuffed with talent both on the pitch and in the dugout, wouldn't have such a clearly debilitating inferiority complex. Back to the drawing board (bank) everyone.

Another argument against the Premier League being The Best League in the World and the Only One that Matters and is the Best is that there has never yet been an instance where the Best Player in the World, or one widely regarded as such, has signed for an English team.

We've had players like Cristiano Ronaldo and Luis Suárez develop into megastars here but never has there been a Zinedine Zidane or a Lionel Messi who has joined the Premier League in their prime. It can only be a matter of time before this happens but as yet we're still waiting. This, of course, doesn't mean that the league is a joke but it does suggest that in certain places the Premier League doesn't have the status it repeatedly insists that it does. Coupled with failure in Europe, you have to wonder whether ambitious players feel that, to truly achieve all they can achieve, they have to avoid England and aim for one of the aforementioned superclubs.

Then there's the playing style. 'But you just said that was one of the best things about it!' you might cry, sat on the bus reading this book, or in your hover car having swallowed this bookpill. Well yes, but the reality is that, as great as the football can sometimes be, at other times it simply has to be West Brom and Crystal Palace failing to find their rhythm and drawing 0–0 on a 'Super' Sunday afternoon. That's the nature of such a lucrative league, where dropping out of it can mean financial peril. Chris Brunt doesn't want to be responsible for Tony Pulis having to sack a load of dinner ladies because he lost his man at a corner and they've been relegated. That pressure can mean that teams are set up primarily not to lose, or play within themselves as they're frozen by it.

This is true of any league at times so let's compare the Premier League with the contenders for the crown it made itself and insists is legitimate . . .

La Liga

'The thing with the Spanish league is that there are only two decent teams in it,' say lots of people who never watch it, like Paul from Pete's school, probably. This opinion doesn't really hold up to much scrutiny though. Barcelona and Real Madrid keep winning the Champions League, after all. Atlético Madrid, the only team to win *La Liga* aside from those two since Valencia in 2004, have twice appeared in the final in the last three seasons and won the Europa League in 2010 and 2012. Current Europa League holders Sevilla have won it three times in a row and Spanish clubs generally dominate in Europe. This is in spite of the money clubs receive being skewed hugely in favour of Barcelona and Real Madrid. Yes, it's ridiculous that they so regularly annihilate the competition but that doesn't mean that the league is easy. Ask Gary Neville. While it is way more predictable than the Premier League, *La Liga* does have a lot that its English counterpart can't compete with: the quality of the teams at the very top; the consistency of skill and technique on display; and that all important mastery of European competition. At youth levels in Spain the focus has long been on technique and that is evident in *La Liga*, with high technical proficiency being the norm even in teams fighting relegation. It is well known inside football that a Spanish footballer's foot has the same level of dexterity as an English footballer's hand.

Serie A

In the early to mid-1990s *Serie A* was the place to be, unquestionably the best league on the planet. The football was generally very defensive yet was somehow also exciting. It seems like a very long time ago. As a child of that era it's odd for me to see Italian football in the situation it's in. Struggling to attract big names and lacking the quality you associate with *Serie A*, it's a shadow of the league it once was, still recovering from the *Calciopoli* scandal. If you somehow missed that, in 2006 Juventus, AC Milan, Fiorentina, Lazio and Reggina were found guilty of rigging games by ensuring that they had favourable referees at crucial times. It wasn't quite match-fixing but it wasn't exactly not match-fixing. I doubt anyone would dare to try this with an English referee. As we've learnt, if you tell Mike Dean who to book he'll put you in a headlock and march you to jail himself. All were punished, with Juventus stripped of their title and the one before it, demoted and given a thirty-point deduction for the next season, eventually reduced to nine. This caused an exodus of disillusioned players from many clubs, involved or not. Juventus were promoted straight back into *Serie A* and have been utterly dominant in recent years. The most frustrating thing about it is that, with the big clubs reeling, it looked like an opportunity for new teams to shake up the establishment. With the two Milan clubs in decline the likes of Roma and Napoli, storied clubs for whom a league title would be an historic but achievable aim, have only Juventus to aim at yet seem incapable of overhauling them. It almost seems unjust. Juventus have made it predictable again, though in a different way from before, and while there is, of course, still a high standard of football, something isn't quite right. Football moves in cycles and it isn't as if it's meandering in irrelevance in the same way that leagues like the Dutch *Eredivisie* is, but the damage done in 2006 still lingers.

Bundesliga

'It's often more difficult to win against our training team than maybe against a team in the *Bundesliga*,' snarked Thomas Müller in 2015, possibly while wearing two monocles and a top hat, holding court at some high society soirée like a Bavarian Oscar Wilde, albeit one with an impossible knack for finding space in the opposition penalty area. Aloof though Müller may sound, he clearly has a point. Since the *Bundesliga* was founded in 1963 – lest we forget – Bayern have won the league twenty-six times, comfortably making them the most successful team in German club football. Though it faces accusations of being a one-team competition, the football is of a very high technical standard and it has a reputation as a very fun league to watch. I can attest to this, having seen Hertha Berlin lose 2–0 to Hannover in the worst game of football I have ever seen live. Despite this the atmosphere was still brilliant – and not just because of Pete's previously mentioned *currywurst* intake, which verged on the feral.

It's probably because fans haven't had to take on second jobs in order to watch their team. The average ticket for the 2015/16 season was just £23, whereas the Premier League's was £53.76. In the modern era it seems impossible that such a successful league would knowingly miss out on such a direct revenue stream but a large part of it comes from what is known as the 50+1 rule. It effectively guarantees club members a degree of control because, to obtain a *Bundesliga* licence, a club has to hold shares of 50 per cent + 1, guaranteeing that it keeps a majority of its own voting rights. This stops third-party ownership and keeps prices low as fans aren't exactly likely to vote to increase their own ticket prices. There are two exceptions: VfL Wolfsburg, owned by Volkswagen, and Bayer Leverkusen, who are owned by the pharmaceuticals company Bayer. These exceptions are allowed because of a rule that grants a company or person the opportunity to have a controlling stake in the club if they have substantially funded it for a period of twenty years. Good news if your company makes time machines, otherwise difficult to break into in the short term.

The Bayer situation is an intriguing one. If we're ever going to get a superhero footballer his origin story will almost certainly begin with an accident in their lab. The naming rights thing also seems at odds with the overall spirit, though clubs do have to be creative with revenue streams, as the discounts the fans get have to be covered elsewhere. There was evidence of this at Hertha Berlin, with adverts for a local pharmacy appearing on the screens every time a player went down injured. You have to wonder how bad an injury has to be before they decide to pull those. You can't be hawking plasters when someone has their leg hanging off. Perhaps in the future the naming rights thing will also happen in England. I can definitely see Mike Ashley thinking that Greggs Newcastle has a nice ring to it.

Though Bayern's dominance is undoubtedly a negative, as it so often makes the league uncompetitive, the *Bundesliga* certainly has a lot going for it. It's a little bit different from anywhere else and is slightly underrated in this conversation. As well as affordability and atmosphere, it can also boast an exciting array of young, home-grown talent and this counts for something. When Germany lost to England at Euro 2000 they collectively said: 'Nein! Never again!' and comprehensively overhauled their youth set-up. The seemingly endless supply of exciting, technically impeccable young talent that now comes from Germany is the result of this period. England's 5–1 defeat of Germany in a 2001 World Cup qualifier can only have compounded this so when you think about it, this basically means that Emile Heskey won the 2014 World Cup.

I'm not even going to include *Ligue 1*. Paris St Germain are simply tyrannical in it, winning the 2015/16 championship with ninety-six points, thirty-one clear of nearest rivals Lyon and Monaco. PSG are so rich even Monaco can't keep up with them. The multibillionaire Dmitry Rybolovlev is their majority shareholder and the whole place is basically just a big pile of money, a made-up hybrid of a grand prix track and a luxury holiday resort where they don't even have to pay income tax and millionaire footballers are viewed as the local peasant class.

So how does the Premier League stack up? Pretty well to be fair. Is it The Best League in the World? It's easy to argue that there isn't a best league in the world but the Premier League certainly holds its own in the conversation. Different people will always have a different definition of 'best' and for me the standard of football is currently higher in *La Liga* and specifically Munich but football is cyclical and there's no reason this won't change. We're just lucky that we live in an era where it's so easy to have access to all of these leagues.

With that in mind this may seem like a Eurocentric list but the bigger South American leagues have long suffered from the best talent making its way to Europe and the league formats make them harder to compare . . .

¿Que?

Many South American league formats are almost unrecognisable from their European counterparts. Brazil is so big that the whole of Europe could fit into it – massive old Russia aside – and that obviously creates complications; complications they've embraced by making everything really, really complicated. There are two championships each year, with many clubs competing in both. The first is the State Championship, which starts in January and ends in May. Clubs play in leagues made up of teams from their own states, which are divided into different divisions. The competing teams range from giants like Santos, São Paulo, Palmeiras and Corinthians to the equivalent of semi-professional sides.

The *Campeonato Paulista* – the São Paulo State Championship – is generally considered to be the strongest so I'll start there. It begins as a league of twenty teams, who each play each other once before the top eight go into a play-off, which then has a two-legged final. That's not so bad, right? It's a little odd but not impossible to follow. However, this is one of two formats used by the various states.

The *Campeonato Carioca* – the Rio State Championship – uses the other format. If it sounds like it involves a singing contest it may as well. It consists of sixteen teams split into two groups of eight with the competition itself split into two sub-competitions. The first one is the Guanabara Cup, where the teams in each group play each other once before the top two of each group go into a play-off with the final determining who wins.

The other competition, the Rio Cup, then follows. The teams from each group now play every team from the other group once with the top two of each new, hybrid group going into a play-off, with the eventual winner of the Rio Cup taking on the winner of the Guanabara Cup to crown the state champions. If the same team wins both then they are state champions without the need for a final, though I'm surprised they don't make them play a three-legged affair against themselves where the third leg is a decathlon for no reason.

After the state champions are crowned the top teams from each state – all of whom have a different number of spots allocated depending on their quality – go into the Brazilian Cup the following year. So to qualify for the cup you have to win a league that then becomes a cup, or win a league that then becomes a cup, that then becomes another league, which also then becomes a cup, which becomes another cup if you didn't previously win both leagues. No wonder they call it a state. Naturally, the state championships also have multiple divisions that include promotion and relegation. To think that at first we all thought the order of League One and League Two was confusing.

It seems like a lot of effort to go to, which gives the impression that it's some beloved tradition, comparable to a five-month, localised version of the third round of the FA Cup. In reality, nobody really cares about it, making the whole thing even more baffling. Attendances are low so the bigger teams receive little revenue and treat it as a kind of pre-season and players from the smaller teams spend six months unemployed. It's a remnant of the days before commercial air travel when having a national league was simply impossible in a country of Brazil's size. It continues as the state federations have a lot of power even though there's a convincing argument that it is actively harmful to the growth and development of Brazilian domestic football. Though this is undoubtedly strange we are talking about a country where Romário is a successful politician so it shouldn't be that surprising.

Things are starting to change, though, with some of the bigger teams starting a breakaway competition due to their frustrations. It is called the Primeira Liga. Sound familiar?

The National Championship then takes place from May to December and is a little easier to follow. It's split into four divisions, Serie A-D, with A-C comprised of twenty teams and D featuring forty. A and B feature the round-robin style we have in Europe whereas C and D are split into regional groups, much like England's National League North and South. The structure is pretty much that of a standard European league now but until fairly recently it also had the eight-team play-off format. Fans miss this and it's understandable. A league that also has a cup final must be a thrilling thing. I'd imagine that they changed it because working out who had won what at the end of every season had become impossible. Brazilian administrators earn their money.

Not to be outdone, Argentina also has a system that looks alien to European fans, particularly as it keeps changing. For a long time there were two championships of equal footing per year known as 'short championships', where each team played each other once in the *Apertura* (Opening) and *Clausura* (Closing) but this came to an end in 2012. It was replaced with a similar format – *Inicial* and *Final* – that had only one overall winner, then in the next season it changed back to having two winners again with the winners of each championship then also contesting what became a separate cup. In 2015 the format changed yet again with the introduction of a thirty-team mega-league, the brainchild of then Argentine Football Association president Julio Grondona, who died in 2014, shortly before a six-month transitional tournament set up to determine who would compete in this league began. Nobody wanted it so when Grondona died they pretty much immediately set about changing it back again, with the aim of reducing it to twenty-four teams by 2018. That's if a breakaway league that's more similar to the European format hasn't simply started without the AFA by then, which is also a possibility. Gah. Changing everything back meant another transitional tournament in the first half of 2016, which consisted of the thirty teams split into two groups. Every team played every other team in their group once, home or away, then one team from the other group twice, home and away. The team from the other group that each side plays wasn't selected at random, they were their *clásico* rivals, deliberately kept apart in the groups, skewing the balance of quality in them, solely so that they could eventually play each other anyway. If a team didn't have a *clásico* rival in the league they just arbitrarily played whoever else needed to pair up. It was so complex that when the AFA released the fixture list it didn't feature the date of the opening round and missed off the penultimate round altogether. Imagine if the Premier League just forgot to mention a round of games in May. At the end of this carnage only one team was even relegated and all this is to get back to a league system they didn't even like in the first place.

Unbelievably, that isn't even the complicated bit. Convoluted though all that is, relegation is where things really start to get odd. It's based on an averaging system known as *promedios*, with relegation actually having its own table. A team's position in this table is determined by dividing the number of points they've won over the last three seasons – that being six short championships – by the number of games they've played in that time. Promoted teams have their smaller tallies divided by the fewer number of games they've played. This means that the worst individual team in a season will often stay up through having points in the bank from previous seasons, as if they've set up an overdraft. This often throws up interesting quirks. Though the league system has changed since then, in 2004 Tallares de Córdoba finished third, with the sixth-best points total and were relegated after losing a relegation play-off final with Argentinos Juniors. If this feels like it makes no sense, it is the same for fans there, who are generally confused by the format.

In the 2010/11 season River Plate managed to get themselves relegated despite good seasons in 2008/09 and 2009/10, showing quite how bad they must have been. As this unthinkable scenario played out radio presenter Atilio Costa Febre, overwhelmed with emotion, tore into River's board of directors for allowing this to happen. 'They fucked us! . . . Rats! Thieves! Where is the money you stole?' he shouted, in reference to the transfer fees River had received from selling their best and brightest to European clubs. Imagine Clive Tyldesley doing that. Ah, South America. Never change.

If you're wondering, yes, it is mathematically possible to win the league and be relegated. In 2012 Tigre found themselves competing for one of the short league titles. Argentina doesn't use goal-difference or a head-to-head record to separate teams who are level on points, instead determining who finishes on top via a play-off. A combination of this and the *promedios* system meant that Tigre came close to being in a situation where they could have played in a play-off for the title as well as a play-off to decide whether or not they'd go into a relegation play-off against a team from the second division. So, they could have played three play-offs to simultaneously win the league and be relegated. No wonder all their players leave.

Even thinking about all that is stressful so to calm down again let's leave South America and head over to the Pacific island of Tahiti. There teams receive four points for a win, two for a draw and one for a loss. When this was introduced in 2005/06 Tahiti FA director

Charles Ariiotima explained: 'We just don't want anyone to be sad.' The system is not unique – it's used in French amateur football – but Ariiotima put it in a particularly adorable way, adding: 'With this system, even if a team loses every game, they won't be on zero points at the end of the season. Football, first of all, is joy.' Maybe when FIFA is finally defeated this is the man to lead whatever takes its place.

22 Guys, One Cup

While South America is undoubtedly king when it comes to confusing rules we don't have to look too far from home to find another competition notable for its quirks in the form of the *Coupe de France*. The FA Cup may be known globally for giving amateur clubs the chance to have a crack at the pros, with 736 teams taking part in 2015/16, but that is nothing. 'Ha! That is nothing!' snorts the *Coupe de France*, for its entrants number in the thousands, the highest on record being 8,506. It is an unfathomable number but it's bulked up with teams from French overseas territories who have their own regional fixtures before sending either one or two sides into the further rounds. It's the equivalent of Bermuda, Anguilla and the Falkland Islands entering teams into the FA Cup. Some places simply send the winners of their own cup, including Tahiti, who are just happy to be taking part as football, first of all, is joy. Ariiotima for president!

Regional preliminary rounds also take place, of course, otherwise it would go on for years, and the professional teams don't enter until the seventh round. Strangely, the domestic amateur clubs enjoy the advantage of always playing their games at home, something the bigger clubs hate. There are no replays and, as some of the teams aren't even from France, this creates the perfect environment for upsets. The most famous example of a territorial team causing such an upset came in 1957 when Algerian side SCU El Biar beat Just Fontaine's then prominent Stade de Reims. In terms of amateur successes Calais RUFC reached the final in 2000 only to lose 2–1 to Nantes. At least they would have had loads of tiny bottles of beer to console themselves with when they got home.

A cup upset is one of the simplest joys of football and the potential for them is what makes cup competition so appealing and exciting, be it in Rio, Paris or Torquay, and it all started with the FA Cup. It's the oldest cup competition there is and it was shown all over the world even before the globalisation of the game, like a precursor to the modern Premier League.

For as long as I can remember people have been saying that its status has been diminished, that it's lost the 'magic' it once had. I know I'm adding to this by mentioning it at all but I want to decry it. The strange thing is that everyone seems to think that everyone else thinks it's lost its magic but nobody actually thinks it themselves. That people keep asking the question perpetuates the idea. It's like when people keep asking you what's wrong when nothing is wrong, you just have a moody face, but they keep asking and then you get annoyed, and then they say that obviously there is something wrong because you're annoyed but there wasn't anything wrong until they annoyed you by insisting something was wrong. *I'm fine.* Just let it go.

The FA Cup may have seemed amazing and life-affirming when you were younger in comparison to now but everything did. I remember when Push Pops came out in the nineties. They were a hard candy that you pushed out of a tube. That was literally it and everyone went nuts. They were a phenomenon. Of course, everything seemed better in the past, but we were easily impressed and our memories are not to be trusted. If you hear someone say 'the FA Cup has lost its magic' it will often really mean 'OH MY GOD I AM OLD NOW'. Of course it's still brilliant. It's football. Do you like football or not? You're over-thinking this. When people talk of the 'magic' they're talking about a combination of their own nostalgia and cherry-picked moments from a competition that's been around since 1871, so of course the past seems better. Also if it were truly magic it would probably be a lamp rather than a cup, and the FA Lamp doesn't have the same ring to it.

One of the most iconic stories from the cup's history is that of German goalkeeper Bert Trautmann, who became an unlikely but much loved star for Manchester City. He fought as a Luftwaffe paratrooper in the Second World War before he was captured and interned in a POW camp in Lancashire. At the end of the war, rather than accept an offer of repatriation, he stayed in England. When he signed for City 20,000 people attended a protest and club captain Eric Westwood, who'd fought in Normandy, had to try to keep the peace, saying: 'There's no war in this dressing-room,' though decades later they would sign human skirmish Craig Bellamy. Eventually winning over the fans with his displays, Trautmann cemented his place in football folklore in the 1956 FA Cup final. When diving for a ball he collided with Birmingham City's Peter Murphy, whose knee hit him in the neck. Back then substitutes weren't allowed so, despite being dazed, he played on for the remaining fifteen minutes, making a series of saves as the Manchester club won 3–1. As Prince Philip gave him his medal he commented that his neck looked crooked – probably also saying something like: 'You can pin this next to the Iron Cross on your lederhosen you damned hun,' – but Trautmann attended the post-match celebrations despite not being able to move his head and attempted to sleep off the pain. It later emerged that he had dislocated five vertebrae in his neck. His second vertebra was cracked in two with the third wedged against it, likely saving his life. So, to recap, he made crucial saves in a victorious FA Cup final with a broken neck, went out on the town to celebrate then tried to sleep it off. Had there been anybody left who didn't respect him by then, surely the keeping of a stiff upper neck in such circumstances would have won them over.

Everyone loves an upset, so much so that they tend to dominate the collective memory of competitions gone by. Footage of Ronnie Radford scoring a screamer for non-league Hereford against top-flight Newcastle United in 1972 on a quagmire of a pitch is as familiar as anything that has happened in recent years as we've all seen it so many times. I was a little too young to appreciate Wimbledon's 'Crazy Gang' beating Liverpool in the 1988 final but it's been so widely covered in the build-up to any game with the potential to be an upset that I feel like I played in it. Everyone has their own fond memories, be it Ricky Villa's goal for Spurs against Man City in the 1981 final, Gazza's free-kick against Arsenal in the 1991 semi, the terrible cream suits the Liverpool team wore to the 1996 final, Ryan Giggs scoring against Arsenal again in 1999, Arsenal winning it rather than getting mugged off.

A particular favourite of mine is the almost forgotten tradition of teams releasing a single before an FA Cup final. It seems mad now but this happened all the time.

Liverpool are responsible for one of the worst offenders with 1988's '*Anfield Rap*', which mashed together elements of the Beatles' '*Twist and Shout*', '*You'll Never Walk Alone*', old-school hip-hop and some truly terrible Scouse rapping. It's almost certainly what inspired Wimbledon's victory. They simply couldn't allow it to be validated.

Manchester United are no better, having released the risible '*Come On You Reds*' with Status Quo in 1994, which incredibly got to number one in the charts when people had to physically leave their houses and buy the single for this to happen. They then followed it with the 2 Unlimited-inspired '*Move Move Move (The Red Tribe)*' in 1996. It is absolutely abysmal but it is undeniably catchy and in many ways this is its biggest crime.

The United team of 1999 are rightly remembered for the incredible feat of winning the league, FA Cup and Champions League but less so for their clear attempt to sound like an Oasis B-side with '*Lift it High (All About Belief)*'. It only got to number eleven, denying them the quadruple. Unsurprisingly, Roy Keane is nowhere to be seen in the video. Why did this happen? Who arranged it? Was someone on the phone as soon as they won the semi, deciding what they wanted it to sound like on a giddy whim? It's not as if these players weren't superstars either. It's the exact equivalent of the current Man United squad reaching the FA Cup final then being bundled into a studio to rip off Ed Sheeran.

Man United are often blamed for supposedly devaluing the cup, though not because of these musical abominations. In 2000 they pulled out of the competition after the FA requested that they instead play in the FIFA Club World Championship. This was in part to help with England's bid for the 2006 World Cup, which went as well as England's World Cup bids generally do, but was seen as an irreversible slight on the proud old competition. Had they and the FA got their story straight they probably would have been fine. They should have simply taken inspiration from Birmingham City, who hold the record for the shortest ever cup run owing to them forgetting to send in their entry form in 1921. 'Oh no. It must have got lost in the post. Well we might as well take one for the team and play in the Club World Championship now. England 2006!'

For me the most galling thing about the modern FA Cup is not sides fielding weakened teams or a supposed lack of interest but the continuing attempts to turn it into something it isn't. The memories people have are of it simply being a football match played by two teams who'd worked hard to get there, not a day of corporate entertainment with some landfill indie band acting as a support act to the game. It's starting to feel like a budget Super Bowl booked by

Chris Evans. These attempts to update it and make it 'relevant' are exactly what's harming it. Don't push it away from its heritage and tradition. That's what we love about it.

I've been lucky/cool enough to experience my team winning the FA Cup on a number of occasions and it's a fantastic feeling that leaves you walking on air. The idea that its status has been diminished suggests that it now isn't of the same standing as the league, but I don't think anyone ever thought that winning the cup was necessarily better than winning the league. They were both great, as they are now. Even if teams do field weakened sides that gives traditionally smaller teams a chance to make history and give their fans a day to remember. Just ask Portsmouth and Wigan.

The Chaaaaaampiooooooons

It used to be that even when your team had won the FA Cup, you'd had the parade and taken advantage of the bragging rights, the fun still wasn't over. That was because you also qualified for the UEFA Cup-Winners' Cup, which pitted Europe's domestic cup winners against each other in a knockout competition. In 1994 Arsenal won it with a narrow win over a Parma side that featured Gianfranco Zola, Tomas Brolin and Faustino Asprilla, making them the Cup-Winners' Cup winners. As a fan of both Arsenal and gibberish this pleased me greatly. Of course, Arsenal then lost in the final the next year, former Spurs player Nayim scoring from forty-five yards out in the last minute of extra-time, but I try not to think about that. About how close it was to going to penalties. About how no team had ever retained the Cup-Winners' Cup. About David Seaman, one of my heroes, sat despondent in the green net. I try not to think about it.

The Cup-Winners' Cup doesn't exist any more. It was swallowed up by an expanding UEFA Cup, which of course then became the Europa League, but European football still holds a lot of magic for me. Some complain that it's boring until the knockout stages and that even then the same teams always feature. Though I see their argument I still love it; the bombastic music, the contrast in national styles, the draw of the biggest and best players on a gigantic stage, even that animated Gazprom ident that somehow feels like both a Christmas advert and a declaration of war. I am an absolute sucker for European football.

The ultimate prize is, of course, the European Champion Clubs' Cup. I say 'of course' but should probably clarify that that is the actual name of the Champions League trophy. The European Champion Clubs' Cup. It sounds like whoever named it was in the process of passing out having just been shot with a tranquilliser dart. Personally, I'd have called the whole competition the League Winners' League, accurate or not.

The European Cup began in 1955 as a straight knock-out competition that featured sixteen teams, picked by French paper *L'Equipe*, who seemed to have been at the centre of everything back then. Real Madrid won the first five and have now won eleven, as you'll know from them never shutting up about it. Benfica did eventually break their spell, beating Barcelona in the 1961 final at the Wankdorf Stadium in Bern, which it is absolutely necessary to mention here.

Some of the finest teams ever seen have been synonymous with the European Cup: from the Lisbon Lions to Cruyff's Ajax, the dominant forces of seventies and eighties Liverpool, Arrigo Sacchi's great Milan side, Cruyff's Barcelona Dream Team and the current Spanish duopoly. In recent years it has certainly become a little predictable but there have been periods like this in the past and surprises still spring up. From an English point of view Nottingham Forest won it twice in a row, 1979 and '80, unfathomable now. Liverpool's comeback from 3–0 down at half-time against AC Milan in 2005 is one of the best games in history. It was like they'd gone back in time to their glory days and I half expected the Beatles to appear and play them out at full-time. Steaua Bucharest won it in 1986, Red Star Belgrade in 1991. Even in a competition with so many strong sides surprises do still happen. They may be rare but if they're not rare they're not surprises. They're the examples that show us all that one day it could be our team.

In the current era of huge TV deals and super clubs it seems that even the Champions League isn't enough for some. Talk of a European Super League simply won't go away. In fact, the Cup-Winners' Cup was abolished after changes made to the Champions League and UEFA Cup that were intended to accommodate clubs who were considering joining such a league in 1998. Damn them for crushing the dreams of my youth. In 2009 Real Madrid overlord Florentino Pérez stated: 'We have to agree to a new European Super League, which guarantees that the best always play the best – something that does not always happen in the Champions League.'

No we don't, you maniac. Though it would undoubtedly be entertaining in whatever form it took it would fundamentally be designed to help the biggest and wealthiest clubs remain the biggest and wealthiest clubs. Football shouldn't work like that. The concept of 'best' is one that's decided on the pitch. Unlikely teams such as Forest and Leicester emerge out of nowhere and do something amazing because the game isn't decided by the status of the team before it starts. You can't just pick a moment in time and decide that the clubs who are the most successful then will be the most successful for ever. This talk comes up a lot, then disappears, and let's hope it does so again, for good, because the idea behind this involves taking the *merit* out of football, defeating the whole point of it. That point is that teams can establish themselves through hard work and smart decisions, that absolutely anyone, however bad their team, has the right to dream that one day the stars will align and they'll have their moment, their time when they know what it's like to be the best, to win, to be at the pinnacle of the thing they love. That means something and it's an idea worth protecting and fighting for.

8. Stadiums

Pete Donaldson

Dewy-eyed traditionalists will have you think that the football stadium is a theatre. A church. A cauldron of unified will.

It's not. It's where men and women go to fart.

It's a place where people's farts go to mingle with other people's farts. Ackee and saltfish waltzing with the gasses of steak and kidney. Dimer Dhokar Dalna mixing with the ghosts of home-made pizza.

This is the true football multiculturalism FIFA will sell you in nice tidy boxes. Football bringing everyone together in gaseous form, no matter your creed or culture. One hydrogen sulphide nation under a football flag. For the fleshy machines that create such noxiousness the truth is a little less idyllic.

Sartre's often misinterpreted saw, '*l'enfer, c'est les autres*' (hell is other people), asks whether we can ever really know ourselves without taking into consideration how we're regarded by others. And sitting on our high-density polyethylene stadium throne and glancing to our left and right, do we really want to know ourselves when everyone around us is so damn objectionable? From the cawing man in the flat cap in front who constantly squawks about where Micah Richards would fit in a four-four-two if he wasn't such a lazy shit, to your screeching, puce-faced neighbour who oscillates between smashing his hands on his thighs and bawling at the referee's blindness, even though he himself sports thick corrective lenses that would put the Hubble telescope to shame. 'Why can't everyone in this stand be like me?' you think. 'Normal. Well adjusted. Above all, fair?'

But then, that's what goes through everyone's head.

This is exactly why revolutions are hard to get off the ground. People abhor other people. Even when wearing the same team colours, with the same love of the game, love of the same feckless boy-millionaires in your hearts, at the end of the day you will always find yourself surrounded by a disparate set of howling know-nothings.

But taking all that into consideration, something still stirs when those familiar battleship-grey, pock-marked cement posts holding up the chalk-white trusses of your home ground come into view. You walk a little taller. The heart swells.

Growing up in Hartlepool on the North-East coast, south of Sunderland and north of Middlesbrough, my first taste of football stadiums and their utilitarian engineering was Hartlepool United's Victoria Park. A rather handsome ground when compared with some of its functional fourth-tier peers, with a capacity of just under 8,000, I spent many a happy afternoon squished into the congregation of denim-jacketed nineties men who themselves had wedged themselves into the Town End terracing.

I'd start the day at the aforementioned Brian Honour Saturday youth club playing five-a-side pick-up matches with kids at least two years my junior (I'd got into football late and people my age were already 'romancing' girls down the park – something I still can't manage and certainly not in a park) and for seven whole pounds you'd get three hours of football on the only sandy all-weather pitch in town and a free ticket to the match.

The ticket in question gave you access only to the decidedly dull family enclosure in the Cyril Knowles Stand (ex-Spurs and celebrated Pools manager who sadly died at 47) but if you waited the steward who manned the gate between the Knowles Stand and the rather more salty Town End would often go and get himself a Bovril of equivalent saltiness, leaving you to stealthily unlatch the gate and leg it to the terracing.

Just call me Hooligan 'Green Street' Donaldson. Whizz with a snooker ball in a sock.

The fencing that circles the ground is still to this day decorated by long vertical pikes, upon which decorative footballs have been impaled. I'm not really sure what this says about the club's commitment to attractive football, but perhaps Hartlepool's league position tells its own tale.

A stone's throw from the town centre (I say stone, I mean a half-empty can of McEwan's lager) the ground in my day was surrounded by vast swathes of waste ground – a perfect locale for a pre-booze-up tactical vomit, or right royal tear-up.

Speaking of kung fu fighting, the only proper scrapping I ever saw was pre and post Darlington derby games. That said, the proximity of the ground to the train station was a godsend for the forever put-upon constabulary. A Darlo fan did once aim a kick at my head after a 4–0 drubbing, missed and ended up managing to kick me in the posterior in the same swing of the boot.

I still don't know how this man, some twenty years my senior, managed to do it, though my memory is hazy after running full pelt into the side of a police horse, who didn't even so much as neigh in response. Horses are trained to expect the unexpected in the North-East.

It's not just the breeze-blocks and mortar that build a stadium experience. In many cases it's all about the approach to the ground. Location is key in a thousand different ways. Clubs lucky enough to have inner-city stadiums trump those whose fans have to trudge the long grass on the verges of the motorways and dual-carriageways to get to their particular cathedrals. To be honest, the march to the ground is often more interesting and colourful than the game.

At the risk of sounding trite, it's this chimerical throng that gives you hope for the future – a young lass in full team colours on her father's back, walking shoulder to shoulder with the fat bloke who sells fruit on the high street with sun-bleached facial tats, while bringing up the rear is that old girl who works in the betting shop who's been attending games since the war. Unity in dichotomy, unity through a common interest and goal. It's intoxicating, heartening and exciting all at the same time.

From the sheer lunacy of witnessing an Arsenal fan planting a dainty flag inscribed with 'SPURS' in some compacted horse crap outside the Finsbury Park mosque, to the wrong 'uns who hawk half-and-half scarves on Wembley Way (seriously, if I was the sheep whose woolly destiny was a scarf with identity issues I'd be furious), these are the images that frequently stick in my mind on the way to the football, and no amount of panenkas and thirty-yard howitzers or pre-match big-telly sizzle reels are going to change that.

The very first match I attended at the cauldron that is St James' Park was a nervy and narrow 1–0 win over Aston Villa in 1996 (Beardsley with a whipped cross from the right, classic Les Ferdinand six-yard bullet header). It lingers in the memory not because of the stomach-churning excitement as I half ran up the steps to the gate, not the thrill of finding myself inside St James' Park watching Tino twist up Alan Wright like a big Alan Wright-shaped kipper, it was the image of an inebriated man of perhaps fifty walking up Barrack Road, spotting a concertinaed can of fizzy pop in the gutter and taking a hefty swing at it with his right peg.

He missed, and missed with some style. Instantly found himself on his back. Magic. The laughter. Subdued concern of his fellow fan, drowned out by the howls. It was pretty much the first time I'd witnessed a grown man make a fool of himself thanks to alcohol at a sporting event, and my love of spectating (and indulging in) that particular sport endures.

Skip forward a good fifteen years and, having watched Newcastle grind out a courageous nil-niller at Upton Park in the World's Worst Away End™, skulking through the back alleys behind the ground, myself and fifty-odd Geordies found themselves walking past the Ahmadiyya

Muslim Association, the administrators of hundreds of mosques in the UK.

Posted at the front door were two stocky chaps, as if to head off any bother from tanked-up football fans. An uneasy hush descended. Let's face it, football fans can frequently be dicks and I think people on both sides of the fence were expecting someone, somewhere to say something a bit off-colour.

Just as I thought the moment had successfully passed without incident, all at once a tall ginger chap behind me started to shout the word 'MUSLIMS . . .' Here we go, I thought, and visibly shrank.

'MUSLIMS ARE A GEORDIE . . . MUSLIMS ARE A GEORDIE . . . A LAH LAH LAH,' he continued.

The crowd eagerly picked up the refrain until the whole lot were chanting. I have never been more proud to be in the middle of a crowd of football idiots.

Nuts And Bolts

But once inside, what makes a truly great stadium? From the Identikit, one-size-fits-all grounds of Madejski and Liberty, to the jagged hotchpotch of Elland Road and the Valley – is there something inherently special about a particular lattice of concrete, steel and PVC? Here are some of the headline grabbers . . . and some that *The Football Ramble* have stuck their heads inside over the years.

Maracanã Stadium, Rio de Janeiro, Brazil

Known to some as the *Estádio Jornalista Mário Filho*, known to me as the 'I will have to figure out which key combination gets me one of those squiggly lines over the vowel' stadium.

Looking at it now after its many refurbishments, the Maracanã in many ways resembles a great ruddy big polo mint, and no amount of romance is gonna dress that one up. Home of both the Fla and the Flu, this stadium is one that's seen many an epic encounter.

Built for the World Cup in 1950, the total attendance for the final that year was a whopping 199,854. One hundred and forty-six. That's all it would have taken to get to 200,000. Hang your heads, Rio, you proper cocked it.

Post-capacity reduction, this stadium is still the largest in South America, save for the *Estadio Monumental* in Lima, Peru – a stadium definitely named in like five minutes. 'Hey guys, what shall we call our *monumental* stadium, bearing in mind it's nearly lunchtime and it's Togosh Tuesday in the canteen?'

The Maracanã has seen many a configuration, scaling capacities both up and down. For the 2014 World Cup and 2016 Olympics, the original seating bowl, in a two-tier configuration, was torn down and replaced with one big footballing tier Italia '90-era Gazza would have been proud of (wordplay doesn't work written down, but I'm imagining most of our listeners read out loud). The concrete roof was removed and, according to Fluminense's terribly informative website, replaced by a fibreglass tensioned membrane, coated with polytetrafluoroethylene.

Side note: polytetrafluoroethylene is the only known solid that geckos can't cling to, making the Brazilian FA's decision to train those thousands of geckos to retrieve lost footballs short-sighted at best. Short-sightedness not bothering the nocturnal gecko, who all have excellent eyesight.

Easily the most recognisable and celebrated stadium in South America, beating off stiff, yet boxy competition from *La Bombonera* in Buenos Aires – the Brazilians have failed to lift a World Cup at this ground in two attempts. From their 7–1 humbling at the hands of the Germans in Bela Horizonte to the ghost that silenced the Maracanã in 1950, Alcides Ghiggia, this is not a happy hunting ground for those hunters tracking the lesser-spotted Jules Rimet or World Cup trophies. I'm sure Pickles the dog would have had more luck.

It's not just soccer and athletics that have found a home at the big polo mint. Concerts are a regular occurrence, too. In January 1998, Tina Turner notably brought her celebrated *'Break Every Rule'* tour to the stadium. Curfew was observed, the bloody liar.

It's worth mentioning that it isn't the only Maracanã in the world – in Panama City there's a rather modest 5,000-seat stadium named after its big daddy. Red Star Belgrade's home is also known as the Marakana and, according to a recent poll, is the least hospitable stadium in the world. I got this piece of information from serbia. com, a website that really isn't doing its job when it comes to attracting tourism.

Allianz Arena, Munich, Germany

German asset management! Financial services! Two concepts that, if they haven't already, may in time cause a painful and involuntary orgasm, so maybe loosen clothing accordingly, or consider cracking out the bromide.

The much maligned but technically quite impressive fluoropolymer panels (more synthetic plastic chat, guys) that hug the contours of this Bavarian horror show are inflated by thousands of fans, for some reason or another. These panels change colour whether Bayern, 1860 or the German national team are playing there, and is known as 'the *schlauchboot*' (the dinghy) by locals.

The designers state that the decision to utilise this 'one weird trick' and go all out for clear plastic panelling is all about getting more natural light on to the pitch, but seriously, the entire stadium looks like a mobility aid you'd stick in your nan's bath.

The Emirates, London, England

In the summer of 1997 London's top scientists came together to see if it was possible to make Arsenal's home ground even quieter.

In 2006 – and at a cost of 290 million – they managed it with the Emirates. Resembling the world's priciest cake tin, the outside walls are adorned with a mural of all the players who made a ton of appearances for the Gunners. Graham Rix isn't up there, though, strangely. Maybe he was on holiday when they painted it.

The players in question are hugging the stadium and can be seen only from the rear, meaning that when the sun and moon set, they're treated to a front-seat view of Steve Bould's back-seat. When Disraeli called London a 'modern Babylon', I only wish he'd been alive to see this.

These murals appeared only after fan criticism regarding the homogeny of the stadium, so a campaign of 'Arsenalification' (their term) took place, which sounds like a word juries have to have explained during rather graphic court cases. They also attached a clock to the south stand, so that fans know when to start their shifts shouting 'Wenger out' into the microphones of Arsenal Fan TV.

Olympiastadion (the Munich one), Germany

Back to Munich we go for a shufty at one proper, mad, plastic and steel wire marvel – the *Olympiastadion*, finished in 1972 and featuring huge sweeping webs of acrylic glass, resembling your bike on its first jaunt out of the shed on a spring morning, spokes covered in glistening spider's webs, long vacated.

Designed to resemble the sloping valleys of the Alps, construction took place on the site of a pit made by Allied bombings, making excavation easier. If that's not turning lemons into lemonade, I don't know what is.

Olympiastadion (the Berlin one), Germany

Christ, there are a lot of *Olympiastadions*, aren't there? This one is the stone arena that gave us the timeless, cathartic image of Jesse Owens socking it to ol' Hitlershits in his back yard. This stadium is now home to Hertha Berlin.

The Football Ramble once went to the *Olympiastadion* to watch Hertha play. I was on my own personal mission to eat as many *currywurst* as I possibly could in ninety minutes. I like to think I turned in a performance of Olympic proportions that the Führer would also have baulked at, being a vegetarian. So in many ways I like to think I'm just as historically important as Jesse.

In the match we attended, Hertha were roundly bummed in the gob after a defensive display that could perhaps best be described as 'out there' and also 'wilful dereliction of duty'. We didn't get back into Potsdamer Platz until 1 a.m., thanks to an oik smashing a window on the *U-Bahn*. Marcus had too much orange squash.

Scary Olympiastadion

Scary *Olympiastadion* loves romantic comedies and junk food, and isn't afraid to tell it like it is.

Baby Olympiastadion

The youngest of the *Olympiastadion* crew, Baby likes nothing better than hanging with her friends, and representing maximum GIRL POWER! at all times.

Ginger Olympiastadion

The fieriest of all the *Olympiastadions*, Ginger loves living with all the other *Olympiastadions*. She just wishes Scary *Olympiastadion* wouldn't leave her clothes all over the house. Oh well, GIRL POWER!

Wembley, London, England

Costing £798 million and the life of carpenter Patrick O'Sullivan, the home of a partially successful national team features a partially retractable roof. This pulls back to avoid shadowing on the pitch, so that people watching at home can enjoy the event, because, of course, that's the primary concern of the FA now. Not the people who actually paid to be there.

Balancing the weight needed for such hydraulic sorcery is the gargantuan Wembley arch, which makes the whole endeavour look a little like one of those sandwich presses you see in Pret A Manger. I hope to live to see the day that the Wembley arch falls with a decisive clunk and a gigantic ham, cheese and mustard toastie envelops the London Borough of Brent.

Exactly one half of *The Football Ramble* have played on the hallowed Wembley turf in an eleven-a-side competition. I won a penalty and then insisted on someone else taking it, a fact that haunts me to this very day. Then I went over on my ankle. The Wembley curse. Don't know what happened in Lukey's match but, having played with him, I imagine he put in a two-footer or three.

Camp Nou, Barcelona, Spain

Originally costing 288 million pesetas back in 1957, which according to this writer's calculator is roughly

BOOBS pounds sterling, the Camp Nou boasts a unique, timeless amphitheatre design, which of course is very much not in keeping with modern tastes so, according to various news outlets, that bloke who made the Gherkin is going to wrap it in plastic so it resembles a massive stupid Berocca.

Team Ramble once visited this stadium back in '09 to watch José Mourinho's Inter take on Pep's Barcelona in the Champions League group stages. With Zlatan benched it was up to Barca's car dealership giant inflatable man Gerard Piqué to open the scoring.

Outside the ground those guys who cool cans of Estrella in the sewers of Barcelona offered us a dose or two of inebriation and Legionnaires' disease. We took them up on their kind offer, which made breathlessly clambering up ten flights of stairs slightly lighter work.

And my word, our seats were in the gods – the gods in question that evening consisting of woozy Catalans shelling peanuts and smoking some pretty heavy weed. Every slick passing move from the *Blaugrana* was met with a rumble of hoots and cackles. To my surprise the wall behind us was only eyeline-high – a 5ft 8in man could have rolled himself over this barrier with very little difficulty and dropped a full fifty metres to his death. But he didn't. Otherwise Marcus would have written this chapter, and it would probably have been a much more informative read. We ended the night dancing in a hostel slash nightclub called 'Kabul'.

Tee-totaller Marcus had an unprecedented three Baileys, and schooled me in Michael Jackson dance moves.

Sapporo Dome, Japan

Located in the north of Japan, where the undrinkable lager comes from, the (literally) mercurial shiny metal blob that is the Sapporo Dome has a secret, but not one of those secrets that shame the entire family for generations and involve swords going into stomachs.

At the flick of a switch – probably one of those awesome ones with a red plastic flip-cap over the top – the football field is ejected outside faster than Jack Wilshere from a nightclub, and the staff get to work unspooling great rolls of artificial turf for baseball matches. Several rows of seats fold into themselves, and the bat and ball game can go on for what feels like fifty dull hours, with commercial breaks.

The baseball team who ply their trade at the Sapporo Dome are the 'Nippon-Ham Fighters', by the way. For those of us who find 'the New York Red Bulls' hard to swallow, remember it could always be worse. The team had been the 'Toei Flyers' for decades and were based in the capital Tokyo, but a pig renderer bought them and moved them more than a thousand miles north and gave them their new, hammy name. You can't stand in the way of progress. Or ham fighting.

Giuseppe Meazza, Milan, Italy

Known to most as the San Siro owing to its location, the Giuseppe Meazza appears at first glance to resemble some mad spacecraft launch pad.

It was named after the man who led Italy to two consecutive World Cups, a player who Luigi Veronelli, noted gastronome and intellectual, described thusly: 'One day, I witnessed [Giuseppe] doing something astonishing: he stopped the ball with a bicycle kick, elevating himself two metres from the ground. He landed with the ball glued at his foot, dribbled over an astonished defender, and then went on scoring a goal with one of his hallmark shots, sardonic and accurate to the millimetre.' From this we can deduce with a fair degree of confidence that Luigi Veronelli was a fucking liar.

I was lucky enough to attend the stadium for the 2016 Champion's League final between the two Madrids, and I noticed but two things. One, the place is falling to bloody bits. And two, you can urinate while still being able to see at least 50 per cent of the pitch.

Food

'A full pocketbook often groans more loudly than an empty stomach'

– Franklin D. Roosevelt.

'From attending the corporate hospitality for a couple of seasons, it is clear why they call it the Theatre of Dreams' – PP Plasma, a leading UK metal profiler and poet collective.

People must be fed. They get ever so grouchy when they're not. From the unlovable eczema-red hot dog sausages in anaemic baps, to the four quid bags of Wispa Bites, the modern football stadium is a haven for bean-counters who get excited about the idea of fleecing yet more money from put-upon punters.

My fortnightly Saturday job during university was a wholly unsatisfying five-hour shift at Filbert Street, home of (the wholly unsatisfying to watch back in 2002) Leicester City. My minimum-wage job was serving food and drink to some of the most deflated football fans I'd ever seen. This was to be Leicester's relegation season from the Premier League, two years since they'd won the Worthington (League) Cup and one since they'd struck out in Europe after just one round. Martin O'Neill had left for Celtic, and the masses took solace in chicken balti pies in their droves.

Even though Leicester has some amazing Indian restaurants on almost every corner, and the balti is very much a staple of British-Asian cuisine, there was still something a bit . . . exotic about ordering one of these. The special bronze foil gave one an affordable yet glamorous thrill – like seeing the mobile phone provider 'Movistar' pop up on your phone screen when you're on holiday.

By the way, if you're ever tasked with pulling out the correct flavour of Pukka pie from a hot oven at speed – here are the foil colour codes:

Chicken balti – bronze.

Meat and potato – brown.

Potato, cheese and onion – gold.

Steak and kidney – silver.

Beef and onion – red.

Chicken and mushroom – gold.

Yes, that's right. Chicken and mushroom, and cheese and onion do indeed share foil trays. Luckily we almost never had enough of the former for it to be much of a problem. If anyone asked I would try my best to slink away and empty more hot dogs into the hot dog machine from their greasy foil packets.

The other part of my job was slicing off great chunks of a hog roast and serving it in baps to the fed-up fans. Every week without fail a chap who looked like John Gordon Sinclair's fat cousin would come up to my friend Justin and me and demand more pork crackling than was allowed (a shard per customer). 'Don't be shy. Your mother wasn't,' he would say. Every. Single. Time. Don't worry, he'd get his extra portion of seared pork skin, but also receive the driest of stuffing, and the soggiest of bun every time. As the old saying goes, 'porking well is the best revenge'.

Once we'd drunk our weight in Coke mixer syrup and eaten as much sweet apple sauce as our stomachs could hold (they couldn't stock-check that stuff, the suckers) we'd have to take the remains of the pig carcass back to the main stand, the tray sloshing about with grease. We were never told why. Maybe Muzzy Izzet wanted to pick at the bones or something. At least once a fortnight we'd be carrying the unwieldy tray past an exasperated Robbie Savage as he was getting a grilling from a *Leicester Mercury* journo.

Drink

The cornerstone of any concessions stand is booze, and a football match is one of the few times you'll hear the word 'concourse' said by anyone – usually by that eighteen-year-old steward who's just told you to get back into the concourse because hiding that bottle of Tuborg in your jacket pocket isn't fooling anyone.

When *The Football Ramble* chipped off to Kiev for the European Championship in 2012 (pre- *Yevromaidan*) I overdid it with what I thought was a special lavender-flavoured Carlsberg. Four pints down, I came to the realisation that I still found the England band strangely obscene and, though I maintain that no amount of inebriation could make that rabble sound anything other than unspeakable, this strange-tasting and above all cheap booze clearly contained no alcohol. I felt cheated, and not just because Marcus had booked us tickets in the Sweden end, which made it harder to cheer for Danny Welbeck's winner, after grisly old beardy-chops Olof Mellberg rolled back the years with a brace.

That said, drinking beer at football stadiums removes much of the fun of drinking beer, much like Carlsberg removed much of my blood-alcohol on that summer's day in 2012. First, the drinks are served in micron-thin plastic glasses. Second, thanks to the maddening queuing system for both drinks and the toilet, you're tasked with throwing a pint of tasteless fizzy lager down your throat in three minutes before the second half kicks off, like some kind of urban bush-tucker trial.

Why can't there be a great big trough everyone pays a quid to stick their stupid faces in, and another trough to get rid of said liquid? Mark my words people, beer troughs and trough urinals are the future. I've drawn up an image for the patent.

In a perfect world, here are some of the things that quite simply should be sold at the football. And the fact that they're not says more about football than me. Or maybe it says something about us both. Or you. Yeah, you.

* * *

Prosecco – it's impossible to get angry-drunk with Prosecco. It makes you giggly, not fighty. You can't take a swing at someone or throw a dart into the away stand if you've got a big chucklesome burp in the chamber.

Haggis – I've actually seen a grown man, presumably with dependants and loved ones, instigate his own 'fifteen-second rule' when a slice of wafer-thin ham slipped from his grasp (he was eating a pack of M&S's finest on its own) and flopped on to the concrete at his feet. I see nothing that suggests a football crowd wouldn't be all over minced pig lung and suet like a rash.

Quiche, but never flan – I'm always proper jealous when I see an old boy open a packed lunch at his seat and unwrap the foil around a fat wedge of quiche. Flan (and there is a difference, people) can seriously *do one*. No place in the modern game.

Those massive comedy lollipops bairns buy at funfairs – I'd bloody love to see a rotter smash one of them over an opposing fan's head. It'd get all stuck in their hair, but wouldn't do any lasting damage. Probably.

Advent calendar – I once saw two grown men sharing one in early December at a Fulham match. God knows what was going on there, but I would have indulged, given the opportunity.

An Iceland Luxury Ultimate King Prawn Ring – Seriously mate, I've got a freezer full of them. No one ever wants to eat them. Help me out.

'The Facilities'

Given an infinite amount of time, typewriters and as many monkeys as you could corral into a room, there is a distinct possibility that the simians would happen upon the complete works of William Shakespeare. Or Shakin' Stevens. Either way, the part of the infinite monkey theorem that no one ever seems to consider is the state of the room after they've finished and presumably received their monkey medals. *There would be piss and shit everywhere.*

Similarly, anyone who's ever been to a football ground will recognise that pervasive, dead-rat-under-the-floorboards *hum* that only a stand full of men can create in an infinitely shorter amount of time. Two hours in fact, sans extra-time.

At the last count around a quarter of Premier League attendees are women and, though I can only speak for the concessions awarded to the un-fairer sex, I do know that heading to the loo at a stadium in a packed concourse with a bladder full of booze is the most unpleasant experience going. That slow, listless shuffle towards the fluorescent stink-box that is the gents makes any right-thinking person shudder. The politics of who's taking the next spot at the trough? The smell of the urinal cakes . . . the men unapologetically letting guffs ring out while expelling hot Tuborg on the other side, all the while shouting their catchphrases 'well, they were fucking shite again' and 'I'm not coming next week'.

Faded 'ladbantz' adverts for deodorant, long-forgotten box sets and testicular cancer charities are Han Solo-ed behind A4 Plexiglas in front of the urinals, the cubicles are treated to hurried Biro graffiti and stickers for hooligan firms some Kazakh nut-job stuck to the cistern three seasons ago.

On top of that, time after time you witness every bloke in your friendship group eschewing the fripperies of actually bothering to wash their hands – following up that decision with a generous offer to buy you a pie, eyeballing you as you jam his piss-tainted pie in your gob.

Look, let's not pretend football fans are even grown-ups any more. I'm proposing nappies for grown-ups. Get them at the turnstile after they've frisked you for knives, drop them off as you leave. I can see the advert now. *Tena – pads for lads.* At least we'd smell better.

Getting 'Made'

Mood lighting around the Allianz is all well and good, but who foots the damn bill for all of this? How does the modern stadium get made?

Well, what usually happens in simple terms is that a football team gets taken over by a person with a big red face who motors about in a helicopter and fancies cementing his or her position as the saviour of a football club on the cheap, without having to guarantee a level of performance from the managers and staff he or she employs.

Invariably, these monolithic chunks of metal and concrete have to be built somewhere accessible and agreeable to the punters themselves, and land is not cheap.

There are two ways to achieve this increase in your match-day profit with an increased capacity, either with a cheeky stadium expansion, or a new stadium altogether. One tactic is to threaten to move the football team out of the area, say into an empty Olympic Stadium (see Daniel Levy), the local borough council (see Haringey) instantly removes all of its clothes and spoons said chairman into submission, showering him with millions of pounds of riot-recovery subsidies (again, Levy and Haringey) and lowering the percentage of affordable housing that will need to be built as part of the deal for a new site (guess who?).

Or you could, over say ten years, systematically buy up and shutter houses in a particular area that impinge upon your plans to expand your stadium, effectively creating an artificial slum in which entire streets lie empty. House prices fall, crime rates dutifully rise and then you can stand and point at the mess, shouting 'Hey city councillor, this road proper stinks. *It like proper hums*. Why don't you threaten the remaining residents with compulsory purchase orders, lowball them with below-market rates and get them shifted? Then we can maximise our own profits by putting more bums on seats in our stadium but at the same time peddle our PR line about being a club dedicated to its community, taking advantage of some proportion of goodwill afforded by collective bereavement due to the unspeakable, unending tragedies its fans have endured in the past?'

See Liverpool.

As always there's a tightrope to walk, community versus competitiveness, and if Man United's domination of the money-rich top division has taught us anything, it's that keeping up with the Phil Joneses puts a smile on the faces of the out-of-towners who come once a season to sit in the pricey seats, if not a roof over local people's heads.

So face it, new stadiums aren't as pricey as they first appear, as long as those at the top of the tree are ballsy enough to indulge in a little brinkmanship. Take Manchester City, for example. Back in 2003 the club accepted £22 million from the local council to help convert the City of Manchester Stadium from an athletics concern to one that could support a Premier League team. The stadium that was built was in part thanks to fingernails and tax collection – scratch-card aficionados filling the lottery grant coffers to the tune of £77 million and the council stumping up a hefty £33 million themselves.

Some time later, the club was able to flog itself to Thaksin Shinawatra, with not a penny flowing back to the council, and then a year later he's made a tidy profit in the region of £20 million from a debt-ridden club and made good his escape. Not bad for a deposed Prime Minister who by now was very much on the run.

Sure, Man City don't own it, but thanks to some super-stealthy renegotiation at the hands of un-stealthily named Mansour bin Zayed bin Sultan bin Zayed bin Khalifa Al Nahyan, their outgoings are now a flat £3 million a year, chump change to our Sheikh, and a much better deal for Manchester City once they get their capacity increase.

Big stadiums mean big-money contracts, from the hawking of naming rights to the supply of concrete and steel to IT provision – this attracts every company with a product to peddle, and the fear of UEFA Financial Fair Play sanctions (FFP) are understandably some way down that list.

Real Madrid were under investigation for some time regarding their deal with Madrid city council over the *Las Tablas* land, the 1998 valuation of it at under half a million euros when it was handed over to the club as part of a payment agreement, becoming a whopping €22.7 million in 2011 when Real Madrid were forced to sell it back to the city. UEFA FFP strictly forbids any form of state aid, but there are some concerns as to the effectiveness and vigour in which those rules are applied.

In short, football is a lovely big sexy quiche, and anyone who's anyone wants to be seen to have sniffed it, be it councils, sponsors or investors.

In the murky world of business, football is (perhaps strangely) regarded as a 'clean' business, with universal appeal and a veneer of respectability, which for many is a PR no-brainer, and owning those grey cement walls and off-white breeze-blocks is the first rung for many.

Pitches Get Stitches

We can talk about the architectural achievements of these modern footballing edifices, but if the pitches aren't tip-top, no one's having fun and players are going to get hurt.

The key to modern football are those wacky half-grass half-plastic hybrid pitches, usually provided by those enigmatic grass boffins over in Germany or Holland. The latter, obviously, being great with grass.

The market leaders by a yard of perfectly coiffured greenery are Desso Sports Systems. Precious few grounds in the Premier League have not been infiltrated by Desso.

Louis van Gaal's first act as Manchester United boss was to install these pitches at their training ground.

Pricey, but way better value than Angel Di María. Rival supplier GreenFields are the official pitch suppliers at PSV Eindhoven, but we can't blame them for Luke Shaw's busted leg.

Mixing artificial fibres with natural grass, a giant sewing machine rocks up one morning and plants green plastic fibres in two-centimetre squares, which would take bloody ages to do by hand. No doubt José will have Juan Mata doing just that by September.

If anyone's under any illusions as to whether the famous Manchester City Football Academy has gone for the full hybrid or full plastic on one of the pitches located to the south of the complex, they probably need their eyes checking for cataracts – it's a tasteful sky blue.

Whichever way you sew it, turf management is pricey at half the price. Jason Booth, the general manager of the 'Institute of Groundsmanship,' weighed in on Hampden Park's owners having to spend a million pounds on multiple real grass returfs in a few short years. 'You can give Queen's Park Cristiano Ronaldo, but if he hasn't got the players around him that can play with him, they're not going to win the league,' he said.

Let's make one thing clear – they totally would. The fact that Jason's doubted it means that Ronaldo would be more than up for the project, too.

Statues

No stadium is complete without the requisite statues and plaques and memorial flowerbeds and slides (one day, Newcastle United, we'll get that proposed slide). Here are some of the more notorious ones . . .

Ted Bates – Southampton FC

Player, manager, president. Ted Bates ploughed his entire life into Southampton Football Club, and they rewarded him with a statue, costing more than a hundred grand, that resembled the old duffer from the film '*Up*' – massive gurning head, tiny body. Spectacular. Bonus points awarded for a passing resemblance to ex-Pompey owner Milan Mandarić.

The King Of Pop – Fulham FC

A classic. People may have mocked this multicoloured shit-show, but we don't see Fulham climbing the table now it's gone from its pedestal, do we? When *The Football Ramble* did a live show in the National Football Museum, the actual deposed statue looked down upon us and gave us a bit of good luck. That luck manifested itself in Marcus getting out of Manchester alive after doing his now legendary 'Manc' impression. The best bit about the statue was definitely the sparkly glove. It resembles chainmail – as if he's working in a metalwork factory. Madness.

Cristiano Ronaldo – Funchal, Madeira

This statue isn't strictly a stadium fixture, being located in Ronaldo's home town of Funchal, yet we couldn't let this opportunity pass without mentioning CR7 and his bizarre lumpy breeches. A lot of papers seemed to obsess over the relative size of our hero's junk, but in all honesty it's more the direction it appears to be hanging. Very direct play from our man in white. Avert your eyes, children of Madeira.

Various – Arsenal

Quite how anyone's conscience would be able to accommodate the act of forcing a sculptor to stare at pictures of Tony Adams for hours on end, I don't know. I think it comes under cruel and unusual punishment, personally. Thanks to the aforementioned 'Arsenalification' of the Emirates, visitors are now treated to some fairly serviceable reproductions of Herbert Chapman (a man who looks like he could take a punch), Dennis Bergkamp, a young Ken Friar (club secretary) and a sleepy-looking Tony Adams. Thierry Henry being very much the pick of the bunch here, depicted performing the knee slide after his fine solo goal against Tottenham back in '02.

Roughly two weeks after it was unveiled, I swear I walked past it and someone had left the shell of a Henry hoover in front of him, and it looked as if he was dutifully in the middle of a bag change.

For Fuck's Sake, Just Put A Ramp In Or Something

I'm lucky enough to live in our nation's capital, a city I have a genuine love of. One of the most prosperous cities in the West has one of the most iconic, celebrated sub-subterranean metro systems, the London Underground. It's a true one-off. I'm proud to be a regular user of its rails.

One of the most disappointing, piss-boiling issues I have with it, though, is watching disabled people try to extract one iota of use from it. Two hundred and seventy stations across the network, only sixty-six of any use to wheelchair users. Admittedly, the network is Victorian and conversion is expensive, but even the new Crossrail network, not scheduled to be finished until 2019, prevents wheelchair users from accessing seven stations. It cost £14.5 billion. Disabled people chucking money at a service they can't use.

And so we end our chapter on a bit of a downer if I'm honest. Though this is a celebration of football, provisions for the disabled at games are nineteenth-century at times, and they need to get better, *and quickly*. The revitalise.org.uk site used a complex scoring system to create a Premier League table of stadiums that provide decent access to their facilities, and those that don't. This was back in 2015, building on work done by the UEFA Centre for Access to Football in Europe and Level Playing Field, both in the business of encouraging more football clubs to up their disabled provision, mainly focusing on seating capacity for the disabled as a ratio of its full capacity, as well as accessible toilets, parking and match stewards with disability training. They also looked at bafflingly easy stuff that would cost a club next to nothing – stuff like website information giving wheelchair users sufficient information on attending a match.

Top of the accessibility tree? The Emirates. Which is how it should be. A new ground, a club with a ridiculously capacious rainy-day fund, nothing more to see here. The home of Southampton, St Mary's Stadium, came in second – adequate wheelchair space, online information, toilets and parking, with ticket concessions to boot.

Bournemouth were third, probably due in part to the reduced capacity, but they scored high in every section, beating Manchester City, Swansea and Leicester at fourth, fifth and sixth.

At the foot of the table, some Premier League stalwarts, and certainly teams with a massive amount of cash flooding through their gates every week. Watford were bottom: not enough seats, not enough staff training or parking – and with a turnover of £17 million in 2013/14. Tottenham Hotspur were nineteenth: too few disabled seats in the ground, not enough info on the website and scant provision for disabled parkers, even with a turnover of £181 million. Everton were in at eighteenth, with no disabled parking and a turnover of £121 million, too few seats available to disabled supporters and very little information available about what they do have. Also just outside the relegation spots were Liverpool, with a 'success' ratio of 47 per cent – a few per cent lower than even Brendan Rodgers' win percentage.

Sorry to end this chapter with a bit of a cob-on. Don't worry, though, Jim's starting the next one talking about the modern England team . . . Oh.

Bottom line is, we're constantly peddled the line that football transcends sex, colour and creed – so to my mind if a club can't provide equal provisions for people less able-bodied, they have failed their remit. Shutter the ground and start again if need be.

9. International Football

Jim Campbell

My earliest football memory is of watching England lose to West Germany on penalties at Italia '90 and it's a foggy memory at that. I remember Ciao, the stick man logo with a football for a head, 'Nessun Dorma', Paul Gascoigne crying, Gary Lineker being revered as some sort of magical saint and hearing that Diego Maradona was an evil cheat who was out to crush everything good in the world. Everything else I learnt later. My first fully formed memory of an international tournament is USA '94, which strikes me as odd because I have evidently edited out Euro '92. In fact, I'm not sure I know anyone of my generation who doesn't remember Italia '90 but does remember Euro '92. Denmark won it! You'd think that would have stood out. England's performance must have been so bad that it induced a trauma our brains blocked out in an act of self-preservation. Maybe we weren't ready for that side of England at such a tender age.

The majority of us will have a World Cup or European Championship as our first football memory. It is an incredibly precious thing, legitimately one of my favourite things about being alive. I find it so much easier to remember what was happening in my life if I relate it to what tournament was happening around the time as those two-year gaps act as markers for the progress you've made as a person. The ubiquity of it also makes it a great unifier. My mum, dad and brother are very casual football fans to the point where none of them supports a team but watching the summer tournaments is still something of a family tradition. They wouldn't be the same without Dad getting annoyed at England for passing backwards, a tradition they've been very accommodating in upholding, and the rest of us giving up on correcting him when he can't be bothered to remember which teams are actually playing. Over Euro 2016 he repeatedly mistook Switzerland for Sweden to the point where he just gave up and settled on calling them Swindon. As Swindon at least play in red this was good enough for me.

There's a lot of fun to be had in international football. It's arguably the most absorbing type of football there is, and to truly reach the summit of it there's really only one place to start . . .

The World Cup

I love the star on the England shirt. You can only have that star if you've won the World Cup and, though I wasn't alive when England did just that, I love the reminder that we're in the club. Sepp Blatter once joked that future tournaments will be contested by teams from different planets and, though this seems worryingly like he's privy to information that we're not, this is the only way it could be contested on a bigger scale. Win the World Cup and you cement yourself as someone who's reached the greatest heights of sporting achievement. The pressure this creates often brings the best out of players who are already at the top of their game, resulting in rivalries that span generations, moments we all share for ever, heroes making history, villains ruining it and, of course, some of the most dramatic matches the world has ever seen . . .

Matches

Brazil 1 Uruguay 2 – the 1950 'final'

The 1950 World Cup was a significant one for football as it was the first to take place after the Second World War. As it was held in Brazil it of course had a confusing format – after the initial group stage there was no knockout round, with the group winners instead going into a further group of four. This maximised the number of games to help cover the cost of hosting the event and it also provided an incentive for the European teams to enter as many had to make the long trip by boat.

In the second group Brazil smashed Sweden and Spain and would play Uruguay last. That this was the decisive game is just coincidence as the format meant that this World Cup technically didn't have a final. Before the game Brazil had four points, with an unconvincing Uruguay behind them on three. This was in a time before Brazil had won a World Cup but so confident was the mood that a spontaneous carnival broke out, essentially celebrating the victory before it had happened as if the game were merely a daft formality. The *O Mundo* newspaper printed a picture of Brazil's team on their front page with the headline 'These are the world champions'.

They had not reckoned with Uruguay captain Obdulio Varela. Incensed by the *O Mundo* headline, he laid copies on his bathroom floor and invited his team-mates to piss on them. In the dressing-room, pre-game, manager Juan López instructed the team to play defensively. Varela waited for him to leave and then gave an impassioned speech about how playing like this would mean certain defeat, pumping up his team before they took to the field. It is estimated that more than 200,000 people were in the Maracanã that day. None of them supported Uruguay.

Early in the second half Brazil scored to incite pandemonium. Varela insisted that the goal was offside and, in an act of tactical filibustering, argued with the referee for so long that both the crowd and the nerves of his own team settled down. In the sixty-sixth minute Juan Alberto Schiaffino equalised for the Uruguayans. Then, with eleven minutes to go, Alcides Ghiggia scored again for them, silencing the great stadium. Uruguay held on to win in an atmosphere of eerie silence. The Brazilian organisers were so stunned and heartbroken that they left Jules Rimet himself on the pitch, wandering around trying to find Varela so that he could award him the World Cup. It's a stark contrast to the presentations we have now, with the big stages and that FIFA anthem that sounds like the music from when someone dies in *The Hunger Games*.

Ghiggia later said: 'Only three people managed to silence the Maracanã: Frank Sinatra, the Pope and me.' People often forget about this latter-day line-up of the Rat Pack, who for me were up there with the originals, though in this case I think he is referring to the game.

West Germany 3 Hungary 2 – the Miracle of Bern

There was a time when it was possible for Germany to go into a World Cup final as heavy underdogs, as they did in 1954. This is because they were up against Hungary's revolutionary Mighty Magyars, who were then Olympic champions and had already beaten the West Germans 8–3 in the group stage. However, German manager Sepp Herberger had fielded a reserve side in that game, hiding the true strength of the team in an era when such cunning subterfuge was still possible. When the final came around at the Wankdorf Stadium in Bern, which it is absolutely necessary to and so on etc, Hungary went 2–0 up in eight minutes and it looked as if another thrashing was inevitable. The fantastically named Max Morlock had other ideas and scored almost immediately, before the also fantastically named Helmut Rahn levelled things up after eighteen minutes. In the second half they faced an onslaught from Hungary before Rahn scored with six minutes left and the world first learnt that when it's business time in football, Germany get it done. The match became known as the Miracle of Bern as the result was so unlikely and because the badly understaffed catering team managed to feed the entire crowd with just five loaves of bread and two fish.

Chile 2 Italy 0 – the Battle of Santiago, 1962 World Cup

To include this game in a series of the best World Cup matches may seem like an endorsement of the violence that took place in it but I'm not a player or a pundit so I don't have to pretend that what happened wasn't fascinatingly spectacular. Before the game Italian journalists had been critical of both Chile and Chilean women, and the early games had been unusually rough, with the first two days featuring four dismissals and three broken legs. It set the tone for one of the most ill-disciplined matches of all time. BBC sports presenter David Coleman famously introduced the highlights thus: 'Good evening. The game you're about to see is the most stupid, appalling, disgusting and disgraceful exhibition of football, possibly in the history of the game . . .'

It was a tough afternoon for English referee Ken Aston. The first foul took place after twelve seconds, leading to a brawl. And when I say 'brawl' I don't mean players leaning on each other's foreheads then falling to the ground, I'm talking serious punches and kicks aimed at the knackers. After eight minutes Aston sent off Italy's Giorgio Ferrini. He wouldn't leave the pitch so police dragged him off. Later in the half Italy's Mario David tried to dispossess Leonel Sánchez and when this didn't work just kicked him. Sánchez responded with a left hook a professional boxer would be proud of. Aston opted not to punish either player and after play restarted David hit Sánchez with a flying kick to the head. He was sent off and, in the aftermath, Sánchez broke Italian forward Humberto Maschio's nose with another left. This guy was in the wrong sport. Incidents continued throughout the match, one of which was essentially a rugby tackle leading to an MMA-style ground-and-pound fight right in front of Aston, with the police intervening three more times. Among it all Chile found time to win 2–0, with one last brawl at full-time that almost certainly carried on in the car park.

England 4 West Germany 2 – the 1966 final

The story of the 1966 World Cup sounds like a lie. England topped a group including France, Uruguay and Mexico without conceding a goal, went on to beat Argentina 1–0 in the quarter-final, Portugal 2–1 in the semi and then beat West Germany 4–2 after extra-time to win the World Cup. The footage of the final is so iconic it almost seems more like a movie. Bobby Moore doesn't even seem like a real person, more an English, football-themed version of Captain America. Whatever mate, didn't happen. Except that it did and we must have used up a hundred years' worth of luck as all of those teams have come back to haunt us apart from Mexico, who we haven't played at a tournament since, so there's time. Mark my words.

The game itself was something special. The noise of the crowd from the footage as the teams walk out on to the pitch is truly stirring. The Germans went ahead after twelve minutes but Geoff Hurst quickly equalised and it stayed that way until half-time, when a marching band entertained the crowd, obviously. In the seventy-eighth minute Martin Peters made it 2–1 before the latest brilliantly named German, Wolfgang Weber, equalised with just a minute to go, meaning extra-time. Eleven minutes into the first extra period Geoff Hurst's shot hit the bar and either bounced down over the line or didn't. Many have claimed to be able to prove this one way or the other but on the day the Azerbaijani linesman Tofiq Bahramov advised the referee that it did. That was 3–2 England. Germany were deflated and Hurst scored again to complete what's still the only World Cup final hat-trick. The controversial goal changed everything and it's worth remembering this when we bemoan our luck as to me it doesn't look like a goal. Please watch it and make up your own mind before reporting me for treason. Still, I don't feel much sympathy given the amount of karmic retribution we seem to have suffered since and we did get a fourth, as well as that lovely star.

Italy 4 West Germany 3 – the Game of the Century

Four years later the World Cup went to Mexico. Games were now broadcast live and in colour owing to technological advancements and it was becoming a bit cool. Where previous tournaments had been noted for their defensive play this all changed in 1970 as a more attacking style came to the fore.

The game actually finished at 1–1 after normal time, then four minutes into extra-time the Germans went ahead through Gerd Müller. Known as *'Der Bomber'* and with legs that were basically industrial hammers made of meat, Müller scored a ridiculous sixty-eight goals in sixty-two games for West Germany. The slang term 'mullered' is thought to come from him as he could strike the ball with such force. This was a poached effort, Müller capitalising on a mix-up in the Italian defence, one of the few occasions in which footage of such a thing has been captured in the wild. Having been behind for most of the game West Germany were now 2–1 up but extra-time is a funny thing. The players are tired but full of adrenaline, space opens up and that often means goals. Four minutes after Müller's goal Tarcisio Burgnich made it 2–2 from a set-piece. Luigi Riva then made it 3–2 to Italy with a brilliantly placed effort after he'd turned his man just inside the box. Müller equalised again, mullering the ball home with his head, and while the replays were still being shown Gianni Rivera got the decisive goal after a slick Italian attack. What for most of the game looked like it would be an embattled 1–0 win had become a 4–3 thriller. Franz Beckenbauer even dislocated his shoulder and played on with his arm in a sling. That's how hard it was to beat West Germany.

The Azteca Stadium now features a plaque that reads: 'The Azteca Stadium pays homage to the national teams of Italy (4) and Germany (3), who starred in the 1970 FIFA World Cup, the 'Game of the Century', 17 June 1970.' While that is very cool it is also slightly creepy as it suggests that the stadium is alive.

Brazil 4 Italy 1 – the 1970 final

Italy were rewarded for their efforts with a final against a Brazil team packed with stars such as Pelé, Rivellino, Jairzinho, Tostão and Carlos Alberto. This was the first time that two former winners had met in the final and, while they're often cagey affairs, this one is rightly heralded as one of the best ever.

Pelé opened the scoring with a leaping header before Roberto Boninsegna pounced on a Brazilian defensive mix-up, in one of many occasions in which footage of such a thing has been captured in the wild. Gérson rifled a second across the goalkeeper to make it 2–1 and Brazil were rampant. Pelé laid off a header for Jairzinho to make it 3–1 – meaning he'd scored in every game – before practically the entire team combined for Carlos Alberto to score one of the all-time great World Cup goals. Tostão won the ball outside Brazil's box then started the move in which eight players were involved. He'd spotted Alberto making a run and, as Brazil passed it around, he ran the length of the pitch. In the footage of the goal you can see him point in Alberto's direction before Pelé releases the ball and he smashes it home.

So much about the match was iconic: the Adidas Telstar ball, with it's black and white pentagonal and hexagonal panels; the yellow of Brazil's kit, visible for the first time via colour television; Pelé's performance; even the grading of the footage, which makes it seem other-worldly, placing it firmly in its era. The style of Brazil's football thrilled the world so much it almost redefined it, so it seems fitting that, with their third World Cup win, they got to keep the trophy. It is the ultimate hat-trick, after all.

Argentina 0 Cameroon 1 – 1990 World Cup

We all love an underdog story – unless it involves an actual underdog because that means you're watching a dog fight and that isn't good at all – and Italia '90 provided a famous one with Cameroon beating the holders Argentina in the opening Group B fixture.

Cameroon were an unknown quantity and it's fair to say that their style was robust. They'd frustrated Argentina with their physicality but when André Kana-Biyik was sent off in the sixty-first minute it looked like this might provide the holders the respite they needed. Nope. In the sixty-seventh minute Kana-Biyik's brother François Omam-Biyik scored with the help of a huge goalkeeping error from Argentina's Nery Pumpido, a name which appropriately sounds like the name of a famous clown. He flapped at Omam-Biyik's header and allowed it to bobble over the line as if to say: 'Ha! A trick! I am the great Pumpido and I have no hands in these buffoonish gloves!'

Argentina then simply could not break them down and the game is perhaps best remembered as much for the result as for the second red card of the game. Late on Claudio Caniggia, the future Roma, Benfica and Dundee striker – deal with it – picked up the ball on the edge of Argentina's area. As he ran into the Cameroon half he was fouled once, then twice, but stayed on his feet. Staggering, Caniggia – who also looked like he'd be in Pearl Jam if they for some reason had a striker – was then absolutely pole-axed by the gigantic figure of Benjamin Massing, who launched his whole body like a torpedo. Even with nine men Cameroon held on and, if you want an example of how much it meant to them to prove people wrong, Omam-Biyik said after the game: 'We hate it when European journalists ask us if we eat monkeys and have a witch doctor. We are real football players and we proved this tonight.'

When Cameroon later met England, Howard Wilkinson, then an FA scout, concluded that England essentially had a bye into the next round, astonishing given that they beat Argentina to top a group that also included then European champions the Soviet Union. They gave England a scare in the quarter-final before losing 3–2, but they changed forever the perception of African football.

France 3 Brazil 0 – the 1998 final

Their multicultural team had lit up the tournament on home soil and united a nation that was struggling with internal divisions so it was only right that France should reach their first World Cup final. Their opponents were Brazil, featuring a 21-year-old Ronaldo, Rivaldo and baby-celebrating dinkmaster Bebeto. Ronaldo had been the star of the competition with four goals and three assists but in the build-up to the final reports emerged that he'd had a convulsive fit. He was left off the initial team sheet then put back on to it just 72 minutes before kick-off. Something wasn't right, but Ronaldo would start.

France were quite simply magnificent. Around half an hour in Emmanuel Petit swung in a corner from the right and Zinedine Zidane put them ahead with a header so powerful it could easily have decked a fully grown Italian man. Just before half-time Petit sent in a corner from the left and he did it again, 2–0. The famous Zidane glide was in full effect, the elegance of his play helping France to dominate the game. By contrast Ronaldo couldn't get into the match, looking like a man who'd recently had a fit. Brazil were encouraged when Marcel Desailly was sent off after sixty-eight minutes but France dug in and Petit scored in the ninetieth minute to finish off a resounding display.

While France celebrated their historic achievement Brazil were left to figure out how such circumstances had come to be. Conspiracy theories emerged. Edmundo, who would have played in Ronaldo's absence, alleged that sponsors Nike may have insisted that he play. There was talk that Ronaldo was having mental health issues, or that he'd had an allergic reaction to a mystery injection. A more extreme theory was that Brazil had sold the World Cup to FIFA, allowing France to win to please Sepp Blatter. The theory went that, in return, Brazil would get breaks in the 2002 World Cup, which they won, and later host the competition, which they did. The idea is a horrible one: that sometimes football isn't real. This was never proven but you can basically say anything about FIFA now because their lawyers are so busy.

Every generation has it's greats – the players who make you feel like your era of football is the best era – and Ronaldo and Zidane were ours. It is a huge shame that the world didn't get to see a fully fit Ronaldo in what was already a fine game but the fiasco shouldn't overshadow France's brilliance. They were exhilarating to watch and fully deserved their win, which was Brazil's heaviest defeat in any World Cup match. At the time anyway . . .

Germany 7 Brazil 1 – the 2014 semi-final

'You're not going to see teams smashing each other at this stage,' said one idiot (me) on an otherwise fine podcast before the 2014 semi-final between Brazil and Germany. Brazil were hosting the World Cup for the first time since 1950 and they were supposed to banish those ghosts. They instead set up a Ouija board and invited in a load of new ones.

They actually started brightly, with Marcelo shooting across goal and just wide but after eleven minutes Thomas Müller opened the scoring from a Toni Kroos corner. In the twenty-third minute Miroslav Klose scored after neat play on the right. Kroos followed suit just a minute later, then won the ball from Fernandinho straight from the kick-off, played a one-two with Khedira and scored again. In dazed shock Brazil allowed Khedira and Mesut Özil to play another one-two in the box for Khedira to make it 5–0 – after 29 minutes. Four of the goals had come in just six minutes. Brazil were in tatters, their confidence a memory as goal after goal had gone in with brutal similarity.

Germany went into the second half intending to respect their beleaguered opponents but André Schürrle still scored twice. After the seventh goal, Brazil fans gave Germany a standing ovation and even cheered their passes. They did get a consolation goal through Oscar in the ninetieth minute but nobody cared apart from the hilariously furious Manuel Neuer.

Sometimes statistics don't tell the story of a game. Brazil actually had eighteen shots to Germany's fourteen. Half of Germany's were goals but Brazil still had eight on target. The other ten were David Luiz trying to knock the moon out of the sky in frustration but it's still amazing.

Sometimes statistics tell the story of a game all too well. Brazil striker Fred had promised to 'kill a lion every day' for the team before the tournament but in his time on the pitch he didn't make a single tackle, cross, interception or run and the majority of his possession was in the centre circle owing to the sheer number of times he had to restart the game.

The defeat ended a run of sixty-two competitive unbeaten home games for Brazil. Germany became the highest scoring team in World Cup history, overtaking . . . Brazil. Klose also broke the record for the most World Cup goals with his sixteenth, taking it from Ronaldo, who was commentating at the time. The hosts were so rattled they even lost the third-place play-off 3–0 to the Netherlands, equalling their previous worst loss at a World Cup.

Rivalries

England and Scotland played the first international football match in 1872. The fixture used to happen with far more regularity than it does now, with a 5–1 win for Scotland at Wembley in 1928 and a 9–3 England victory in 1961 standing out, as well as Scotland winning 3–2 in 1967, then claiming to be unofficial world champions, which is officially not how it works. International teams are notoriously bad neighbours – I wouldn't want to live next door to one – and proximity is always a factor in giving a rivalry some added spice. As is history . . .

England and Germany

The cliché about Germans having no sense of humour is proven a nonsense by how funny they think this is. Given world history it's a natural rivalry and, though they have issues with Geoff Hurst's goal in 1966 and we have the ultimately meaningless 5–1 World Cup qualifying victory from 2001, the traffic has largely been one way down the *autobahn*. They even started singing *'Three Lions'* ironically until it became a popular song in its own right, with them changing the lyrics to 'Four stars on a shirt . . .' You have to concede that they've even won that. They're really not that bothered about us, instead caring much more about . . .

Germany and the Netherlands

In a sporting sense this began at the 1974 World Cup final, the loss of which was a huge blow for Dutch national pride given the resentment that still lingered from the events of the Second World War. They would get a measure of revenge when they beat West Germany in the semi-final of Euro '88, with Ronald Koeman celebrating by pretending to wipe his arse with German midfielder Olaf Thon's shirt.

One of the most famous incidents from their meetings occurred in a tetchy second-round affair at Italia '90. Frank Rijkaard hacked down Rudi Völler, who'd recently hit peak-Völler and looked like one of Hans Gruber's generic henchmen from *Die Hard*. Rijkaard was booked and responded to this by spitting into Völler's mullet. After the ensuing free-kick they had another altercation, Rijkaard pulled Völler's hair, both were sent off and Rijkaard spat in Völler's mullet again. I don't care how annoyed you are, Frank, you don't spit in a man's mullet.

England and Argentina

It is apt that two countries that love steak as much as England and Argentina would have beef with each other. In a sense it's odd as it's intercontinental. You don't get Norway and Peru kicking off at each other, for instance, but this one has its reasons. While here we may think back to the Falklands War and Maradona's Hand of God as the major catalysts, it really began at the 1966 World Cup. In Argentina that meeting between the sides is known as 'the Robbery of the Century'. Geoff Hurst scored the only goal, with the Argentina players protesting that it was offside. Their captain, Antonio Rattin, was also sent off, his second yellow being for dissent, though the German referee spoke no Spanish and would later claim that he simply didn't like the way Rattin looked at him, as if that's a good reason. The ref was accompanied from the pitch by policemen. Argentina claimed it was a plot between England and West Germany to knock them out, Alf Ramsey later called them 'animals'. It was *on*.

Brazil and Argentina

Arguably the biggest rivalry in world football, this has always been mad. In 1939 Argentina's players were so incensed by the awarding of a late penalty to Brazil with the score at 2–2 that Arcadio López assaulted the referee and was removed from the pitch by police, as is unbelievably common in the history of international football. Brazil's José Perácio struck the ball into an undefended net as the entire Argentina team had left the field in protest. It seems like every other game they've played is known as 'the Battle of This' or 'the Shame of That'.

The last time they met at a World Cup was in 1990 and it resulted in what was known as the Holy Water scandal. Brazil defender Branco had been tasked with marking Diego Maradona and was doing a good job until he was handed a bottle of water by a member of Argentina's coaching staff during a break in play. He later said that, after drinking from it, he began to feel drowsy and was finding it harder and harder to keep up with El Diego, who went on to set up Claudio Caniggia for the game's only goal. This may sound like a sour conspiracy theory but the person who made the claim about the drugged water bottle was Diego Maradona. Argentina manager Carlos Bilardo denied this and it may actually be a brilliant strategy. 'They're on to us . . . Get Diego to say we did it and then nobody will believe it.' This is exactly why the man can do and say whatever he likes.

Moments

Given that the World Cup happens only once every four years every notable moment becomes one that is remembered for ever. Let's start at a beginning . . .

USA '94: the Opening Ceremony

The 1994 World Cup was supposed to launch football as a sport to be taken seriously in America. MLS arrived in the same year and the national team performed admirably so, to a degree, it worked but on very early impressions you'd be forgiven for thinking it wouldn't. Keen to show what the USA was about by injecting some razzmatazz into the opening ceremony, somebody decided that the best way to do that would be to get Diana Ross to sing her hit *I'm Coming Out* and take a penalty, except that, as any English person can tell you, taking a penalty isn't as easy as it looks. She actually started well, with a stuttering run intended to fool the goalkeeper, but then scuffed it wide before the goal collapsed. We assume that the goal was supposed to collapse but maybe it just couldn't take the awkwardness. To be fair to Ross she carried on like a pro but let people stick to what they're good at. You wouldn't have had Romário belting out the 'the *Star Spangled-Banner*' before the final.

Mwepu Ilunga's free-kick

Zaire became the first sub-Saharan team to represent Africa at the World Cup when they qualified for the 1974 edition. Sadly, they're best remembered for what appeared to be a clownish moment against Brazil; while lined up to defend a free-kick, Mwepu Ilunga burst out of the wall and kicked the ball away. The referee booked him and Ilunga looked astonished.

Stunned and amused, the entire world thought that, even though he was a professional footballer, he didn't understand the rules. In reality Ilunga was deliberately trying to get himself sent off in protest as the Zaire team had discovered that their government had decided not to pay them bonuses they'd been promised. This is not the act of some spoiled millionaire; those players would not have been rich men and had been part of an historic achievement for their country.

They'd initially learnt of this before their game with Yugoslavia and, in protest, made little effort, losing 9–0. Having also lost 2–0 to Scotland, Ilunga said that the government sent presidential guards to threaten them, saying they'd not be allowed back into the country if they were to lose 4–0 to Brazil. They eventually lost 3–0 and, with this in mind, it was an incredibly bold show of defiance. All the same, if he wanted to get sent off he would probably have been better off with a blatant handball . . .

The Hand of God

. . . though even then the referee might have missed it. As I've already touched on, this moment goes a long way to defining the English national team's modern self-image; that of the wronged champions of honesty and sporting integrity, undone by teams who just won't play properly. In the 1986 quarter-final between England and Argentina in Mexico City, the 5ft 5in Diego Maradona leapt to challenge the 6ft 1in Peter Shilton for a Steve Hodge back pass, punched the ball into the net and ran away in manic celebration. It was so blatant, so obvious as to have been utterly ridiculous, yet the referee gave it.

Maradona later said: 'I was waiting for my team-mates to embrace me and no one came . . . I told them, "Come hug me, or the referee isn't going to allow it."'

In Argentina there is a phrase, *viveza Criolla*, which when translated literally is the suddenly bigoted *Creole's cleverness*. It is the idea that sly cunning is something to be proud of; that beating the system is to be applauded regardless of the means; that it is good to dominate another by displaying quick wit. The English are not like this. We have aneurysms at the mere thought of not realising that we've been undercharged for things. Maradona basically saw himself as a kind of gleeful, gaucho Robin Hood, but a Robin Hood who revelled in being a bastard. That he would cheat so proudly and openly was perhaps the biggest shock of it all. Then, just to really rub it in, he got the ball in the middle of the pitch, dribbled around half the England team including Peter Reid, who probably had a flash forward to the hotel bar, and scored one of the all-time great World Cup goals.

When asked how he scored the first goal, he said: 'A little with the head of Maradona and a little with the hand of God.'

Bastard. Brilliant, brilliant bastard.

Roberto Baggio's Penalty

England didn't make it to USA '94, which probably spared us some trauma, but the silver lining for me was that my favourite player from abroad, Roberto Baggio, was on show. He started slowly, Ireland stunning Italy with a 1–0 win in the first group game, which concerned me as I wanted him to be brilliant. I needn't have worried. He soon lit up the tournament with two goals against Nigeria, one against Spain and two against Bulgaria as Italy made their way to the final, where they met Brazil. It wasn't a classic, going to penalties after it had finished 0–0. Even the first two penalties, from Márcio Santos and Franco Baresi, were missed. Both Brazil and Italy scored their next two, Dunga then scored for Brazil and Daniele Massaro missed. Baggio was up. Score and they stayed in, miss and that was it. He missed, blazing it over. There was that moment, that horrible moment, when it sinks in. Even though the entire tournament had built to that moment it felt sickeningly sudden. Even with no England I still had to be disappointed by a penalty shoot-out, which only got worse, to the point where I'm certain that penalties will somehow be involved in my death. It seemed especially harsh as Baggio was and is one of the good guys in life. He is a UN ambassador and has done incredible things. He played an active role in the Burmese pro-democracy movement, which helped secure the release from house arrest of opposition leader Aung San Suu Kyi and was the World Summit of Nobel Peace Laureates' 2010 Man of Peace. As if being known as 'the Divine Ponytail' wasn't brilliant enough.

Kevin Keegan's Commentary

It's 1998. It's England v Argentina. It's gone to penalties. Obviously. Brian Moore and Kevin Keegan are commentating. David Batty steps up . . .

Moore: 'Now, you know him better than anybody. Do you back him to score? Quickly, yes or no?'

Keegan: 'Yes.'

Batty misses.

Moore: 'Oh and he hasn't!'

Keegan: (Anguished noise)

This is Moore's fault. You don't jeopardise England's chances by introducing the variable of Kevin Keegan's luck.

Roy Keane

When Ireland flew to Japan for the 2002 World Cup the squad sat in second-class while members of the FAI sat in first. Just imagine how this news would have been processed by Roy Keane. He soon expressed frustrations about what he saw as amateurish preparations in an interview with an Irish newspaper, leading to manager Mick McCarthy confronting him in front of the squad. McCarthy accused Keane of pretending to be injured for the second leg of Ireland's play-off with Iran. Over to you, Roy.

'Mick, you're a liar . . . You're a fucking wanker. I didn't rate you as a player, I don't rate you as a manager and I don't rate you as a person. You're a fucking wanker and you can stick your World Cup up your arse. The only reason I have any dealings with you is that somehow you are the manager of my country! You can stick it up your bollocks.'

The notable phrase from this is, of course, 'stick it up your bollocks'. How does one do this? It's impractical if nothing else. Surely the anus is a more traditional insertion point in such a situation? When mulling this over it's important to remember the full quote. If McCarthy were to follow Keane's instructions he would already have the World Cup up his arse, so would need somewhere else to stick the situation, like his bollocks.

Keane was sent home, presumably in second-class.

Zinedine Zidane's Head

Zidane's magnificent dome has already featured heavily here owing to the effect it had on the 1998 final but that's only half the story. In 2006 his career was winding down and the World Cup final against Italy in Berlin was to be his swansong. It seemed fitting and many hoped that his final act as a player would be to win it again.

It started well when, after seven minutes, he converted a penalty, conceded by Marco Materazzi. Twelve minutes later Materazzi connected with a corner to make amends and level the scores. They would stay level, meaning extra-time.

At one point during this period Materazzi had hold of Zidane's shirt. The Frenchman said to him, with what Materazzi later described as 'super arrogance': 'If you really want my shirt, you can have it later.' Materazzi said something and Zidane butted the Italian in the chest, knocking him flying. I remember being so shocked that it took me a moment to even register its significance. He, of course, had to be sent off. That was it, his career was over. It wasn't out of character – it was the fourteenth red card of his career and his second at a World Cup – but this was the World Cup final, with ten minutes of his career to go. Italy won on penalties.

The BBC hired a lip-reader to interpret Materazzi's words and it was reported in the British press that he'd called Zidane 'the son of a terrorist whore'. This was on the day, unknown to Materazzi, that Zidane's mother had been taken ill and to hospital. The Italian furiously denied this, clarifying that what he'd said had simply been the innocuous on-pitch banter: 'I'd prefer the whore that is your sister.' Oh God. He sued the newspapers, saying in a further interview: 'I am ignorant, I don't even know what an Islamic terrorist is.

My only terrorist is her,' pointing at his baby daughter. Statements like that make it easy to see how this happened.

Adel Abdessemed, the French-Algerian artist, made a statue of Zidane head-butting Materazzi, which went on display outside the Centre Pompidou in Paris in 2012 before being moved to Doha. Conversely, this means that Materazzi has a statue of himself being head-butted, which must be annoying.

Heroes and Villains

Make an impact at the World Cup and it immediately becomes legend, preserved like a mosquito in amber that you can later extract DNA from in order to play God and start your own footballer-themed amusement park. 'Over on the left here in the One-Hit Wonder enclosure are Saeed Al Owairan, who dribbled around loads of Belgians to score a wonder goal in 1994, and Oleg Salenko, who scored five goals for Russia in one match against Cameroon in the same year. Over here is Rivaldo and it's feeding time! You're in for a treat, ladies and gentlemen. Try not to hit him when you throw the food . . . Oh you have, and he's gone down clutching his face, just like against Turkey in 2002. He's now trying to get you thrown out of the park, but ignore him. What disappointing behaviour from an otherwise wonderful attraction.

Moving on to one of our Champions enclosures, here we have the 2010 Spain squad and yes, they *do* press in herds . . .'

Were I to curate such a park these are the heroes and villains I would populate it with. Welcome to World Cup Park . . .

Heroes

Pelé

The star attraction, Pelé is the only man to win three World Cups. He won his first in Sweden aged just seventeen, scoring twice in the 1958 final (fulfilling a promise he'd made to his father in the wake of 1950), then again in 1962 and, of course, 1970. He's still Brazil's all-time leading scorer despite having retired in 1977. It is a given that Pelé is one of the best players of all time but I wonder how many people assume this without actually having seen much footage of him. He was *ridiculous*. He was lightning fast, powerful, could dribble past people so easily they'd question whether or not they actually existed, and he could score from anywhere.

Santos would effectively go on world tours to capitalise on his popularity. He is also excellent entertainment value as he always seems to be doing weird stuff, such as when he started turning his hair into diamonds and selling it in 2014. Using a complicated high-pressure, high-temperature hair-diamonding process I frankly do not understand, he had 1,283 diamonds made out of his own hair – one for each goal he scored – to commemorate the 2014 World Cup. To commemorate the 2014 World Cup and to make lots of money.

He also talks a fair bit of nonsense, famously saying that Nicky Butt was the best player at the 2002 World Cup. Romário, no stranger to guff himself, once said: 'Pelé is a poet when he keeps his mouth shut.' To be fair to Pelé, poets can function perfectly well with their mouths shut, they simply write things down, but only a fool would say this to Romário's face.

Héctor Castro

When Héctor Castro was thirteen he had an accident with an electric saw and cut off his right forearm. As we know, people from the past were really tough so, despite having only one arm, Castro still forged a very successful playing career. Known as *El Manco* – 'the Maimed' – he scored eighteen goals in twenty-five games for Uruguay, including one in a 4–2 win over Argentina in the first World Cup final, in 1930. Seriously, 'the Maimed'. Saying that kind of thing would get you exiled to Qatar these days.

Pickles

This technically didn't happen at the World Cup but it's got a dog in it and the publishers recommended including a bit with a dog as people like that. On Sunday, 20 March 1966 some callous bounder had the temerity to *steal* the World Cup after it had been put on display at a stamp exhibition in Westminster, as England likes to parody itself as often as possible. The thief was brilliant because he managed to evade constant security but also an idiot because he ignored stamps worth £3 million, which in 1966 could have bought you a former colony. A ransom demand for £15,000 appeared, with the removable lining from the trophy, at the home of FA chairman Joe Mears. He contacted police, who set a trap for the thief. However, when they arrested him he didn't have the trophy.

Enter Pickles the collie. Out for a walk with his owner David Corbett, Pickles was dogging about in a hedge in South London when he dogged upon an item wrapped in newspaper. Corbett realised what it was, handed it in to police and gave all the credit to Pickles, who briefly became a star. When England won the World Cup he attended the celebrations, he was on *Blue Peter*, was given free dog food for a year and even had the titular role in a movie called *The Spy With a Cold Nose*, alongside Eric Sykes and June Whitfield. He was also awarded the silver medal by the National

Canine Defence League. Silver! What did he have to do to win gold, play in the final? If you're wondering, the National Canine Defence League is now the Dog's Trust, and not a group of dogs who solved crime, which would have made their under-appreciation of Pickles' achievements even worse as he actually was a dog who solved a crime.

Salvatore 'Toto' Schillaci

Footballers are fundamentally the same as we are but the hype around football presents them as gladiatorial super-beings, so when somebody makes it to the top via slightly unusual means we root for them all the more. It reminds us that it's possible to succeed if things don't immediately go to plan.

Schillaci wasn't exactly a nobody when Italia '90 came around – he played for Juventus and had been their top scorer in a season in which they won the UEFA Cup and the *Coppa Italia* – but in the season prior to that he'd been playing in *Serie B* and grew up in poverty in Palermo, never even attending school.

He'd not been a regular in the Italy squad before the World Cup but once it began he was a sensation. He came off the bench to score against Austria and forced his way into the starting line-up. He scored against Czechoslovakia, lashed home a fantastic goal against Uruguay, scored against Ireland and then Argentina, each goal accompanied by a wild-eyed, manic celebration.

The Italians couldn't believe their luck and neither could he. From such difficult beginnings he'd become the unexpected star of the World Cup on home soil. Italy went out in the semis and in the end Schillaci played only sixteen times for Italy, with injury and loss of form contributing to his decline. Still, his peak was so profound, so exhilarating and so timely that few players have shone so brightly at such a perfect time.

Ronaldo

Redemption is a rare thing in real life. It's kind of like walking away from an explosion that you caused and not even bothering to look back: it happens more in movies than in reality.

The events of '98 had been tough on Ronaldo and in 2000 he ruptured his right knee ligament, leading to a lengthy absence that meant he missed Brazil's entire World Cup qualifying campaign. His career looked in danger of becoming a sad tale of what could have been.

Once the tournament began, though, he was back, scoring an obscene eight goals, including a whopping none against England – the only team who stopped him scoring – and two in the final as Brazil won their fifth World Cup. Pelé had predicted that they wouldn't get out of their group, which featured China, Costa Rica and Turkey.

Villains

Not everyone in football can be Ronaldo, only two people can, making this a bad example but whatever. As my park is essentially a zoo and a zoo is essentially animal prison it seems only fair that I also incarcerate some of the World Cup's greatest monsters . . .

The Disgrace of Gijón

You know how the final group games are all played at the same time and it's annoying because you have to choose which one to watch? You can blame West Germany and Austria. In the 1982 World Cup in Spain they were in a group with Algeria and Chile, who'd played the day before in the final round of group fixtures. Results meant that should West Germany win either 1–0 or 2–0 then both they and Austria would go through; a bigger win would dump Austria out at the expense of Algeria.

West Germany went 1–0 up after ten minutes of sustained attacking, then after that . . . not a *bratwurst*. Both sides passed it around in their own halves, hitting the occasional long ball to nobody and making no effort to score. The German commentator Eberhard Stanjek felt so ashamed of the tactics that he refused to com-mentate. Spanish fans in the stadium chanted for Algeria, Algeria fans waved money at the players and one German fan even burned the national flag. As admi-rable as all of these protests are, the best condemnation of the event must belong to Spanish local newspaper *El Comercio*, who printed their match report in the crime section.

Harald 'Toni' Schumacher

Disgrace was all the rage in 1982. In the semi-final between France and West Germany in Seville, French substitute Patrick Battiston ran on to a through ball from future disgrace Michel Platini, only for the West German goalkeeper Toni Schumacher to storm out and leap hip first into Battiston's head. Battiston went down hard and stayed down, but incredibly the referee gave a goal-kick.

Unconscious, Battiston had lost two teeth, cracked three ribs and needed oxygen on the pitch before he was removed by the Spanish medical team, who had a very strange get-up. It was the sort of look you would imagine an early member of the Village People would have had if his gimmick was that of a Nazi paramedic.

Battiston's injuries were so bad that he slipped into a coma and part of what made this so shocking was

Schumacher's behaviour after the incident. When he heard that Battiston had lost teeth, he said: 'If that's all that's wrong with him, I'll pay him the crowns.' Schumacher has always insisted that the foul was not intentional and later apologised to Battiston in person, an apology the Frenchman would accept. Battiston has back damage to this day but recovered enough to continue his career, winning a redemptive European Championship with France in 1984.

Luis Suárez

Luis Suárez certainly has some *viveza Criolla*, even without all the biting. In the 2010 World Cup in South Africa his Uruguay side faced Ghana in the quarter-final. With the score at 1–1 in the final moments of extra-time Ghana launched a free-kick into a chaotic box. Stephen Appiah shot at goal and Suárez blocked it with his leg, Dominic Adiyiah headed it back and Suárez pushed it away with his hand, which isn't allowed. He was sent off and Asamoah Gyan crashed the resulting penalty against the bar. Off the pitch, Suárez wriggled with delight and Uruguay won the penalty shoot-out that followed.

There are two ways to look at this: outright cheating, or an act of quick thinking in which Suárez took a risk that paid off. He took his punishment and Ghana did have the chance to score the penalty, after all. What didn't help was Suárez revelling in his villainy. Afterwards he said things like 'I made the best save of the tournament', and 'the Hand of God now belongs to me'. His actions led to him being recognised as the World Summit of Nobel Peace Laureates' 2010 Man of Evil.

FIFA

FIFA's current motto is 'For the game. For the World', which sounds grand but ultimately means nothing. Before that it was simply 'For the good of the game'. Changing it was one of the most honest moves they've ever made because, in reality, they are a stain on the sport.

Even if the next two World Cups, in Russia and Qatar, go without a hitch they will forever be tainted by controversy owing to doubts about the legitimacy of the bidding processes and the impracticalities and abysmal human rights record of the latter. Even Sepp Blatter didn't want the World Cup to go to Qatar and if *he* thinks something is too suspicious then surely it is automatically a new benchmark for corruption.

Like many, we've long bemoaned the ridiculous nature of FIFA – their World Cup courts set up to try people accused of commercial infringements in South Africa in 2010; the shady allegations of corruption that are always being thrown their way; and their ludicrous, self-aggrandising movie, *United Passions*, in which they paint themselves as noble and heroic ... administrators. The irony is that their recent history would make a much better movie, a tense political thriller in which people in suits have serious conversations in offices.

In 2015 it all started to fall apart, with the FBI arresting surprised old men in hotels all over the world. They had so much dirt on former CONCACAF official Chuck Blazer – a man who had access to two apartments in Trump Tower paid for by CONCACAF, one for him and one for his cats – that they demanded he help them in their investigation or face prosecution. He wore a wire in order to record FIFA executives. Sepp Blatter even resigned, though not until after proving that he could still win a farcical election in which he ran unopposed, fiddling as FIFA burned. Even then he maintained: 'I did not resign, I put myself and my office in the hands of the FIFA congress.'

He definitely did resign, the tit. After that former FIFA vice-president Jack Warner started to crack, posting a video in which it became abundantly clear that he thought an article by satirical US website the Onion about FIFA organising a snap World Cup in the USA was actually real. He then started saying mad things that implied he had dirt on everyone and would take them down.

Later still Blatter and UEFA chief Michel Platini were banned from all football activity for six years after it was deemed that they couldn't satisfactorily explain what a payment of £1.3 million that had been made to Platini was actually for. Both still insist they did nothing wrong and have shown a complete lack of contrition, odiously spluttering about what an outrage it all is.

They're supposedly in a period of reform but with the sheer scale of the wrongdoing that has already been uncovered and the farcical nature of the 2022 World Cup it's impossible to have any faith in them. The reality is that they are not fit for purpose and something else needs to take their place. It's difficult to make a proposal on what this is – and I'd be surprised if anyone would be bold enough to challenge FIFA even now – but the national associations would have a lot of power if they banded together and started again.

The Future

There we have it then, the World Cup. Not even the dastardly deeds of that lot can spoil it; the sheer diversity of its multifaceted brilliance. This is not supposed to be a definitive collection of games, moments, dogs, heroes and so on. It is just some of the ones I think are the most interesting. If at this point you feel like any of your favourites are missing and you're annoyed at me for such an affront then bad luck. This is a book, not the internet. You can write some abuse at the bottom of the page if you want but I'll never see it so you'll just be defacing your own property. You'll get over it anyway – there'll be some football on soon.

That's one of the great things about football; it just keeps on going, finding new ways to be beguiling, wonderful and surprising and, as massive as it is, it's still growing. Even in America, its final frontier, the sport finally seems to be taking hold as a younger generation embraces it. This growth is also happening in Australia, China, India, the Middle East. Maybe the era we live in now, even with the wealth of history we have to call upon, is just the beginning. Maybe as the world develops there will be footballing superpowers from Asia and from Africa. Perhaps picking a favourite in future World Cups will be impossible as the global standard will be so high. Let's hope so, because whatever anyone says, it's still as good as it gets.

10. Grassroots Football

Luke Aaron Moore

grassroots *(noun, used with a singular or plural verb) – 'the common or ordinary people, especially as contrasted with the leadership or elite.'*

While we've spent the majority of this book detailing and, in part, ridiculing the finer points of the professional game, this bears little to no resemblance to football as most of us play it every week. Football at the very top is always ripe for derision, parody and more than the odd humorous comment, but that doesn't mean that amateur football is any less entertaining and interesting, despite its lack of investment and attention from the mainstream media.

Clearly, although the grassroots game bears no real resemblance to the pro game aside from the fact that they're in essence the same sport governed by the same laws, the professional game nevertheless informs the football that we all play regularly among our friends or for our local side. For every Cristiano Ronaldo tantrum, Giorgio Chiellini slide tackle and Lionel Messi mazy run there are several million of us trying, and failing, to replicate them on a bumpy pitch at playing fields all over the country every single week. Football at the grassroots level has its own style, though, its own unwritten rules and culture and its own universe in which the players operate and function.

I played football at what could accurately be described as 'the lowest level of organised football possible' for years, and I honestly enjoyed every second of it. These days, although my playing days are behind me, I often head over to the playing fields near my parents' house on a Sunday morning when I'm visiting to watch the local league teams playing, usually in all weathers, with a huge amount of passion and enthusiasm for the game.

What manifests itself almost every time is a hugely enjoyable, engrossing melodrama in which everyday men are cast in the role of hero (occasionally), villain (more often) and bit-part accessory to both glory and failure on an almost minute-by-minute basis. I genuinely enjoy watching football at this level over any other for a mixture of reasons, including the fallibility of the protagonists, nostalgia and realism. It is impossible to feel far removed from the game when you can hear and feel almost every kick from just a few yards away.

At this juncture I should state what I consider to be the 'grassroots' game. It is a level of football that players, managers, administrators and officials take part in purely for the love of the pastime, the camaraderie between them and their fellow players and the stories it weaves for them all to share for years to come, rather than any financial recompense they may, or in most cases, may not, receive. Referees at this level are paid a derisory amount for their time, but I refuse to accept they do it for a legitimate income – the amounts on offer are simply too small. They, like the players, are doing it because they (some would argue perversely) enjoy officiating and enabling games to go ahead.

This is football as we experience it, not viewed from a distance through a TV set, computer or expensively priced seat at a purpose-built stadium. Football may be watched by billions around the world, but it is these enthusiastic yet limited men that make up the lifeblood of the game in this country. Because what's the use in watching the pros strut their stuff on the big stage if we can't attempt, and fail, to replicate it when still half-drunk from the night before on a muddy field on a windy January Sunday morning?

Players

There are, to my mind, only a handful of types of player at this standard of football. Whereas the top level contains not only many different types of player, but even specialisms within positions themselves – for example, John Terry and John Stones may both be centre-backs, but anyone who's watched them both will realise they are very different players – amateur football is nowhere near as complicated.

It's tempting to reduce this down even further to 'good players' and 'bad players' but I think that might be just a touch too reductive. Nevertheless, there isn't much to go on and a lot of it rests on speed, fitness and effort, the latter of which can vary from 'literally all the effort in the world that a human being can muster' to 'won't even try for a single, solitary second even if his life depended on it'. Seriously, the whole gamut is covered when it comes to just how much or how little grassroots players will try on a Saturday afternoon or Sunday morning, as well as how effective/ineffective they'll be.

The Big Unit

If you've ever walked past a patch of grass that a football game is being played on then you've seen the Big Unit. That's because he's the size of a house. You would have almost certainly have heard him, too, because he is the loudest one on the pitch (apart from the other team's Big Unit, of course).

Big Units tend to be older, have filled out somewhat in their advancing years and spend the entire game pointing, shouting and fouling. They are sometimes captain as well, for there are two types of Big Unit – the first is just big and fat and dominant (not usually captain material), the other is talented, too, but has had to accept a deeper (and slower) role as his fitness has decreased as rapidly as his weight has increased over the years.

These guys are critically important in any team, not only because they spur a team on through respect/fear (and there's a fine line somewhere in between those two things) but also because they tend to be older, have their own manual labouring business that sponsors the kit, and are almost always generous at the bar.

The Nippy Winger

The Nippy Winger is always young, always really fast and, for some reason, almost always the brother of someone else in the team. He can't tackle, in fact he's never really attempted to do so, but he is really important to the team and here's why.

In professional football full-backs are hugely influential. They play two positions, both working back to cover in defence and also launching a thousand attacks. Think Kyle Walker.

In grassroots football no one is Kyle Walker. No one is even Murray Walker. As a result, the full-back positions are invariably taken by people who can't play anywhere else or players who are filling in as a favour and don't have a position nailed down elsewhere in the team. Therefore, there is a direct correlation between how nippy and skilful and fast your wingers are, and how demoralised the other team's full-backs, and by extension their defence generally, are going to become.

Ideally, you'd have two Nippy Wingers in your team, but no one I've ever played for has ever managed that, apart from one iteration of our university side for a season, but they were wing-backs and neither of them ever bothered defending and so it didn't really work anyway.

If you do have two wingers, the un-Nippy one always wants to cut inside and never take any one on because he is, in reality, the third best striker available and he just wants to play up front.

The One Who Should Really Be Playing At A Much Higher Level

I've played with a few of these chaps in my time, and not a second has gone by when I haven't been thankful they were on my team and not the opposition's. These types play for you only because they can't be bothered with the endless semi-pro grind of a Tuesday and Thursday training session followed by a game in the arse-end of nowhere on Saturday. And when they turn out for your team it's fucking brilliant.

I can remember a guy moving to our area halfway through a season, straight from the academy at Plymouth Argyle. He scored something like twenty-seven goals from midfield from January to April, and it was like someone had enabled a video-game cheat in real life.

The unquestionable highlight was when an opposition manager saw how good he was and instructed a defender to man-mark him for the entirety of the game. When our superstar had to be subbed off because he wanted to leave early (he had probably scored six by that point), the boy tasked with marking him actually followed him off the pitch. Our man had to turn to the defender and quietly whisper to him 'Er, I'm being subbed off now mate', to which came the reply 'Oh, cheers', before the ersatz Martin Keown happily jogged back on to the pitch with a grin, safe in the knowledge that his ordeal was over and he would hopefully never see his tormentor ever again.

The Trier

Everything is done at a hundred miles an hour in a lung-busting fashion and no injury is too much to bear for the Trier. Friction-burns on rock-hard August pitches are their calling card, strained muscles are their currency and broken legs (usually their own, but sometimes other people's owing to their take-no-prisoners tackling style) are their trophies. Every team needs at least two of these, and if you're blessed enough to be playing alongside one in central midfield you can essentially spend the game doing whatever you want (see the Prima Donna). They cover every blade of grass on the pitch, they usually have limited ability, and they are almost always really nice people, too.

Everyone who isn't a Trier has played with/against one, and if you haven't and you're reading this still wondering why no one tries as hard as you at football, you *are* one. God bless the Triers and all who sail alongside them, for no game has ever been won without them.

The Prima Donna

Let's be absolutely clear here, these men are bastards. They don't have to be alice-band-wearing, tackle-dodging stereotypes – some just have longer hair and value their jobs enough not to want to break their leg on a Sunday – but you'll know a Prima Donna when you see one.

They moan. They don't track back. They refuse to take the kit home and wash it, and the one time you manage to shame them into doing so they bring it back all damp and the colours have run. They don't turn up for away games that are more than ten miles away. They refuse to drive and insist on being picked up.

OK, fair enough, they score a free-kick or two each season and they can occasionally pull off a Cristiano-esque turn that they've spent all week practising in the garden, but other than that they are of no value. Give me one Trier over three Prima Donnas any day of the week.

You remember earlier when I was talking about players who 'won't even try for a single, solitary second even if their lives depended on it'? Yep, you got it.

Everyone's lives would be a whole lot easier if we just made a group pact not to put up with any of his shit. But we all do though, don't we? Because remember that goal Jonny scored back in 2012, against the Market House Tavern? Yeah, it was a while ago now but he could do it again at any point, so chase back and win the ball back for him like a good boy, won't you?

Again: these men are bastards.

Goalkeepers – The rare beasts

The hen's teeth of Sunday league football. You have more chance of finding a previously undiscovered, uncontacted tribe living in your local woods than you do of finding a decent, reliable keeper available on a Sunday – especially if we're talking about one that can actually reach the halfway line with a goal-kick.

At a slightly higher level – Saturday football for instance – it's not as hard to come across a potential Safe Hands, but Sundays? Not a chance.

If you ever find one, I suggest having a local solicitor draw up an all-encompassing employment contract to ensure that he doesn't disappear a few weeks into the season. When I think back to the lengths some of the teams I've played for over the years have gone to to nail down a regular 'keeper, it's laughable. And I would always make the phone calls to help the manager in his quest because I knew that, as the tallest member of the team, I'd have to deputise if he didn't turn up. Seriously, two things are for sure if you're a tall Sunday league player: one, you're helping put the net up *and* take it down afterwards; and two, you're going in goal if the 'keeper doesn't make it. Back in the day I could never relax until I saw Danny the Keeper's red Peugeot 205 arrive in the car park. That car was like my last chopper out of Saigon.

Managers

Managers of grassroots football teams are an absolute goldmine of character and entertainment. When you watch a game on TV and marvel at, laugh at and recount some of the things managers say in frustrated and angry post-match interviews, just remember that there are thousands of similarly-aged men all over the country also experiencing those emotions, without the money or TV cameras to console them. They don't even have more than a handful of players who can string two passes together a lot of the time, but still they plan and think about Sunday's game all week. And, unlike their Premier League counterparts, they also have to tell their players where the next game is, get the kit washed by somebody, find a goalkeeper and then work out who's going to play and who isn't, assuming more than eleven players actually turn up. If there's a sub available, he then needs to be convinced to run the line, something he won't want to do, and if there isn't a sub available then the manager is probably going to have to run it himself.

Yet still they do it, every single season. I've known Sunday league managers who are well into their sixties and have been doing it since before I was born. One used to come into the supermarket where I worked almost every Saturday and talk about his team for the following morning like he was Arrigo Sacchi crossed with Béla Guttmann. It was clearly the most important thing in his life. And some of the funniest football moments I've ever witnessed have come via the actions of these wizened, hardy old chaps who have seen more terrible players than they've had pints of lager. And all of them have had a lot of pints of lager.

For instance, a manager of mine was once so incensed by a terrible first-half performance from our team that he spent all 15 half-time minutes ranting and raving on a variety of subjects that didn't really make any sense, peppered and punctuated with several insults that would make a docker blush, all while standing under a sign saying, and this is no word of a lie: 'Half-time is a time to create positive energy' – Glenn Hoddle. I didn't dare smile at the time, but I was sure to point it out to all the boys afterwards.

Marcus tells a great story about a manager of his who used to go to town on his players at the interval, lining them up one by one and screaming at them: 'You're shit! You're shit! You're even shitter!' and then wonder why he rarely got a positive response.

It's tempting to suggest that these are put-upon men, using this one day a week, God's day, to expunge and relieve the pressure that's been building up all week in one foul swoop by shouting and screaming at an assembled throng of football-kitted man-children, before Monday rolls around and the whole process starts again. But I think that would be unfair. Sometimes they're real gems. I've learnt a lot over the years from football managers I've had about character and about responsibility, and also about how to hold your own in a pub – all valuable skills for a young British man to learn I suppose.

These men are unwitting father figures, and it's a responsibility they largely ignore, but when you get a good one that doesn't threaten to kill you if you give the ball away again, you really want to play for him. He's your Brian Clough. And if he likes you enough, he might just give you his player-of-the-year nod at the end-of-season awards at the Red Lion. And everyone knows that's the second best one you can win, just below the Ballon d'Or of grassroots awards, the players' player.

While we're on that subject, here is the approved and confirmed order of end-of-season awards, arranged by kudos:

1. *Players' Player of the Season* – as I've said, the Ballon d'Or of grassroots football awards. It doesn't get any better than being voted the best by your team-mates, even if sometimes this gong can be tainted by a bit of dressing-room politics and based on how much of a good bloke you are.

2. *Manager's Player of the Season* – always great to get the nod from the gaffer, but can come with resentment from the rest of the squad, especially those who play in the same position and can't get in the team as a result. The cry-babies.

3. *Top Scorer* – this sits below manager's player because only a certain amount of players can realistically win it. That said, though, my centre-back partner once won this in the best Sunday league tribute to Steve Bruce I've ever witnessed. I think he bagged something like sixteen goals, without taking a single penalty. He was at least five years too young to be considered a Big Unit, but he was well on his way at that point. He is almost certainly one now.

4. *Clubman of the Year* – this one is reserved for people who don't really contribute on the pitch very much, but are nevertheless a good egg. It's kind of nice to win it, because it's always lovely to be appreciated, but you wouldn't choose winning this over any of the big three above it, and there's a sort of unwritten rule that good players don't win this one. How do I know that? Well I've won it a few times myself. So there's all the evidence you'll ever need.

5. *Most Improved Player* – admittedly this one doesn't exist as much in adult football, it's more of a kids' thing, but whichever way you slice it it's a total insult. It's impossible to win this without first being terrible at football to start with. Trust me here, again I'm talking from a position of experience.

Referees

Referees at the pro level have been discussed at great length elsewhere in this book and, as I've already stated, I think it's clear as to why they choose that particular profession. It's harder to ascertain why men volunteer to referee at grassroots level – for two hours of being shouted at by everyone within 100 metres of you, both players and onlookers alike, before you head home to be shouted out again for being out all morning and not cutting the grass like you said you would.

Seriously, refereeing at this level is like being Bill Paxton's character in the movie *Twister*, but instead of cars and cows flying all around you from all angles, it's young men dressed in football kits. Except it's even worse than that. And I'm fairly sure Bill got paid more than £45 for his time and there wasn't dog shit all over the set when he was trying to run.

There are only three reasons I can think of for these hardy fools actually bothering to turn up and do this thankless, horrendous task. One, they are masochistic deviants who find being abused on a football field by several men on a Sunday morning socially more acceptable than one or two other insalubrious alternatives to fulfilling that need. Two, they hate their home life so much that any time out of the house is a bonus. And three, they actually believe in the game of football and want to further it by offering their own precious time for the betterment of other people's leisure.

Thinking about it, it must be the first or second of those reasons. The third one is just too weird to contemplate.

Lexicon of Terms

In addition to the types of player one encounters at this level of football, there also exists a constantly evolving language that ostensibly serves to get across instructions and encouragement in the most pithy and efficient way possible. In reality, it is a series of nonsensical statements barked between players to at least make it sound like they know what they are doing. They rarely do.

I've compiled a selection of my favourites below. They are some of the more vocal contributions I've experienced in my time of playing at the very bottom of the football pyramid, and if you play yourself you'll recognise at least a few of them, I'm sure. And if you don't play but fancy going down to watch a local game, I guarantee you this will be the soundtrack to what you see.

'On his toes!'

Translation: 'Get tight to the man or he will hurt us with his ability'

This, in essence, means get as close as you can to your opposite man when he receives the ball so he can't do anything with it. Of course, the guy shouting it is probably guilty of not being anywhere near his man to stop the pass in the first place and knows full well that if you do get 'on his toes' then you're going to get turned inside out because the kid is about ten years younger than you and isn't hungover. Meaningless.

'Seconds!'

Translation: 'We've not won that first header/tackle, so let's try and win the ball second time around'

We didn't win the first header because, with the exception of our 25 stone centre-back, no one else can head it and, even if they could, they all have headaches from the night before. On one team I played for, this term was rendered absolutely obsolete by a guy who we'll call 'A.J.' who used to tirelessly shout it every minute for the entirety of the game. It was almost like it became the soundtrack to the ninety minutes – the ball goes out for a throw in, 'SECONDS!'; the goalkeeper makes a save, 'SECONDS!'; you've been subbed off, 'SECONDS!'

He also used to shout 'A.J.'S HEAD!' every time there was a goal-kick, too, despite being about 5ft 9in in his boots, so maybe he just had a form of amateur footballer's Tourette's – a lot of people do.

'Let's all have a squeeze!'
Translation: 'Move up the pitch for this goal-kick/clearance
    so we're not defending too deep'

I used to love this one because it was regularly shouted by two very good goalkeepers I used to play in front of, and it was a welcome variation on the frankly maniacal 'OOOOOOUUUUUUTTTTTTT!!!' that most goalkeepers shout.

'Let's all have a squeeze' is a lot more gentle and interesting (even though it was also screamed at top volume), and it makes the 'keeper in question actually sound a bit more professional. The two best goalkeepers I played with both used to shout this, and that can't be a coincidence. If you're reading this as a goalkeeper, think about including this in your armoury of shouts. Defenders will respect you more, trust me.

Martin 'Hutty' Hutt and James 'Pav' Paviour (when you can actually find grassroots goalkeepers, they always have nicknames. No one knows why) were both dominant alpha males of the first order, Pav especially. The man is on record as being proud of the fact that he's 'the loudest person in any room he's ever been in'.

Pav's other favourite goalkeeping shout was 'NEXT JOB!' after you'd made a tackle or clearance and he would also bellow this over and over again at deafening volume. A genuinely very good goalkeeper was Pav, but he's right up there on the list of men I'd least like to be stuck in a lift with, for reasons of size, sweatiness and volume.

The only goalkeeper's shout that I've ever heard of that's better than this is something Marcus told me about a 'keeper he once played with. When striking the ball for a goal-kick he used to scream 'MMMMMEGAKICK!' every time, but I never heard that with my own ears and, to be frank, it's a funny thing to say, but it sounds like the call of a man who perhaps belongs on the very fringes of our society.

'Where's the talking, eh?'

Translation: 'We're not talking to each other and helping each other with friendly advice and the opposition team may take encouragement from our silence'

It is a long-held belief among the grassroots football fraternity that any lack of ability can be more than made up for by shouting, encouraging and casually demeaning the other side. As a result nothing strikes more fear into the heart of a Sunday side captain than the dreaded wall of silence from his team-mates.

He (or other, more vocal members of the team) will continually ask this half-question, half-plea as if everyone starting to make a lot of noise will suddenly turn the tables in favour of their team and close out that much-needed win.

You'll notice that this particular soundbite from the grassroots lexicon is always followed by a sort of call to arms disguised as a half-hearted question. The 'eh?' in this instance is very important because it invites a response.

Variations on this theme include 'There's no talking, is there?' 'They've shut us up, haven't they?' And 'Why are we so quiet, lads?' All pathetic and all belonging to a captain who's lost control of his team and fears a heavy defeat. This is almost never shouted when a team is winning.

'Time! Loads of time!'

Translation: 'You have lots of time and space now you're in possession of the ball to do whatever you want with it'

You'll hear this a lot, especially towards the end of the game when players are tired and have essentially stopped working back to defend. The problem is that if there's one thing you don't want to give to the majority of players at this level it's time – time to misplace a pass, time to shank it out for a throw, time to take a bad first touch and then slide in late on someone, time to scuff a shot straight at the keeper, time to trip over the ball, time, time, time.

'Turn on it!'

Translation: 'You have time to turn and face towards the goal with the ball with a view to launching an important attack'

A variation on 'Loads of time!', this is nevertheless slightly more specific and ambitious and will usually be reserved for a player with some attacking prowess and talent. Whereas 'Loads of time!' can serve to calm down a nervous left-back who has possession of the ball inside his own half, 'Turn on it!' tends to be used more to encourage an attack-minded player to go and do some damage.

Invariably they turn the wrong way and are instantly tackled.

'Travel!'

Translation: 'Don't pass it, move forward with the ball at your feet'

Depending on where you are on the pitch, this can also be 'Carry it!', 'Move with it!' or 'Bring it!' and is again usually reserved for players who aren't treating the ball like a bomb to be got rid of at the earliest opportunity. You may bark this at a tricky winger who has space in front of him, or an ageing, cultured centre-back who likes to take a touch, but never a bambi-on-ice, hoof-it merchant who 'gets rid' at all costs. Never shout 'Travel!' at someone like that. Because it's going to end with a dispossession and the ball in the back of your own net.

'They're fighting among themselves, aren't they?'

Translation: 'We should take encouragement from the fact that the other team are arguing'

Whenever you hear any cross words between two members (or more) of the opposition you must always leap on it with abandon and interpret it as them 'fighting among themselves'. It means they're not focused on the job at hand, they are therefore not concentrating and your team are then primed to strike, just as long as you let everyone on your side know in case they haven't noticed it themselves.

All this amazing, A level psychology that you've learnt over years on Sunday league pitches is almost instantly undone, however, when you forget where you are and tell your centre-back partner to 'Fuck off!' when he asks you who you were supposed to be marking on that corner they just scored from. Now who's fighting among themselves, eh? Fuck off, mate.

'Nil-nil boys! Nil-nil!'
Translation: I have no idea.

This is a tricky one because I estimate I've played more than 200 games at what I would call a grassroots level and I've never quite got to the bottom of this one. It's used a lot, whatever the scoreline, and the only thing I can hazard a guess at is that it's a call for improved concentration and to act like the game is still 0–0 with all to play for.

But I've heard it shouted when a team is 6–0 down, which at the time just pissed me off. And I've also heard it while 6–0 up, too, which also pissed me off because it made me feel like my team weren't enjoying the win – we're 6–0 up with ten minutes left, pal. Why would we act like it's nil-nil?

Curiously, I've never heard this shouted when the game is actually 0–0.

'Pride and ball!'

Translation: 'The only thing that matters in the current situation is your personal pride and the football we're playing with'

Not heard too regularly, this makes it in by virtue of the fact that it's so ridiculous. I just absolutely love the idea of a grown man shouting, at the top of his voice, 'PRIDE AND BALL!' during a game. It's the Sunday league equivalent of 'THIS IS SPARTA!' Your team's not going to lose today because you've got pride, and you fucking well want the ball. That's all that counts. Pride and ball. Pride and ball. PRIDE AND FUCKING BALL.

'Heads on!'

Translation: 'If we don't concentrate here, we're going to be beaten'

Never mind that all you can think about is the eight pints you had last night, which you could well be reacquainted with at any moment, or that you've double-parked your Golf and you're fairly certain you're going to get a ticket, even on a Sunday, if you don't move it. What's needed right here and right now is 100 per cent concentration or the nippy little striker is going to score yet another goal – as if concentration is going to make up for the ten yards of pace and eight years he's got on you.

If you just concentrate here, you'll be fine. But try not to concentrate on that curry that you also had last night, or things could get very messy. Get your 'head on', yeah?

'Box 'em in!'
Translation: 'They have a throw-in in their half. Why don't we attempt to stop them getting the ball into our half?'

Because this game is just an endless exchange of massive hoofs up the pitch, from one end to another, that's why. It's all very well asking a professional team to execute a complicated *gegenpress*, in which every player knows their role and can force the opposition into endless mistakes in their own half, awarding you possession in a dangerous area. But Dave's mate Ash the Bash has only come along because we were short and, although he says he's a striker, you're wondering if he's ever played the game before.

There is basically zero chance of anyone boxing any-one in, unless it's the car park in which case it's you that's stuck there and it's going to take you an extra half an hour to get out later. An extra half an hour holding your leg in that position to try to stop the friction-burn from the unwatered pitch you slid on sticking to the car seat.

'Box 'em in' is as redundant as it is ridiculous.

'Cuppa tea with that slice?'

Translation: 'He's sliced that shot so wildly that it's actually reminded me of a slice of cake, something that is traditionally enjoyed in this country with a cup of tea'

When a defender has a running battle with a striker, he takes great pleasure from said striker missing the target with a shot. If it's missed that badly, because he's sliced it, all the better. The defender, if he's really obnoxious (and most of them are, this writer included), can then laugh and deliver a witty line like the one above, all the while looking over at some pals or a girlfriend on the touchline with a wink.

Never mind that it was your fault he was open for the shot in the first place, and never mind that in the second half, when you're knackered, he's going to make your life hell for forty-five minutes by scoring a hat-trick, this is *your* time. Go on, laugh at him. Ask him if he's going to fetch the ball after that or if he wants a cup of tea with that slice. Because you're not just an overweight centre-half who can't play anywhere else in the team because you're too slow, you're a comedian. You're wasted on this football pitch, you should be performing on a stage. But not in a theatre production that involves repeating any sort of footballing skill or athletic ability.

'We're making them look good!'

Translation: 'We're playing so badly at the moment that the other team, who we implicitly consider to be terrible, are actually starting to look like a better team than us'

This is a good one because it works on two levels. Not only does it imply that your team has a few notches of performance level higher than this, but it manages to also state, *at the same time*, that you don't think the other team are very good. It also implies that it's only the fact that you're all playing so badly that is enabling the opposition to be ahead.

It's intended to rile the other team and inspire your own troops at the same time. This almost never works.

Matching the lexicon with the type of player

This is easy, and there are a few general rules:

1. Big Units shout and scream, all of them, all the time, as do some goalkeepers
2. Nippy Wingers never say anything
3. The Ones Who Should Be Playing At A Much Higher Level are a mixed bag, but can occasionally be withering
4. The Triers only ever say 'Seconds!'
5. Prima Donnas only say the negative ones, in between their own personal moans

Ah, grassroots football. With your terrible pitches and your obvious lack of any sort of facilities and your hamstring-ruining double-banker games at the end of the season due to fixture pile-ups and your reluctant linesmen and your discarded electrical tape littering the abandoned dressing-room and your smell of Deep Heat and your raucous laughter in the pub afterwards and your aching, limping legs on a Monday.

Playing football with your mates at the weekend is a form of escapism, and some would argue the best form of escapism at that. Aside from the few beers that invariably take place after the game it's an inherently healthy pursuit; it takes place outside, involves exercise and inspires bonding, camaraderie and positive shared experiences for men all over the country, something that is severely lacking in other areas of their lives, for the most part.

Some of the best memories of my adolescence and young adulthood have come from playing football with my pals on a Saturday afternoon or a Sunday morning: that time a few of us jumped into the back of a team-mate's van before he drove home and made spooky, weird noises until he stopped halfway back to investigate, at which point we all jumped out and wrestled him to the floor while he screamed in terror; the friends I made when I travelled to New Zealand to play for a team there and how they didn't judge me or ridicule me for not being good enough to get in the team very often; the lessons you learn about mucking in and working hard for each other and how much more you enjoy your weekend if you win a game. It's all fairly pointless, trivial stuff when taken in isolation but, as part of a young man's whole life, they are key components of coming of age, growing and finding one's way in the world.

And for me, that's what football is when you boil it all down and study what's left. It's not just sport; it's friendship and it's belonging. Whether that's through the shared team you support, or the rival team you deride, the shared team you play for, or the rival team you play against, with football we all have a place in the world, a position in the world, a purpose.

Bill Shankly once said football is much more important than life and death. It obviously isn't. But for billions of people around the world, it's a lot more important than just about anything else.

Now, let's all have a squeeze, shall we?

Acknowledgements

The majority of you know *The Football Ramble* as the four men on the microphones each week, but there is a fifth man in our number – Jon Teague. It is no exaggeration to say that he takes leadership and responsibility for anything and everything that occurs when the mics are faded down (and also one or two things when they're faded up), from organisation of live shows to the securing of commercial agreements, not to mention his tireless work to improve our frankly appalling diary management. We wouldn't be in the position to write our first book (or indeed do anything much) without him. What's more, he does all of this for minimal credit and recognition. Jon, we salute you and your incessant and relentless Spurs knowledge. Thank you, sir!

Thanks also must go to our Dutch uncle, Ben Bailey Smith, and our adopted son, Joel Grove, as well as our online king Matt Isherwood and queen, the Always

Excellent Kelly Welles. Cheers also to acast for having our backs, everyone at Penguin Random House but particularly James Keyte and Ben Brusey, as well as Paul at Absolute Radio. Ed Davis must be thanked for providing the subtitle – it was a spot-on observation and we couldn't agree with it more.

This book is also for Chris Applegate and Chris Wildey, no longer of this parish but forever somehow a part of it.

The Football Ramble would also like to individually thank:

Jim Campbell

I would like to thank my amazing wife-to-be, Holly, for always being inspiring and understanding of a man who spends so much time at the behest of this ridiculous game. Thanks also to Mum, Dad and Andrew for always being supportive.

Thanks to Marcus, Luke, Pete and Jon Teague: I can think of no better people with whom to effectively spend most of my time in a cupboard. Extra thanks to Jon for doing the grown-up work like contracts and hanging rivals off bridges.

Thanks to Rupert Fryer for his invaluable help with understanding how the South American league systems work, or rather helping me to get a grasp on how actually they don't.

Last but by no means least, thanks to you, our readers and listeners. I wouldn't say that we couldn't do it without you, we could, but if we did it would just be pathetic by now.

Luke Aaron Moore

Thanks first and foremost to my beautiful Mimi, you're everything to me.

Also to my wonderful family but particularly my late Uncle Les, who set the football fire blazing within me in the first instance. May it never be quenched!

Thanks to JT for everything – you're not only a brilliant colleague but also a true friend. Thanks particularly for your help with the Media and Referees chapter, it was invaluable.

Thanks also to Thomas Moss, Dan Poulton, James Sullivan and Duncan Haskell for constant inspiration and Andy Brassell and James Horncastle, two men who wear their ridiculous football knowledge lightly enough to still be great company.

And to all our listeners for accompanying us on this wonderful journey. You're the best co-pilots we could ask for.

Marcus Speller

Thanks first to my marvellous family Speller, aka the wind beneath my wings.

Also to Jamie, Paul and Ruth for making excellent sounding boards, as well as Laurence McKenna for the endless positivity and guidance.

I am especially appreciative to Jonathan, David and all the chaps at *The Blizzard* for the football knowledge, encouragement and ice cream.

A great big thank you from the very bottom of my heart to all of you for journeying with us on this football ramble. We couldn't and wouldn't do it without you.

And lastly, of course, my fellow Ramblers – Jim, Jon, Luke and Pete – without whom none of this would exist and thus life would be a lot less fun.

Pete Donaldson

Thanks to Chankles, Alex G and his rabble, Matty, Marc, Al Z, Mam and Dad and Christine Fish. The Nonstuff crew and Les Ferdinand. Love ya x